PLAYING THE GAME?

CRICKET'S TARNISHED IDEALS
From Bodyline to present

MARK PEEL

First published by Pitch Publishing, 2018

Pitch Publishing
A2 Yeoman Gate
Yeoman Way
Worthing
Sussex
BN13 3QZ
www.pitchpublishing.co.uk
info@pitchpublishing.co.uk

ISBN 978-1-78531-437-7

Typesetting and origination by Pitch Publishing
Printed and bound in India by Replika Press Pvt. Ltd.

Contents

Acknowledgements

I 'D like to thank the following for helping with my research: Rodney Cavalier, Geoffrey Dean, Tim Munton, John Murray, Peter Parfitt, Pat Pocock, Ivo Tennant and John Woodcock.

I'd also like to extend my thanks to the Library and Research Manager of the MCC Library at Lord's, Neil Robinson, and to the MCC Archivist, Robert Curphey, for all the help over many visits; and to the staff at the Central Library, Edinburgh; the National Library of Scotland; the Melbourne Cricket Club library; and the New South Wales State Library.

I am most indebted to my agent, Andrew Lownie, for all his efforts on my behalf; to Graham Hughes for his invaluable copyedit; and to Jane Camillin, Paul Camillin and Derek Hammond at Pitch, along with Duncan Olner, Dean Rockett and Graham Hales, for all their work in bringing the project to fruition.

Mark Peel

Introduction

F EW passages of Test cricket have proved as riveting as the confrontation between Michael Atherton and Allan Donald during the fourth day of the fourth Test between England and South Africa at Trent Bridge in July 1998. Needing 247 to win, England had reached 87/1 when Atherton deflected a Donald bouncer to wicketkeeper Mark Boucher and was given not out by New Zealand umpire Steve Dunne, much to Donald's consternation. Convulsed by fury, Donald then threw everything at Atherton in a blistering six-over spell which Atherton survived unscathed, living to fight another day. The spectacle captivated the nation, especially as Atherton carried on the good work the next day to see England through to a highly satisfying eight-wicket victory; but one person disturbed by the physical and verbal confrontation was Colin Cowdrey, one of England's greatest batsmen and former chairman of the International Cricket Council (ICC).

In a stellar career between 1950 and 1976, Cowdrey, an England captain on 27 occasions, was the essence of decorum both on and off the field. Raised by a cricket-loving father and tutored by austere schoolmasters whose word was law, he learned to revere the game and embrace its finest traditions. With his natural modesty and charm, he was a cricketing idol to many, and although not averse to a touch of gamesmanship in his unwillingness to always 'walk' for a thin edge to the wicketkeeper, this was a minor flaw in relation to a life of service to the game. It was entirely appropriate that, given his concern about declining standards of cricketing etiquette, he was the driving force behind MCC's Spirit of Cricket, a preamble to the recodification of the Laws of Cricket in 2000, commending the values of fair play and respect for one's opponents. It was an appeal that won support from the majority of the English cricket establishment and many cricket lovers the world over. Yet for all the efforts invested in spreading its message, it has had only limited effect in restoring cricket's lost soul, so that after a particularly acrimonious Test match between Australia and India at Sydney in January 2008, Jeremy Cowdrey, Colin's second son, felt moved to write to the *Daily Telegraph* to ask whether the Spirit of Cricket still meant something important or was just an empty phrase.

To Michael Atherton, the former England captain turned cricket journalist, it was the latter, 'a myth promulgated by Victorian moralists rather than an accurate reflection of the game as played by human beings rather than Gods'.[1] Yet even if we accept this view, and that of social historian Derek Birley that 'Cricket, in particular, had been plagued by nostalgia since people first began to think it worth writing about', the Victorian ethos of fair play won allegiance not only on the playing fields of Eton, but also across broad swathes of the Empire.[2] 'From the eight years of school life this code became the moral framework of my existence,' wrote renowned West Indian writer and political activist C.L.R. James, who grew up in Trinidad at the beginning of the last century. 'It has never left me.'[3] Many others in the Caribbean thought the same. 'I always saw cricket as a noble sport and I tried to play in the true spirit of the game,' recalled Gary Sobers, the great West Indian all-rounder.[4]

It was the same ethos which had always inspired Bill Woodfull, the Australian captain in the bodyline series of 1932/33, and which he articulated with devastating effect to MCC manager Pelham Warner during the Adelaide Test, when he said that one side was playing cricket and one wasn't. It was to combat the genius of Don Bradman, Australia's run-making machine, that England captain Douglas Jardine had resorted to the tactics of bodyline: intimidatory bowling at the head and upper body (see Chapter 1). He justified such tactics by claiming that they in no way contravened the laws of the game, and on this he was supported by most of his countrymen back home. It was only when bodyline made a brief but bloody appearance in England in 1933 that opinion quickly changed, prompting an amendment to the laws that outlawed fast short-pitched balls aimed specifically at the batsman.

Following bodyline, England–Australia Tests returned to more traditional standards of rivalry, but beneath the outward bonhomie the bitterness lingered. Bradman, for one, never forgot the humiliation heaped upon his compatriots by Jardine, and when Australia unearthed two exceptional speed merchants in Ray Lindwall and Keith Miller post-war, it was England's turn to feel the heat, none more so than their revered opener Len Hutton (see Chapter 2). Beginning with a fusillade of bouncers on a treacherous wicket at Brisbane in the first Test of the 1946/47 series, they rarely let up thereafter. In England in 1948, Bradman's final tour, the popular Miller was roundly booed at Trent Bridge for bowling persistently short at Hutton and Denis Compton. In the opinion of Compton's team-mate Bill Edrich, Bradman was the best captain he'd encountered, 'but nearly all cricketers agree that, since 1945, Australia under his captaincy had shown more ruthlessness, more cold-blooded determination to win, even at the cost of happy relationships, than any country has displayed, in 1932/33 or on any other occasion at all'.[5] In time, Hutton fought back with Frank Tyson in Australia in 1954/55, as did Ray Illingworth with John Snow there in 1970/71, proving that any side with the necessary firepower would deploy it to the maximum effect.

During the later 1950s, the cricket world had been preoccupied by the vexed question of throwing, a question that Bradman, by now Australia's leading cricket administrator, called one of the most complex because it was so open to opinion and interpretation (see Chapter 3). Confronted with evidence that was often ambivalent, umpires and administrators tended to turn a blind eye to suspect actions, leaving bowlers such as South Africa's Cuan

McCarthy and England's Tony Lock free to ply their trade. By the time of England's ill-fated tour of Australia in 1958/59, every state except Queensland had a fast bowler with a suspect action. Not wishing to disturb the waters – Australia hadn't complained about the ill-prepared Test wickets in England in 1956 – MCC suffered in silence against the throwers. They did, however, warn their hosts that they intended to confront the matter on their return, and the Australians, appreciating the gravity of the situation, attended the Imperial Cricket Conference at Lord's in July 1960. (They were normally represented by proxies.) The conference vowed to rid the game of throwing, and Bradman, in his role as chairman of selectors, returned home determined to act. It was a task he accomplished with his customary efficiency, culminating in the no-balling of Australian opening bowler Ian Meckiff for throwing against South Africa at Brisbane in November 1963 and his retirement from the game.

By then, Lock had rectified his action and South Africa's Geoff Griffin had retired after being repeatedly called on his team's tour of England in 1960, leaving West Indian Charlie Griffith and Derbyshire's Harold Rhodes as the prime suspects. Although the former was called only twice during his career, it was enough to condemn him following a life-threatening injury he had inflicted on Indian captain Nari Contractor. Various opponents labelled him a 'chucker', particularly for his bouncer and yorker, helping to embitter the West Indies' relations with England and Australia at a racially sensitive time. Three decades later, the throwing controversy was revived around the genial personality of Sri Lankan spinner Muttiah Muralitharan, when once again it proved extremely difficult to resolve satisfactorily.

In the 1960s, most cricketers continued to abide by an accepted code of sportsmanship which, above all, placed the authority of the umpire as paramount – but this was a decade of rapid change, when traditional authority and age-old certainties gave way to a dynamic youth culture addicted to greater freedom. In this more liberal climate, with greater social and recreational activities available, the stagnant cricket of that era was fast losing its popular appeal (see Chapter 4). It needed the onset of the one-day game, with its monetary rewards and more extensive television coverage, to revitalise cricket – but in this new competitive environment, players marched to a more discordant drumbeat. Spurred on by the greater financial rewards now available, the 1970s generation, opinionated and materialist, was less bound by the conventions of the past. Led by Australian teams at both national and state levels, players increasingly resorted to gamesmanship, verbal abuse and dissent, placing additional pressure on the umpires (see Chapter 5). The advent of Australian entrepreneur Kerry Packer's World Series Cricket, with its gladiatorial atmosphere, partisan crowds and lucrative rewards, only accentuated such trends: West Indian Colin Croft barging into New Zealand umpire Fred Goodall, Australia's Dennis Lillee aiming a kick at Pakistan's Javed Miandad, and Greg Chappell, the Australian captain, instructing his brother Trevor to bowl an underarm grubber to win a one-day match against New Zealand (see Chapter 6).

In an era when fast bowlers became fitter and stronger, nothing compared to the abundance of West Indian pacemen during the 1970s and 1980s (see Chapter 7). Their fitness and skill couldn't be faulted, but their sluggish over rate, their preponderance of short-pitched bowling and the physical threat posed to batsmen raised uncomfortable questions about whether they were flouting the spirit of cricket. These questions had rarely been asked in Australia in 1975/76, when the West Indians were on the receiving end of a fearful onslaught from the Australian fast bowlers Dennis Lillee and Jeff Thomson. Yet once the boot was on the other foot, the West Indians were accused of brutalising the game. After seeing them overwhelm England in the Caribbean in 1986, the *Sunday Times* cricket correspondent Robin Marlar wrote that current West Indian cricket had become 'a missile out of control which will kill cricket, all cricket, including their own. Even protected, the England players bore bruises which would horrify the toughest among us, and bring tears to their maiden aunts.'[6]

A couple of years later in Australia, the West Indies won convincingly, but once again their style of cricket left most of the critics cold. According to Keith Rigg, an Australian batsman in the 1930s, the West Indian bowling was worse than bodyline because there was no let-up and many more batsmen were hit; while to Australia's captain, Allan Border, his team could think only of survival as opposed to playing shots.

'The West Indians took a long time arriving at the top, repeatedly suffering the kind of humiliating indignities it is now inflicting on its erstwhile masters,' countered Tony Cozier, the respected West Indian cricket journalist. 'Clive Lloyd is not the only one who still rankles when his side's developing excellence is somehow interpreted as endangering the game.'[7] They pointed to the tacit approval they had received from umpires the world over – but, while this was essentially true, it merely exposed the ambiguity of the law on intimidatory bowling, which was difficult to police and open to different interpretations. It wasn't until the ICC placed a limit of two bouncers an over in 1994, and the decline of West Indian dominance, that batsmen could breathe a touch more easily.

Amid the turbulence of the 1980s, few countries created such an impression as Pakistan. Once the novices of the international game, they emerged from their chrysalis a talented, swashbuckling team whose flair and ingenuity were matched only by their disregard for cricketing protocol. Touring there had always been an exacting experience given its Islamic culture and the vexed question of its umpiring – but, in an age of instant communication, such grievances received unprecedented exposure, never more so than on England's tour in 1987/88 (see Chapter 8).

After two rancorous tours to England in 1982 and in 1987 when they had criticised the home umpires, the Pakistanis were in no mood to accommodate England's request to change the officials. In the first Test at Lahore, Mike Gatting's side were undone by the genius of Pakistani leg-spinner Abdul Qadir, aided by some dubious umpiring. When opener Chris Broad was given out caught behind off spinner Iqbal Qasim in the second innings, the decision so outraged him that initially he refused to walk. His defiance brought widespread condemnation, although not from the England management. The most they did was to reprimand him, while reserving most of their spleen for the umpiring, insinuating that it had lacked impartiality.

Their resentment was further fuelled by the appointment of the egregious Shakoor Rana, an umpire renowned for niggling touring sides, for the second Test at Faisalabad. England batted first and took command on the second day, but, after an afternoon of petty wrangling with Shakoor in Pakistan's first innings, Gatting went head-to-head with the umpire in an ugly finger-wagging confrontation that shocked the cricket world. Many England supporters sympathised with their captain given the provocation he had endured, but his demeanour, according to former *Wisden* editor Graeme Wright, ignored more than cricket's code of the umpire's word being law. 'It overlooked an essence of English cricket that appears to be a weakness and is in fact its great strength: there is more to the game than the game itself.'[8] Repeated gripes about Pakistani umpiring convinced Pakistan captain Imran Khan that independent umpires should officiate all Test matches, and when England and Australia opposed his proposal because it would deprive their officials of standing in home Tests, he accused them of opportunism. Independent umpires in Pakistan's home series against the West Indies in 1986/87 and India in 1989/90 had helped keep the peace, a welcome contrast to the discontent the world over caused by mediocre umpiring. It was the increasing failure of umpires to hold the line against disorder on the field that prompted Colin Cowdrey, the first elected chairman of the ICC, to propose one independent umpire for each Test, accompanied by a new Code of Conduct and an international match referee (see Chapter 9). The reforms, introduced in 1992, heralded an orchestrated fightback by the custodians of the game, but, in truth, progress was painfully slow as their bark proved greater than their bite.

Few of the game's ills proved more taxing to deal with than that of verbal abuse towards opponents, often referred to as sledging. Comments, witty, barbed and mildly insulting, were nothing new on the cricket field, but they were normally uttered on the spur of the moment and were rarely personal. In the early 1970s, this all began to change when the abuse became much more coordinated, frequent and offensive. Originating in Australian domestic cricket, it was given wings by their national cricket team and soon spread its tentacles to most forms of the game, right down to club level. While its practice was abhorred by traditionalists everywhere, contemporary opinion was more indulgent, viewing it as an acceptable part of the game, provided it wasn't too personal, although exactly what constituted a personal harangue was very much open to interpretation. With umpires unwilling or unable to intervene – some of the chat among the close-in field was out of earshot – those teams that prided themselves on being good scrappers led the way in mouthing profanities, none more so than the great Australian side of the 1990s (see Chapter 10).

Following the decline of Australian cricket in the mid-1980s, it took several years of hard graft under Allan Border's leadership to restore its fortunes. Criticised for being too friendly with the opposition on their 1985 tour of England, Border returned there four years later, a feistier figure intent on sacrificing all civilities to the greater cause of winning. The rumbustious approach helped his team to a 4–0 triumph, unleashing a golden era in Australian cricket, but one tainted by conduct unbecoming to a great team. When Australia, once again under Border's leadership, retained the Ashes in England in 1993, *Wisden* felt moved to admonish them for their vocal abuse. The next year in South Africa, in Border's final series, two of his leading players, Merv Hughes and Shane Warne, were fined by the match referee for obscene and offensive language towards an opponent.

Under Border's affable successor, Mark Taylor, the boorishness diminished, only to be revived under the next captain, Steve Waugh. After a plethora of disciplinary lapses by his team at the beginning of 2003, fast bowler Glenn McGrath then became embroiled in an unseemly confrontation with West Indian batsman Ramnaresh Sarwan in the Antigua Test that May. The backlash in Australia was so widespread that its cricket administrators vowed to wipe the slate clean (see Chapter 14). In concert with the players, they introduced a Spirit of Cricket protocol committing Australia to playing the game fairly, and for the next 18 months they broadly lived up to that resolution without losing their winning ways until the 2005 tour of England. There, in a spectacular series full of captivating cricket, they lost the Ashes for the first time in 16 years, prompting accusations back home that they had gone soft. Determined to regain their former ascendancy, the Australians thereafter played with an aggression that, protestations aside, appeared out of kilter with their new-found ideals. Several players faced disciplinary sanctions, but as far as the team were concerned it was a price worth paying for a record-breaking run of 16 Test wins between 2006 and 2008. It was in the last of those Tests, against India at Sydney, a particularly unsavoury match in which gamesmanship and abuse abounded, that they fell under critical scrutiny. According to defeated Indian captain Anil Kumble, in echoes of Bill Woodfull in 1932/33, there was only one side playing cricket – his side – and, in a significant show of support, most of the Australian public agreed with him. According to Mark Nicholas, the former Hampshire captain turned cricket writer and commentator, Australian captain Ricky Ponting's vision of fair play didn't extend beyond the Australian dressing room. 'His reluctance to connect with views contrary to his own crystallises the problem faced by the game. The players don't fully realise what the true spirit is. "Hard and fair" is a cliché that tells us nothing. They see their approach as the norm. No one has had the guts to suggest otherwise.'[9]

Yet if Australia had violated the spirit of the game with their uncouth behaviour, the Indians were little better. Their disciplinary record was the worst in international cricket over the previous decade, and when the two teams had competed in a recent one-day series in India, Australian all-rounder Andrew Symonds, a man of partial Afro-Caribbean descent, had been subjected to monkey chants by sections of the crowd. Symonds had also allegedly been called a monkey by Harbhajan Singh, India's feisty off-spinner, and during the Sydney Test several Australian fielders were convinced they had heard him repeat the slur. Having had Darren Lehmann, one of their players, suspended for using racist language in a match against Sri Lanka in 2003, the Australians were insistent that Harbhajan was brought to book now that they were the injured party. Match referee Mike Procter, the former South African all-rounder, found against Harbhajan and suspended him for three Tests, whereupon the Indians took umbrage. They threatened to abandon the rest of the tour unless the ruling was reversed, and Steve Bucknor, one of the umpires responsible for several questionable decisions at Sydney, was replaced for the next Test. By flexing their muscles so crudely, the tourists forfeited much of the sympathy they had previously elicited in Australia, but their brinkmanship had its desired effect. Fearing a massive financial loss, Cricket Australia, the sport's governing body in that country, danced to the tune of the powerful Board of Control for Cricket in India (BCCI), replacing Bucknor and ensuring that Harbhajan was charged with the lesser offence of using offensive language. Left floundering amid the turbulent currents of high politics and finance, the ICC had once again failed to restore cricket's good name.

While the West Indies were shaping the cricketing weather in the 1980s and Australia in the 1990s, England were left to dangle in the wind, their flabby defences cruelly exposed by the power of the elements. After yet another Ashes defeat in 1997, their leading batsman Nasser Hussain lamented the lack of a hard-edged ethos in county cricket and called on his countrymen to emulate the Australians in their approach. Two years later, on becoming captain, Hussain and new coach Duncan Fletcher set about putting the roar back into the English lion (see Chapter 17). A new swagger and aggression appeared, which reaped rich dividends under Hussain's successors, even though it did little to advance the spirit of the game. While England led the world in 2011/12, their style of cricket won overwhelming support from their partisan supporters, but when on the receiving end of a verbal and physical battering by the Australians in Australia in 2013/14 they found that sympathy was in short supply. They had been hoisted by their own petard.

In July 2014, England fast bowler James Anderson, a veteran of many an Ashes altercation, clashed with Indian all-rounder

Ravindra Jadeja during the first Test at Trent Bridge. After a mutual exchange of insults, Indian captain M.S. Dhoni, Jadeja's partner at the time, accused Anderson of physically assaulting Jadeja and, against the advice of his superiors, insisted that he should be charged under the ICC's Code of Conduct. The charge was thrown out by the Australian commissioner because of a lack of evidence, but the case did highlight the latent antagonism between the two sides. While Anderson was encouraged by his captain to continue to display aggression, he did tone down his sledging without any ill effect on his bowling.

On 24 November 2014, the world of cricket was plunged into grief by the tragic death of Australian batsman Phillip Hughes, struck on the neck when playing for South Australia against New South Wales. At his funeral, Australia captain Michael Clarke talked of the need to take stock and learn from Hughes's ability to bring cricketers the world over together. Yet these fine sentiments lacked substance when, days later, Australia played India in an ill-tempered series in which several players from both sides were fined for various misdemeanours. Australian boorishness was again on display during the World Cup Final against New Zealand in March 2015, proving graceless victors against opponents who had rediscovered the art of playing cricket with a smile. Undaunted by their defeat, New Zealand, under charismatic captain Brendon McCullum, vowed to keep playing their brand of enterprising cricket devoid of personal abuse – and on their tour of England that summer, they lived up to expectation, so much so that they won plenty of new friends (see Chapter 18).

Another encouraging pointer was Pakistan's more courtly approach under dignified captain Misbah-ul-Haq – yet these were but flashes of sunlight in an otherwise capricious climate. The unrealistic expectations that Victorian moralists placed upon the game have become increasingly difficult to uphold in an ever more competitive era. With the Spirit of Cricket meaning different things to different people, the game remains riven by moral confusion, reflecting the uncertainties of the age we live in.

Chapter 1

'Well bowled, Harold'

CRICKET has always been a controversial game, and never more so than during England's 1932/33 tour of Australia, when Douglas Jardine's side challenged the very bounds of sportsmanship. The sequence of events of the infamous bodyline series are too well known to recount in detail, but what's of interest is how the ethical foundations of the game cracked all too easily.

Following the evangelical revival in early 19th-century Britain, the cult of athleticism took root in its elite public schools from 1850 onwards, with physical exercise turned into a moral virtue. According to historian Jeffrey Richards, the whole ethos of athleticism could be summed up in three words – 'play the game' – which meant abiding by the spirit of the game, as well as the laws, so as not to gain an unfair advantage over an opponent. 'This morality was synonymous with that of the chivalric knight – magnanimity in victory, dignity in defeat, hatred of injustice, decency and modesty in all things.'[10] Yet according to distinguished sports historian J.A. Mangan, the idealistic world of Tom Brown seldom matched the reality of late 19th-century public schools, where kindness was often lacking. 'The playing fields were the place where public schools put into practice their own distinctive brand of Social Darwinism; in games only the fittest survived and triumphed.'[11]

This paradox between sporting ideal and reality was later re-enacted on many a foreign field. Imperialists saw cricket as a means of civilising the Empire and reconciling the natives to

British rule, but its high moral tone concealed a more ruthless competitive streak. 'Beneath the stuffy, benign image of public service cultivated by British imperialism lay a more strident belief in the mission of the English people,' wrote historian Richard Holt. 'The English, after all, had been the first to personify the nation in the robust shape of John Bull; they were also the first to have a national anthem. Sports were not just the source of high-minded ideals, they were inseparably associated with the more down-to-earth, assertive and patriotic Englishness.'[12] W.G. Grace was an English national hero not because of his moral conscience but because of his forceful personality and will to win. According to Simon Rae, one of Grace's biographers, it was his highly competitive cricketing upbringing in the family home in Gloucestershire that bred in him a single-minded ruthlessness that overrode considerations of propriety and fair play. Notorious for his excessive appealing, abuse of opponents and hectoring of umpires, W.G. never walked, never recalled a batsman even when he knew he had been unfairly dismissed, and would exploit any chink in an opponent's armour to his own advantage. Playing for the Gentlemen against the Players in 1874 and standing at the non-striker's end, he obstructed the bowler, James Lillywhite, as he was about to catch his brother, Fred Grace; in 1893, he persuaded Nottinghamshire batsman Charles Wright to throw him back the ball, only then to get him dismissed for handling the ball; and in 1898, bowling for Gloucestershire, he caught and bowled Essex batsman Percy Perrin on the half-volley.

Grace reserved some of his most blatant gamesmanship for the Australians. At Sydney, playing for his XI against a Combined Fifteen from Victoria and New South Wales in 1873/74, he led his team off in protest when the crowd took exception to some dubious umpiring; then, against Victoria, he so abused the umpire after he'd awarded a boundary to the home team that the umpire refused to continue officiating. 'He had gone to Australia pledging to "maintain the honour of English cricket, and to uphold the high character of English cricketers" and it cannot be said he did either,' wrote Rae. 'In fact he quickly exhausted almost limitless funds of personal goodwill towards him and his team.'[13] In the Oval Test of 1882, Grace ran out Australia's Sammy Jones, who, having completed a single, left his crease to repair the wicket – a breach of sporting etiquette that infuriated Australia's legendary fast bowler Fred Spofforth, especially since he had earlier spared England captain A.N. Hornby from a similar fate. Having told Grace that he was a cheat, Spofforth then decimated England for the second time in the match, his 7–44 propelling Australia to a historic 7-run victory, a win that heralded the birth of the Ashes.

Grace's second tour of Australia, in 1891/92, was no less acrimonious than his first, his lack of courtesy off the field matched by his gamesmanship on it. In the second Test at Sydney, he persuaded the umpire to give debutant Walter Giffen out by claiming a catch on the half-volley, and, when batting, he waved a glove at the umpire in response to a confident lbw appeal. Despite Grace's shenanigans, England lost the match and the Ashes, a blow which did nothing to lighten his mood. Against the Twenty-Two Juniors of Sydney, he so insulted umpire E.J. Briscoe with stinging barbs about his performance that the latter stood down immediately.

Grace's gamesmanship wasn't the only instance of sharp practice in these early contests for the Ashes. According to Australian journalist and cricket writer Malcolm Knox, 'the truth is that Anglo-Australian cricket up to 1914 was cricket in the raw. Cricket was never a gentleman's game. It was a highly competitive affair played with desperation for the highest stakes.'[14] On England's 1901/02 tour of Australia, their captain, Archie MacLaren, refused to lead his team out if New South Wales played their Aborigine fast bowler, Jack Marsh, who was suspected of throwing. During the first Test at Sydney in 1903/04, the controversial run-out of Australia's Clem Hill so irked the crowd that England captain Pelham Warner had to be restrained by his opposite number, Monty Noble, from leading his team off the pitch. In the Headingley Test of 1909, it was the turn of the Australians to be incensed when England's Jack Hobbs was given not out for hitting his wicket, the umpires ruling that he had completed his stroke. The verbal tirade directed at him so disconcerted Hobbs that he gave his wicket away two balls later. In the Sydney Test of 1911/12, England batsman Phil Mead was run out while backing up without a warning; and, during that same series, England fast bowler Frank Foster riled the home crowds with his leg-theory bowling that often struck the Australian batsmen painfully on the upper thigh.

Australia's answer to W.G. Grace was Warwick Armstrong, a 21-stone giant of a man whose prickly personality and uncompromising leadership did much to shape his country's cricket during the early part of the 20th century. 'In what cricket historians now refer to as the Golden Age, the twenty years from 1894, usually depicted as the high summer of amateurism and sporting chivalry, Armstrong was the ultimate pragmatist,' wrote his biographer Gideon Haigh. 'He cheerfully played as a professional when it suited and was not averse to overt gamesmanship, verbal aggression, intimidation of umpires, disputation over playing conditions, even cheating the odd batsman out.'[15] He thought walking (the custom of the batsman leaving the crease voluntarily when out) foolhardy, he frustrated batsmen by bowling wide of the leg stump, and at the Oval in 1909, he kept debutant Frank Woolley waiting for 19 minutes to face his first ball while he bowled looseners, known as trial balls, to fielders. More significant, as captain of the victorious 1921 Australians, he deployed his formidable pair of quick bowlers, Jack Gregory and Ted McDonald, to devastating effect as they battered England into submission, a humiliation not forgotten during the bodyline series over a decade later.

After enduring heavy defeats by Australia in the first three post-war series, England finally regained the Ashes in 1926 and retained them in Australia in 1928/29, before losing them at home in 1930. This defeat was overwhelmingly due to the genius of Don Bradman, Australia's new batting sensation, his series aggregate of 974 runs coming at an average of 139.

Although the figures of Jardine and Bradman loom large in the bodyline saga, they should be seen in the context of a world that

23

had become ever more strident, an Empire under threat from her Dominions and a game that increasingly favoured the batsman at the expense of the bowler. As professionalism took hold in the 1920s and winning became ever more obligatory, batsmen, helped by ever-better wickets to bat on, forfeited adventure for accumulation, increasingly using their pads to combat swing. Confronted with this glut of runs, the bowlers began to fight back. Leg theory – leg-stump bowling to a strongly packed leg-side field to keep scoring in check – and short-pitched bowling became more commonplace by 1930, but up against the genius of Bradman on Australia's featherbed wickets, something more outlandish was needed if England were to bring him to heel.

The instigator behind bodyline was Jardine, England's captain since 1931, whose imperial upbringing in India and classical education at Winchester and Oxford made him the archetypal amateur in appearance and manner, although not in his approach to the game. A cold, aloof man, his ruthless desire to win knew no bounds, especially against the Australians, for whom he harboured a barely concealed antipathy. This antipathy intensified on tour there in 1928/29, when he became the object of vociferous barracking from the partisan home crowds, increasingly keen to assert their own national identity. 'As he strode out to bat, a tall, angular, acidulated and seemingly aloof Englishman, with a gaudy cap rampant and a silk handkerchief knotted around his throat,' wrote Jack Fingleton, the Australian batsman turned journalist, 'he walked into the vision of many Australians as the very personification of the old-school tie.'[16]

Jardine hadn't played against Bradman in the 1930 Tests, but, believing him to be suspect against the high-rising ball, not least against fast bowler Harold Larwood during his 232 on a drying wicket in the Oval Test, he hatched a plan in concert with Larwood and his opening partner, Bill Voce.

Although leg theory and short-pitched bowling had been on the rise, the novelty of Jardine's tactics lay in bowling at the head and upper body to a close leg-side field, waiting for the catch from the defensive prod, in addition to having two men back for the hook. For these tactics to succeed, it needed bowlers of raw pace and relentless accuracy, and in Larwood and Voce, both ex-miners, Jardine had the perfect practitioners. Larwood was one of England's greatest-ever bowlers, combining a perfect action and phenomenal speed with swing, bounce and accuracy. A success in Australia in 1928/29, he had toiled against Bradman at home in 1930 and was clamouring for revenge against a batsman he didn't like. His partner, Voce, was less hostile – but his left-arm in-swingers, delivered from a great height, and the bounce he extracted, made him no soft touch. With support from the pace of Gubby Allen, the Australian-born Middlesex amateur who refused to bowl bodyline, and Yorkshireman Bill Bowes, combined with Hedley Verity's left-arm spin, this was a formidable England attack.

Given Jardine's hard-nosed character and steely 'professional' resolve, his attitude wasn't entirely surprising. More enigmatic was the role of manager Pelham Warner, a former captain of victorious MCC teams that toured Australia in 1903/04 and 1911/12, the chairman of the England selectors and self-proclaimed guardian of the game's best traditions. When Bowes caused ructions at the Oval in August 1932 by bowling bodyline at Surrey's great maestro, Jack Hobbs, then aged 49, Warner shared in the general indignation. 'I am a great admirer of Yorkshire Cricket,' he wrote in the *Morning Post* the next morning. 'I love their keenness and the zest with which they play, but they will find themselves a very unpopular side if there is a repetition of Saturday's play. Moreover, these things lead to reprisals, and when they begin goodness knows where they will end.'[17]

Later Warner was to pen a more damning critique in *The Cricketer*, the magazine he'd founded in 1921.

> Bowes should alter his tactics. He bowled with five men on the on side and sent down several very short-pitched balls which frequently bounced head high and more. That is not bowling. Indeed, it is not cricket, and if all fast bowlers were to adopt his methods there would be trouble and plenty of it.[18]

Warner's hostility to Bowes didn't prevent him from picking him for Australia, and once there he made little effort to stop the bodyline tactics. Some historians have attributed this inaction to Warner's loyalty to Jardine and MCC; others have depicted him as a duplicitous personality quite willing to ditch his ideals in pursuit of the victory he craved. Whatever the case, his inertia greatly undermined his reputation.

Bodyline made its first appearance in Australia against an Australian XI at Melbourne, the penultimate match before the first Test, in which neither Woodfull, the Australian captain, nor Bradman made much of an impact against Larwood and Voce. Larwood was rested for the next match against New South Wales, but his absence provided few consolations to the home team as they were pummelled by Voce, many taking painful blows on the body. Jack Fingleton, opening for New South Wales, recalled several members of the MCC close-in fielders offering condolences to his team-mates, 'but a continuation of such courtesies would, in the circumstances, have been hypocritical and embarrassing to the giver and receiver alike.' He battled through his ordeal to make a gritty undefeated century, but his achievement was overshadowed by a feeling of hurt at the methods employed by his opponents. 'It was the consciousness of a crashed ideal.'[19]

'I was revolted by that particular day's play,' recalled Herbert Evatt, the renowned Australian High Court judge and later leader of the Australian Labor Party. 'It made me feel that I never afterwards wanted to see a single day's play of that series.'[20]

It was a feeling shared by Fingleton's mother. A dedicated follower of the game, she refused to watch another day that summer, including her son's first Test against England.

The first Test at Sydney saw Australia, without Bradman because of illness, exposed to the full force of bodyline, and, despite a magnificent undefeated 187 from Stan McCabe in the first innings, they lost by ten wickets. *The Referee* (Sydney) accused Warner of double standards and called on him to 'stop this short-pitched body theory that he so strongly abhorred before he left England', but, for the most part, the Australian reaction was relatively restrained, not least from the Australian Board of Control, which rejected Bradman's plea to 'do something'.

The critics of bodyline lay low after the second Test at Melbourne, which Australia won by 111 runs. The match was notable for the return of Bradman, who overcame his first-ball dismissal in the first innings with an undefeated century in the second. On a docile wicket that doused the fires of the England attack, Australia gained a narrow first-innings lead and after Bradman's century, and, led by leg-spinner Bill O'Reilly, who took ten wickets in the match, they dismissed England for 139.

With the series all square, the teams resumed battle at Adelaide, the city of churches, in one of the most unpleasant Tests of all time. The trouble began on the second afternoon when Australia, on the fastest pitch so far in the series, began their reply to England's 341. A vicious delivery from Larwood at the end of his second over hit Woodfull over the heart. As the Australian captain doubled up in pain and the 50,962 crowd turned hostile, Jardine walked up the wicket to Larwood to congratulate him in full earshot of Bradman, the non-striker. Yet what really riled them was the switch to the bodyline field at the beginning of Larwood's next over, the first ball knocking Woodfull's bat out of his hands. As Larwood and Voce kept up the intimidation, hitting Woodfull several more times, the England players feared that the fury of the crowd would give rise to a riot. It said something for the conventions of the time that at no stage did anyone enter the playing arena.

After his dismissal for 22, Woodfull, the Methodist schoolmaster and devotee of Corinthian values, was nursing his injuries in the Australian dressing room when he was visited by Warner to sympathise with his lot. 'I don't want to speak to you, Mr Warner,' Woodfull told him. When Warner asked why, he replied, 'There are two teams out there; one is playing cricket, the other is not. It is too great a game to spoil. The matter is in your hands.'[21]

It was a crushing rejoinder to one of the game's white knights. 'Warner – the epitome of all the game stood for,' wrote his biographer Gerald Howat, 'the quintessence of sportsmanship and high ideals; the chevalier of cricket – had been identified with a rejection of the very standards he had devoted his life to upholding.'[22]

Woodfull's altercation with Warner, leaked to the press, intensified anti-English feeling when the match resumed after the weekend. Australia, 109/4 overnight, rallied through Bill Ponsford and wicketkeeper Bertie Oldfield until the latter, on 41, sustained a hairline fracture of the temple when trying to hook Larwood, then bowling to an orthodox field. As the highly popular Oldfield staggered from the crease, clutched his head in both hands and fell to his knees, pandemonium broke out around the ground as 32,000 spectators gave vent to their fury. Thankfully, Oldfield was soon back on his feet and able to walk unassisted from the ground.

The barracking and abuse continued throughout the rest of the Australian innings, and intensified when Jardine walked out to open England's second innings in his multi-coloured Harlequins cap and silk cravat. Undeterred by his hostile reception, Jardine composed a sedate 56 as England scored 412, setting Australia 532 to win. Despite a thrilling cameo of 66 by Bradman, making room for himself outside the leg stump to hit into the wide open spaces on the off side, and a spirited undefeated 73 from Woodfull, the home side lost by 338 runs.

The fury of the Adelaide crowd was matched by the indignation of the Australian press. 'Today the man who plays cricket in a fine sportsmanlike way that nobody in the world can excel is W.M. WOODFULL, captain of the Australian Eleven,' reported the tabloid newspaper *Smith's Weekly*. 'All the honours are with him and none are with Warner or Jardine.'[23]

In response to this pressure, the Australian Board of Control released the contents of a cable it had sent to MCC deploring the tactics of its team.

> Body-line bowling has assumed such proportions as to menace the best interests of the game, making protection of the body by the batsman the main consideration. This is causing intensely bitter feeling between the players as well as injury. In our opinion it is unsportsmanlike. Unless

stopped at once, it is likely to upset the friendly relations existing between Australia and England.[24]

According to Fingleton, even Australians recoiled at the clumsy, blustering manner in which the Australian Board of Control cast aspersions on MCC's sportsmanship, since the charge of bodyline was a vague one, and MCC, true to form, bristled at such allegations.

In an age of sparse communication – letters took the best part of a month to arrive, there were no radio or television broadcasts, and no English national daily sent out their own cricket correspondents because of economic austerity – it was difficult for people back home to ascertain the true nature of bodyline and the furore it generated. Jack Hobbs, working for the *News Chronicle* and *The Star*, was the one witness who could have opened the nation's eyes to its perils – but, reluctant to criticise Jardine, his county captain, and his fellow professionals, not least in the face of Australian protests which he found irksome, he chose to overlook such matters. Bruce Harris, the correspondent of the London *Evening Standard*, knew little about cricket, and, as an apologist of Jardine, he tended to follow his line. *Reuters* correspondent Gilbert Mant was privately critical but kept his reports strictly factual, and although Warwick Armstrong, the former Australian captain, expressed reservations in the London *Evening News*, mainly on aesthetic grounds, his main gripe concerned the failure of Bradman and his team-mates to combat Larwood. The *Daily Herald* accused Australia of being poor losers, and Percy Fender, Jardine's predecessor as captain of Surrey, writing in the *Daily Telegraph*, dismissed the charge that bodyline was dangerous; it was just that the Australians couldn't play it.

The Times pronounced rather pompously: 'It is inconceivable that a cricketer of JARDINE's standing, chosen by the MCC to captain an English side, would ever dream of allowing or ordering the bowlers under his command to practise any system of attack that, in the time-honoured English phrase, is not cricket.'[25]

Unwilling to grasp the gravity of the situation confronting it, Lord's – recalling the damage inflicted on English cricket by

Gregory and McDonald in 1921 and assuming the Australian Board was making a mountain out of a molehill – replied in suitably lofty tones.

> We, Marylebone Cricket Club, deplore your cable. We deprecate your opinion that there has been unsportsmanlike play. We have fullest confidence in captain, team and managers and are convinced that they would do nothing to infringe either the laws of Cricket or the spirit of the game. We have no evidence that our confidence has been misplaced. Much as we regret accidents to Woodfull and Oldfield, we understand that in neither case was the bowler to blame. If the Australian Board of Control wish to propose a new Law or Rule, it shall receive our careful consideration in due course.
>
> We hope the situation is not now as serious as your cable would seem to indicate, but if it is such to jeopardise the good relations between English and Australian cricketers and you consider it desirable to cancel the remainder of the programme we would consent, but with great reluctance.[26]

Confronted by MCC's uncompromising response and reluctant to abandon a tour which had captured the public's interest and filled their coffers, the Australian Board felt compelled to partially back down. On the day before the fourth Test at Brisbane, they sent a second cable withdrawing their comments about 'unsportsmanlike play' and reiterated that the tour would continue, which it subsequently did with relatively little discord in comparison with Adelaide.

After England won the final Test at Sydney by eight wickets to take the series 4–1, Woodfull congratulated Jardine on his success, but not one of his players attended the farewell dinner for the England team or saw them off at the quayside. 'It was a jarring reminder of the bitterness that had marred the tour,' wrote Laurence Le Quesne in his book *The Bodyline Controversy*, 'and it can have left the minds of few of the MCC party entirely at peace.'[27]

'At the end of that season the nerves of all the Australian batsmen had worn thin,' wrote Fingleton. 'I do not think there was one single batsman who played in most of those bodyline games who ever afterwards recaptured his love for cricket.'[28]

Jardine returned to England to a hero's reception, with several MCC committee members there to greet him on his arrival at Euston station. He was reappointed captain of England for that summer's series against the West Indies, and was cheered to the rafters when he walked out to bat for MCC against the tourists at Lord's. Convinced that bodyline was a figment of Australian imagination, MCC dismissed the Australian Board's attempt in April 1933 to amend Law 48 outlawing deliveries intended to intimidate or injure batsmen. The Board continued to press their case, however, their persistence paying off as the exposure of the English public to the perils of bodyline that summer induced a change of opinion.

Aside from the West Indian quicks, Learie Constantine and Manny Martindale, the main exponent of bodyline was Bill Bowes. Having infuriated the crowd at Cardiff by hitting Glamorgan batsmen Maurice Turnbull and J.C. Clay, Bowes caused further uproar by knocking Lancashire's Frank Watson senseless at Old Trafford. In the Varsity match at Lord's, Cambridge fast bowler Kenneth Farnes, bowling bodyline, hit several of his opponents, including Peter Oldfield, the Oxford number eleven, bowled off his jaw, and opener David Townsend, who broke his wicket after being struck on the neck. Seven MCC members, including the cricket journalist Sir Home Gordon, wrote to *The Times* to denounce such tactics and warn that they risked destroying the spirit of the game.

Three weeks later, during the second Test against the West Indies at Old Trafford, public opinion took a further turn when Constantine and Martindale bowled bodyline. Jardine stood firm with a courageous century, but Walter Hammond, England's premier batsman, wasn't so fortunate. Hit on the chin as well as the back as he ducked into a ball from Constantine, he expressed his disgust at these tactics as he left the crease. *Wisden* called this kind of bowling 'objectionable' and assumed that those watching it for the first time would have deemed it contrary to the spirit of the game. Warner, no longer a Test selector, also spoke out. Writing to the *Daily Telegraph*, he regretted that the West Indies had resorted to bodyline, which he described as intimidation that often gave rise to serious injury. He accepted that bodyline was legal but questioned its value if it generated controversy and bred ill-feeling, as it had between England and Australia. Should it continue, he thought, the courtesy of combat would disappear from the game and would be replaced by anger, hatred and retribution.

Fourteen out of 17 county captains agreed not to employ bodyline, and celebrated journalist Neville Cardus wrote that he had yet to meet a cricketer that summer who wanted to see that form of attack. 'Everyone is getting to hate the sight of the leg-trap and the short bumper. Bodyline would vanish tomorrow if cricketers here governed the game.'[29] At a joint meeting of the Advisory County Cricket Committee and the Board of Control for Test Matches, attended by the county captains, that November, MCC accepted that any direct attack by the bowler upon the batsman would be declared an offence against the spirit of cricket. The Australian Board pushed for something stronger, but the most that MCC would countenance was a formal understanding that the Australian tour of England in 1934 would be played in the right spirit.

Such an understanding was helped by Jardine's resignation from the England captaincy, after leading MCC in India in 1933/34, on the premise that he had no wish to play against the Australians. With Larwood also unavailable because of his refusal to renounce bodyline, as requested by the president of MCC, the series passed off without serious incident. Australia, again under Woodfull, won 2–1, but they did experience hostility in their match against Nottinghamshire, not least from the crowd. Infuriated by MCC's shabby treatment of their hero Larwood, they rallied fully behind Voce, who took 8–66 in Australia's first innings bowling bodyline. When he began their second innings with another bombardment, Woodfull told the Nottinghamshire secretary that the county had breached the agreement underpinning that summer's tour. If Voce took the field the next day, Australia would refuse to play, an ultimatum with which Nottinghamshire complied. The county did resort to one final salvo of bodyline, against Middlesex at Lord's – Voce knocking Len Muncer, a lower-order batsman, unconscious and hitting another player. Appalled by such pugilism, the Middlesex committee protested vehemently, and the recriminations were such that Arthur Carr, Nottinghamshire's uncompromising captain, was dismissed and the county committee resigned. More importantly, MCC finally convinced themselves that legislation was necessary to outlaw this dangerous form of fast bowling. An amendment was made to the law banning 'persistent and systematic bowling of fast short-pitched balls at the batsman standing clear of his wicket'.

MCC gave umpires the power to deal with bodyline. They ruled that once the umpire adjudged a bowler to be bowling in such a manner he should caution him, and should he continue to transgress, the umpire would instruct the captain to take him off immediately and prevent him from bowling again during that innings.

Although the bodyline series stands out as the most notorious in the history of cricket, it shouldn't be seen entirely in isolation. While Larwood and Voce's assault on Australia was seen by many Englishmen as payback for the punishment meted out to them by Gregory and McDonald in 1920/21, so its legacy remained a powerful one. Bradman never forgot the humiliations of that summer, and once he had the necessary firepower to retaliate in the form of Ray Lindwall and Keith Miller post-war, he showed little mercy to England's batsmen. Other countries were to feel the full force of the whirlwind until they could respond in kind, such as the havoc wreaked by the West Indian quicks on all and sundry during the 1980s.

Chapter 2

Bradman's Revenge

FOLLOWING the rumpus over bodyline, the announcement that Gubby Allen had been appointed captain of the MCC team to tour Australia in 1936/37 was warmly welcomed by the new Australian captain, Bradman. Not only was Allen his friend, he was a fourth-generation Australian, born in Sydney, who'd publicly dissented from bowling bodyline. A pillar of the Lord's establishment since his appointment to the MCC committee, he fully appreciated that the ultimate purpose of the tour was to bury the hatchet of the previous one. For that reason, he was reluctant to pick Voce, but, deferring to the wishes of the selectors, he insisted that the Nottinghamshire fast bowler apologise for past misdemeanours and promise to avoid any repetition of 1932/33.

Despite criticism in certain quarters orchestrated by Jardine in the *Evening Standard*, Allen kept the faith and appeared rewarded when Voce took 6–41 in Australia's first innings in the first Test. On a rain-affected wicket, he took another four wickets in the second innings, including Bradman for nought, as Australia were skittled for 58.

Another rain-affected wicket in the second Test at Sydney, a second duck for Bradman and more wickets for Voce culminated in another overwhelming victory for England, giving them a 2–0 lead in the series. The local critics were unimpressed with their team, and Bradman's captaincy came under fierce scrutiny as rumours circulated of dissent in the camp, but he deflected some of the criticism by declaring that not enough credit had been given to the quality of England's performance, his magnanimity much appreciated by Allen.

In the third Test at Melbourne, it was England's turn to suffer from the elements in their first innings. After they had reduced Australia to 181/6 at the end of the first day, heavy overnight rain made the pitch close to unplayable, and, after the home side declared at 200/9, England struggled to 76/9 before Allen called a halt, hoping to give the home side a taste of the afternoon's horrors. His ruse came too late, as Bradman sent in his numbers ten and eleven to weather the final overs and held himself back to number seven when the match resumed after the weekend. At 97/5, England appeared back in the game, but the Australian captain had other ideas. Sharing a partnership of 346 for the sixth wicket with Fingleton on a much-improved wicket, his 270 ensured his side an overwhelming victory.

Unenterprising batting by England in their first innings on a perfect Adelaide wicket lost them the early initiative in the fourth Test. Establishing a narrow lead, they had to contend once again with Bradman. As he rose to the challenge, his 212 in Australia's second innings and sublime spin bowling by 'Chuck' Fleetwood-Smith, who took ten wickets in the match, enabled his team to square the series.

Prior to the final Test, MCC took exception to some short-pitched bowling by Victoria's Laurie Nash, who had previously never played for the state, and when he was drafted into the Test squad Allen warned Bradman about a bouncer war. Bradman assured Allen this wouldn't happen under his captaincy, and the Test passed off without incident. Taking advantage of a placid Melbourne wicket, Australia batted first and scored 604 (Bradman a vintage 169) before rain consigned England to bat on a drying wicket. Undone by O'Reilly, they lost by an innings, a disappointing end to a series that had begun so auspiciously. Now it was the turn of the crestfallen Allen to compliment his opponents on their victory, the first time that a side had emerged triumphant after being 2–0 down, and pay tribute to Bradman's magnificent form with the bat. King George VI sent congratulations to the captains on the excellent spirit in which the Tests had been played, and Lord Gowrie, the governor-general of Australia, was similarly effusive about the level of sportsmanship by both sides, which had gone a long way towards re-establishing Anglo-Australian relations.

On 3 September 1939, British prime minister Neville Chamberlain declared war on Germany, and one hour later Robert Menzies, his Australian counterpart, followed suit out of loyalty to Britain. In a war where close to one million Australian men and women served – in Europe, north Africa, south-east Asia and the Pacific – and over 50,000 were killed or wounded, nearly all the cricketing fraternity enlisted. War brought the two nations closer together, and this shared camaraderie seeped through to the cricket field with the coming of peace in Europe. In this climate of celebration and hope, the Victory Tests between England, captained by Walter Hammond, and the Australian Services XI, captained by Lindsay Hassett, their one Test player, perfectly reflected the national mood. Keen to restore a semblance of normality to their lives, vast crowds flocked to the Tests, the first at Lord's 11 days after VE Day. Included in the Australian side was medium-pacer Graham Williams, who had just been released after four years as a prisoner-of-war in Germany. His plight had become common currency, and when this emaciated figure, 68lb below weight, came in to bat, Lord's rose to him in a show of silent solidarity that brought tears to the eyes of fellow pilot Keith Miller.

For all the intense rivalry on the field – the series was drawn 2–2 – the matches were played with a smile, not least by Australia's new sporting prodigy, Keith Miller, one of the most charismatic cricketers ever to grace the game. Not only did both teams change in the same dressing room, they travelled to the ground together and stayed at the same hotel. By common consent, this was cricket at its most rewarding and a model for how future Ashes series should be conducted. 'This is cricket as it should be,' commented Hassett. 'These games have shown that international cricket can be played as between real friends – so let's have no more talk of "war" in cricket.'[30]

Such hopes ignored the weight of history because, since 1880, the fight for the Ashes, the greatest prize in cricket and one of the greatest in all sport, had left little room for sentiment, especially once Bradman decided to continue playing. A fierce competitor at whatever he turned his hand to, Bradman's war as an invalid – he was discharged from the Australian Army in 1941 with acute fibrositis – and stockbroker in Adelaide had left him immune to the camaraderie of service life that had united so many English and Australian cricketers. With bodyline and England's mammoth 903/7 at the Oval in 1938 still fresh in his memory, Bradman had a few scores to settle once normal business resumed in 1946/47. MCC's tour of Australia was dubbed the 'goodwill tour', but the simmering animosity between Bradman and his opposite number, Hammond, soon put paid to that, especially given the events of the first morning of the first Test at Brisbane.

Entering at 9/1, Bradman looked a shadow of himself as he progressed tentatively to 28 before cutting a wide ball from Voce to Jack Ikin at second slip. In the opinion of the England team, and many Australians, it was unquestionably a clean catch, but Bradman, convinced that it was a bump ball, stayed rooted to the crease and was given not out on appeal by umpire George Borwick, a reprieve that infuriated his opponents. Hammond told Bradman in no uncertain terms what he thought of his behaviour at the end of the over, and any hope of a new *entente cordiale* in Ashes cricket vanished in that one instance.

To add to England's woes, Bradman went on to score 187 out of an Australian total of 645, at which point a fierce tropical storm on the third day, and an even more ferocious one on the fourth evening, reduced batting to a lottery. On a spiteful wicket left open to the elements, England had to face a revitalised Australian attack led by one of the most formidable combinations of raw pace in Ashes history. At last Bradman had the bowlers to repay England in kind for bodyline, and he wasn't going to miss his opportunity. According to Malcolm Knox in his book *Bradman's War,* Lindwall and Miller proceeded to target Len Hutton, England's premier batsman, and his wounded arm, injured on commando training during the war. Anticipating what lay in store for him as he came out to bat at Brisbane, Hutton told Miller that his wife sent her love, alluding to a friendly encounter between the two families a year earlier. Miller grinned but said nothing before proceeding to bombard the Yorkshireman with bouncers. After dismissing him for seven, he inflicted similar punishment on his friend and fellow serviceman Bill Edrich, who took some 40 blows on the body during his innings of 16, before Miller took pity on him, as he later recalled.

> All the England players were war boys and they were my best mates. [At one point] I'm bowling and there was little Billy Edrich [facing]. He was the toughest little guy you could ever meet, a lovely man, Bill, and he got a Distinguished Flying Cross over Germany in the early part of the war, when it was like winning a Victorian Cross.
>
> And I'm bowling ... and I keep hitting him, ... and so I started to ease up, started to slow down, till in time, thought 'we'll win this anyway and that's it' ... so I slowed down. ...
>
> And when Don says, 'Oh, Nugget [Miller's nickname], bowl faster, it's hard to play that sort of stuff on this pitch ...', I just thought 'We've just finished one war and it's like walking into another war'. And that really turned me completely against Test cricket as it was played then. That took the sting out of me, as far as playing cricket and enjoying it. Test cricket suddenly went from a sport to a war.[31]

According to Fingleton, Lindwall and Miller bowled more bouncers than Larwood and Voce ever did during bodyline, although they weren't directed at the body.

After England were beaten by an innings and 332 runs, they looked for better fortune in the second Test at Sydney. It failed to materialise. Batting first in benign conditions, they failed to take advantage and were dismissed for 255. Rain on the second day forced Australia to bat on a drying wicket. Unable to bat at number three because of a leg strain, Bradman encouraged Sid Barnes,

Australia's opener, to appeal constantly against the light, tactics which incensed the crowd and Hammond. 'It was certainly within the laws of the game,' wrote Charles Williams, one of Bradman's biographers, 'but the intention of the law was equally certainly pushed to the edge.'[32] Eventually the umpires relented, despite there being no obvious deterioration in the light, and England were deprived of helpful bowling conditions. When the match resumed after the rest day, the pitch had improved immeasurably, and Bradman came into his own as he and Barnes both scored 234, putting on 405 for the fifth wicket. With a lead of well over 300, the consensus was that Bradman would declare at the end of the third day, but instead he irked the England dressing room by batting on before declaring at 659/8.

'Don, who had not experienced the horrors of total war, who had not been privileged to witness the average Englishman's stoic reaction to them, was determined to grind his old cricketing enemy into the dust if he could,' wrote eminent Australian cricket writer R.S. Whitington. 'England, if Bradman had his way, was not merely to be defeated but annihilated and humiliated.'[33]

Heavily defeated at Sydney, England did manage draws in the next two Tests at Melbourne and Adelaide, but the latter brought Denis Compton, England's finest batsman after Hutton and a good friend of many an opponent, into conflict with Bradman. As Compton and wicketkeeper Godfrey Evans battled to save the match during an obdurate ninth-wicket partnership in their second innings, Bradman took exception to Compton turning down singles when he spread the field so he, Compton, could keep the strike and protect his partner. When Bradman confronted Compton about this, Compton told the Australian captain that if he set his field properly he would bat normally.

Later, Bradman objected to Compton scuffing up the pitch when advancing down the wicket to spinner Colin McCool, pointing out that Australia still had to bat on the wicket, to which Compton replied: 'I am terribly sorry but I'm playing for our side.'

'Don was the King as far as I was concerned,' Compton later wrote, 'but there was a win-at-all-costs streak in him that could turn him into less than a likeable opponent,'[34] a view with which Evans concurred. 'This tension on the field really grew out of Bradman's interpretation of the spirit of the game. He was out to win, and at all costs.'[35]

Adelaide marked Hammond's last Test against Australia. Well past his pomp, stricken by lumbago and beset by personal problems, he cut a lugubrious figure throughout the tour, disdaining an invitation to dine with Bradman at his home and only speaking to him when tossing. Norman Yardley, the vice-captain, led the side in the fifth Test, a match they lost by five wickets to cap a miserable tour. 'The winning hit closed the nastiest and most acrimonious season I've ever experienced in thirty-nine years of cricket and fifteen years as an umpire,' commented Jack Scott, who announced his retirement from officiating.[36] According to Fingleton, the goodwill series had done little for the spirit of the game and much of this was due to Bradman. 'He was a good and a shrewd leader, but not a generous one ... It was Bradman's job to win for Australia, undoubtedly, but he could have made one or two gestures to such an opposing side. Particularly should he have ordered his fast men, Lindwall and Miller, to cut down the big crop of bumpers.[37] It seemed to me, however, that Bradman, when confronted with an MCC cap, could neither forget nor forgive the bodyline tour.'

Much to the delight of the English public and financially pressed counties, Bradman opted for one final tour there in 1948. The Australians came bearing 17,000 parcels of food to distribute to austerity Britain and were well regarded wherever they went. The fact that they won the Test series 4–0 and completed their five-month tour unbeaten proved a real fillip to Bradman, who didn't allow his attachment to the old country to distract him from his relentless pursuit of victory.

With England lacking fast bowlers to match Lindwall and Miller, Australia were handed a massive boost when MCC changed the new ball law so that a second new ball would become available after 55 overs. This enabled Bradman to unleash Lindwall and Miller with the new ball, then switch to defensive tactics with his support bowlers before they returned fresh with a second new ball.

In the first Test at Trent Bridge, the Australian fast bowlers were soon in their element, dismissing England for 165 before their batsmen spent the best part of two days accumulating a massive first-innings lead. With limited bowling resources at his disposal, England captain Norman Yardley implemented his own version of leg theory to contain Bradman and his vice-captain, Hassett, much to Bradman's displeasure. At one point, he turned to Edrich and remarked, 'This game is developing into a farce.'

'You've got yourself to blame. You started it,' replied Edrich, alluding to Bradman's negative use of Ernie Toshack, in particular, with the old ball.

For all his frustration, Bradman maintained his concentration to reach his century, the slowest of his 29 in Test cricket, as Australia finished on 509. They then took two early wickets before Hutton and Compton offered some resistance. Intent on breaking the partnership before the close of the third day, Miller began bowling four bouncers an over in the fading light, a move that incensed the Trent Bridge crowd, still indignant at the way their hero Larwood had been hounded out of Test cricket post-bodyline. When Miller struck Hutton on the shoulder in the penultimate over, his fifth bouncer in eight balls, the crowd erupted and roundly booed him as he left the field at the close of play. Irked by Bradman's evident pleasure at the discomfort Hutton and he were experiencing, Compton approached the Australian captain in the pavilion afterwards.

> 'Well, Don, I said, with probably more than a touch of sarcasm in my voice, 'I saw you enjoying yourself just now. I can't really understand why and how you were. ... – I thought you used to say that this wasn't the right way to play cricket – bouncers and all that ...'
>
> He wasn't smiling any more. From his answer I had the impression that he was a little uncomfortable but, being Bradman, was very definitely not going to show it. 'You've got a bat in your hand, haven't you,' he answered. 'You should be able to get out of the way of them anyway. ... I

used to love it when I played against bouncers. I used to hook them.'[38]

An appeal by the Nottinghamshire secretary to the crowd for normal civilities to be observed on the match's resumption after the weekend had its desired effect, aside from the occasional bout of exasperation whenever Miller bowled short. On the final day, it needed a vicious Miller bouncer to finally dismiss Compton for 184, hit wicket after slipping when taking evasive action, and break England's resistance. Left a mere 98 for victory, Australia won by eight wickets.

Although Miller was unable to bowl at Lord's, the rest of the attack, led by Lindwall, accounted for England cheaply in both innings, Australia winning by 409 runs. The England selectors responded, as only they sometimes could, by dropping Hutton, a decision that provoked incredulity. In the third Test at Old Trafford, England had the better of the match thanks to another epic century by Compton. Forced to retire hurt early on when hit by a Lindwall bouncer, he returned to the fray at 119/5 and withstood any further punishment that the Australians inflicted upon him. His 145 enabled England to recover to 363 all out.

Throughout the series there had been mutterings about Sid Barnes's position at short leg, perilously close to the bat. The England team thought it gamesmanship designed to distract the batsman, but, with no umpire ruling it unfair play, he continued to stand there in this most exposed of positions. At Old Trafford, his luck ran out when Dick Pollard, the hefty Lancashire tail-ender, smashed a ball into his stomach. He collapsed and had to be carried off by four policemen.

Without Barnes to open, the Australian innings never gained momentum and they were all out for 221. With defeat a distinct possibility, the Australians, led by Miller, who was bowling his first spell since Trent Bridge, retaliated with a fearsome display of short-pitched bowling against England's Cyril Washbrook and Bill Edrich. Edrich thought the Australians overdid the bouncers, but, whatever the rancour on the field, it didn't degenerate into verbal abuse. 'It is in this respect (if only in this respect) that Test cricket of 1948 may be seen as a gentler sport than in later times,' wrote Knox. 'Whatever they felt, players strived to maintain a friendly face. The tenor of the time was to maintain public composure, and the Englishmen saw themselves as proving their moral superiority over Australians by not complaining about the bouncers.'[39]

Although Washbrook and Edrich played England into a winning position, heavy rain washed out play on the fourth day and delayed the start on the fifth, leaving Australia less than three hours to bat, something they easily achieved.

The last two Tests, both won by Australia, passed peacefully enough. The crowd gave Bradman a fitting send-off in his farewell Test at the Oval, their admiration for him rather more pronounced than that of the England players, and he returned home the captain of an invincible team to a knighthood. No cricketer was more deserving of such an accolade in terms of personal accomplishment. His batting stands alone in the game's pantheon, and his record as Australia's captain, unbeaten in five series, ranks among the best – but his ruthless desire to win, while entirely within the laws of the game, wasn't always in its spirit. Those who looked to the resumption of Ashes cricket post-war as an opportunity to inject a more generous tone to the rivalry were to be disappointed. 'It remained a hostile game, a ritualisation of conflict between nations,' wrote Knox. 'For those who did well in it, this was the way it should have been played, and they were glad that it had lost none of its hostility. But that brief moment of hope, embodied in the Victory Tests and the Australian tour of New Zealand in 1945/46, was snuffed out by a reality just as crushing as that which, in the form of the Cold War, snuffed out a generation's ideals of a peaceful post-war world. Old habits die hard.'[40]

The passing of the Australian captaincy from Bradman to Hassett ushered in an era of good feeling, while in no way undermining the competitive nature of the cricket. The Victorian Hassett was a charming, unassuming man with a pawky sense of humour, and the Australian side he led to South Africa in 1949/50 was considered a triumph in every respect. According to Dudley

Nourse, his opposite number, Hassett made his team one of the most popular to grace his country. Despite winning 4–0, they struck up a wonderful camaraderie with their opponents and were the perfect ambassadors both on and off the field.

The goodwill continued when MCC toured Australia in 1950/51. The excellent rapport between Hassett and his rival captain, Freddie Brown, not always the easiest of men, extended to the players on both sides. While Miller's late nights out with Englishmen such as Compton and Evans were the stuff of legend, Arthur Morris struck up an equally firm friendship with England's opening bowler Alec Bedser and his twin brother, Eric. Aside from meeting up every year, they wrote regularly, and when Alec Bedser died in 2010, the 88-year-old Morris flew halfway around the world to speak at his memorial service, bearing a letter from Australian prime minister Julia Gillard to read. She wrote:

> What a wonderful tribute to cricket and the goodwill between England and Australia that two men who began their relationship as on-field adversaries in 1946/47 should become such friends. As you both served the Allied cause in the Second World War, there is little cause for wonder that your cricket on the field was necessarily tempered by what you had seen of the consequences of war. The courtesies of the immediate post-war era are an example to sportsmen of every era as, surely, they are for anyone who is involved in public office. Your generation is properly remembered as heroes. One of the very finest of those heroes you farewell this day.[41]

Despite the occasional umpiring error, the series attracted very little controversy, such was the chivalry on display. Hutton accepted his fate without demur when given out caught off his pad off Jack Iverson in England's first innings in the second Test at Melbourne, and Brown refused to blame the officials for his side's narrow defeat. In the fourth Test at Adelaide, Brown appeared to be out first ball, caught by Miller at short leg, only for Miller to indicate that he'd taken the ball on the half-volley. In the same match, Australian off-spinner Ian Johnson walked for the only time in his career, despite being given not out for a caught-behind, in order to give England fast bowler J.J. Warr his one and only Test wicket; and his team-mate Bill Johnston took pity on Compton, who was experiencing a total run famine in the Tests. 'You poor old cobber. I'll give you one off the mark,' he whispered to the Englishman as he came in to bat in the second innings. He was as good as his word as he served up a rank long-hop, only for Compton to thrash it straight to Sam Loxton at midwicket.

With England unfortunate to be 4–0 down in the rubber and beset by injury, their spirited efforts won the appreciation of the home crowd, and few begrudged them their victory in the final Test in Melbourne, their first against Australia since 1938.

'From my point of view, and the view of the Australian team, this has been the happiest of Test series,' Hassett told the cheering crowds in front of the pavilion. 'Players of both sides mixed together and enjoyed each other's company on and off the field.

'Playing against Brown has been a delight. He deserved all the praise he has received. As a captain to play against, he has been perfect in every sense.'[42]

In 1951/52, Australia hosted John Goddard's West Indians, fresh from having beaten England on tour there in 1950. Despite the 'White Australia' policy, which prohibited coloured immigration, Hassett's side made a point of getting to know their visitors and spend time with them off the field. The mutual respect, however, didn't stop Lindwall and Miller from going about their business. Knowing the strength of the West Indian batting, led by Frank Worrell, Everton Weekes and Clyde Walcott, they were unsparing in the use of the bouncer as they dismissed their opponents relatively cheaply in both innings in the first Test at Brisbane.

A further onslaught by Lindwall and Miller in the second Test at Sydney prompted *Wisden* to complain about their tendency to bowl too short. Their most intimidating spell, however, came in the final Test at Sydney – again won by Australia to take the series 4–1

– when Lindwall bowled four successive bouncers to the injured Weekes. It was an act of hostility that upset West Indian skipper Goddard and drew fire from a host of former Australian players such as Bill O'Reilly, who thought that the umpires should have intervened, and illustrious cricket commentator Alan McGilvray. McGilvray recalled Lindwall taking exception to his criticism and threatening to hit him on the nose. 'Hit me and I'll fall down,' McGilvray replied quietly. 'But I'll get up a gentleman, and you won't be.'

Recognising that his views placed him in a minority of his compatriots, McGilvray continued: 'It is often a source of amazement to me how blind patriotism colours people's thinking on simple matters of right and wrong. I had no doubt in my mind that the treatment Miller and Lindwall dealt to Weekes was wrong in concept and hurtful to the game in its execution. I could find few who agreed with me.'[43]

There was further trouble the following year when Jack Cheetham's South Africans, after winning the second Test at Melbourne, were humbled by Lindwall and Miller in the third Test at Sydney. 'I thought we had come to Australia under a gentlemen's agreement that there would be no bumpers,' manager Ken Viljoen complained to Jack Fingleton after the match. Fingleton replied that the matter had nothing to do with him but he reckoned he knew the person responsible for perpetuating bumpers in Australian cricket. Ironically, South Africa were soon to unearth their own pacemen who could mix it with the best, as a plethora of fast bowlers from Peter Heine through to Dale Steyn would testify.

Hassett's genial leadership helped ensure that all the proprieties were observed during the 1953 Ashes, despite some questionable tactics by England. The appointment of the obdurate Hutton as her first professional captain injected greater resolve into the team. On the receiving end of three successive Ashes defeats, he vowed to play the Australians at their own game with an uncompromising never-say-die approach. Such tenacity enabled England to escape with draws in the second Test at Lord's and in the fourth Test at Headingley when defeat loomed large. While the reprieve at Lord's was down to a gallant fifth-wicket stand between Willie Watson and Trevor Bailey that kept Australia at bay for most of the final day, Headingley was much more controversial.

Trailing for most of the match, a mixture of bad weather and Bailey's defensive batting had prolonged England's second innings into the final afternoon. During this time, the Australians came into conflict with Frank Chester – England's leading umpire, but now past his prime. Already aggrieved by a reprieve that Chester had given England's Reg Simpson when he was clearly run out in the first innings, they were convinced they had Compton caught at slip off Lindwall on the final morning, but Chester (at square leg) ruled that the ball hadn't carried. It wasn't just his decisions that alienated the Australians, it was the sneering manner with which he dismissed their appeals, and Hassett requested that he should not be appointed for the final Test, a request MCC adhered to.

At Headingley, Australia needed 177 to win in 115 minutes. (There were no mandatory 20 overs in the final hour then.) They fairly took to their task. After 70 minutes, they had scored 111/3, at which point, with a further 66 needed in 45 minutes, Bailey entered the attack and bowled wide down the leg side to a packed on-side field. Already exasperated by Bailey's time-wasting when batting, the Australians were disgusted by his latest ploy. Unable to hit much of his bowling – he conceded just nine runs in six overs – they finished 30 runs short at 147/4. Although they joined the England team for a post-match drink, they felt cheated of victory and, according to Compton, they had every right to be. 'It wasn't cricket. The Aussies were furious. Their anger was justified.'[44]

The Australian mood didn't improve when they saw the wicket for the fifth and final Test at the Oval. On a strip prepared specifically for England spinners Jim Laker and Tony Lock, Hassett's men capitulated to them in their second innings, their sense of grievance heightened by their suspicion that Lock had thrown them out with his quicker ball. After England's win by eight wickets to regain the Ashes for the first time in 19 years, Hassett was the essence of grace in his post-match speech on the balcony, but in private Australia once again felt hard done by. A dressing-room clock was smashed as they drowned their sorrows in copious quantities of champagne.

Following their triumph over Australia, England's tour to the West Indies that winter was given added billing. Given their 3–1 defeat by the West Indies at home in 1950 and the formidable challenge that awaited them, the selectors, unlike on previous tours to the Caribbean, selected their strongest side apart from the unavailable Alec Bedser.

With tensions running high in the Caribbean because of the growing movement for independence from the mother country, in addition to traditional island rivalries, the tour called for the highest degree of tact and diplomacy. Unfortunately, with a weak player-manager in Charles Palmer and an overwrought captain in Hutton, the leadership failed to rise to the occasion. With his siege mentality, Hutton discouraged his players from socialising with the opposition, and their churlish response to traditional West Indian hospitality conveyed a very bad impression. 'Never once, however, did the members of the MCC party show that they wanted our hospitality, and their attitude distressed us beyond words,' wrote Worrell, a staunch Anglophile from his time in the Lancashire League.[45]

This insular attitude helped promote a critical view of all things West Indian, from the organisation to the crowds and, most important of all, the umpires. By no means was all the umpiring poor, but with officials at the mercy of volatile crowds – Jamaican umpire Perry Burke's family were attacked after he had given out local hero J.K. Holt Jr in the first Test at Kingston – it isn't surprising that some erred in favour of the home team.

That said, MCC did themselves no favours by overreacting to decisions and by their general petulant behaviour both on and off the field. One of the worst offenders was fiery Yorkshire fast bowler Fred Trueman, on his first tour and with a point to prove. Against Combined Parishes in Jamaica, he upset the locals by hitting their idol George Headley, brought home from the Birmingham League by popular demand at a cost of over £1,000, and was given a police escort as he left the field.

Headley's bruised arm kept him out of the first of two matches against Jamaica. Returning for the second one, he again was shown no mercy by Trueman as he gave him plenty of short stuff. 'The crowd ain't going to like that, man,' Headley told him. 'No, but it'll go down a storm in Sheffield,' Trueman replied.

Later, during the first Test at Kingston, Trueman compounded his felony by bowling several bouncers at the 44-year-old shortly after he came to the crease. A shadow of the great player he had been in the 1930s, Headley was twice dismissed cheaply by Lock, in the second innings to his quicker ball, which led to Lock being no-balled for throwing shortly afterwards.

Soundly defeated in the first two Tests and slated for their ultra-cautious approach, England resolved to be more decisive from then on. They beat British Guiana by an innings, but controversy once again predominated when Trueman took exception to Cec Kippins's umpiring. Unhappy at the standard of umpiring in the game, Hutton asked that neither official should stand in the Georgetown Test. His request was granted, and their replacements, models of impartiality, were most unfortunate to be the catalyst for an ugly riot as the West Indies struggled to stay in the game. Replying to England's 435, the home side had slumped to 139/7 before an eighth-wicket stand of 99 between the injured Holt and local hero Clifford McWatt gave them hope. With many a bet dependent on the 100 partnership, McWatt's dismissal, run out going for the elusive run, upset the highly partisan crowd. Bottles were hurled towards the square-leg umpire, who had rightly given McWatt out, the game was halted and mounted police moved in, but Hutton remained defiant amid the tumult. He refused to leave the field and was rewarded with a further wicket that night. On the fourth day, he made the West Indies follow on and England went on to win the match by nine wickets.

The discord continued in Trinidad when Trueman smashed the jaw of popular leg-spinner Wilf Ferguson in the colony match after words had been exchanged between them. The *Trinidad Guardian* described his action as 'frightfully unsportsmanlike' and the *Evening News of Trinidad* regretted Trueman's failure to apologise.

For this and other misdemeanours, he lost his good-conduct tour bonus and rarely played for England over the next four years.

It was during the fourth Test at Port of Spain that England's petulance was most in evidence. Consigned to field first on a batsman's paradise, they appeared to have made an important breakthrough in the final over before lunch when opener Holt edged Compton's googly to Tom Graveney at slip. The catch looked obvious enough, but Holt refused to walk and umpire Ellis Achong gave him not out, much to the disgust of the England players. Graveney threw the ball to the ground and swore; Compton waved his arms and berated the umpire, reactions which affronted the crowd and the umpire, who filed a formal complaint. When they further blotted their copybook by making sarcastic asides to Achong's colleague, Ken Woods, after he ruled in Weekes's favour for a caught-behind appeal, their boorishness caused much public comment among locals brought up to believe that English cricketers were perfect gentlemen. Sir Errol Dos Santos, the president of the West Indies Cricket Board, expressed surprise at their demeanour, and, in an open letter to Hutton in the *Trinidad Guardian*, Yorkshire journalist J.S. Barker, by then a resident of Trinidad, deplored their attitude. 'That England should lose a well-deserved reputation for sportsmanship is a far more serious matter than the loss of a cricket match, even a Test Match, and will be remembered much longer than and in far more important fields of life than the cricket field.'[46]

Barker's view wasn't shared by many of the English journalists, who mostly sympathised with the constraints under which Hutton was operating and applauded his batting, not least his 205 in the final Test at Kingston, which helped England to win by nine wickets and square the series. Yet for all their tribulations and the inconsistency of the umpiring, the disparaging attitude of the England team grated on their hosts. According to Walcott, some of the language directed towards the West Indian players was appalling, and he attributed much of the blame to Hutton for giving his players a licence to offend. 'The reputation for sportsmanship of previous English touring sides lay in tatters by the end of the tour.'[47]

Had West Indians behaved in the same way on tour, he suggested, they would have run the risk of being sent home.

As a postscript to these events, the Australian tour to the West Indies the following year was everything that the MCC tour wasn't. Going out of their way to socialise with their opponents, taking the local journalists into their confidence and respecting the umpiring, Ian Johnson's side proved highly popular, so that even their 3−0 win in the Test series in no way diminished the esteem in which they were held. Gary Sobers, then a young 18-year-old, recalls sharing a room with his good friend Collie Smith before the second Test in Port of Spain when there was a knock on his door and an order to open it. He did so, tentatively, only to find Lindwall and Miller outside inviting them to have a drink and chat. Most evenings thereafter they would repeat the routine, and at the end of the tour Miller gave Sobers his bat.

Following the turmoil in the Caribbean, Hutton's tour to Australia in 1954/55 passed off more smoothly. Due to some excellent umpiring, the potential for controversy was much reduced as England recovered from an innings defeat in the first Test at Brisbane to win the series 3−1. Yet while on-field protocol was observed and players such as Edrich, Compton and Evans resumed their traditional off-the-field revelry with their Australian counterparts, Hutton played hard with his opponents. 'Remember, lad, one day we'll have a fast bowler,' he was heard to mutter at Lindwall during one previous confrontation when he was facing the music, and now that bowler had arrived. Frank Tyson was a 24-year-old tearaway who had shattered the jaw of the doughty Edrich that summer and caused jitters in dressing rooms on the county circuit. Innocuous at Brisbane, he cut his run down and became a different proposition in the next Test at Sydney. Hit in the face by a Lindwall bouncer, he bowled even quicker, although he rarely resorted to bouncers, and in Australia's second innings he won the match for England by taking 6−85.

In the third Test at Melbourne, he was even more fearsome, taking 7−27 in Australia's second innings of 111, giving England victory by 129 runs and a 2−1 lead in the series. With Brian

Statham a wonderful foil at the other end, Hutton was in his element. Taking a leaf out of Bradman's book, he set defensive fields and slowed down the over rate to preserve the energy of his quick bowlers, as well as frustrating Australian stroke-makers such as Neil Harvey. The tactics didn't endear him to his hosts, especially at Melbourne, where, in intense heat, England managed only 54 eight-ball overs on New Year's Day. Throughout the series, England on average managed 11.5 eight-ball overs an hour, the lowest ever in Tests to that time, compared with Australia's 14 an hour. In the fourth Test at Adelaide, notable for England's five-wicket win to retain the Ashes, their over rate deteriorated even further, with Hutton repeatedly stopping Tyson just before he began his run-up to make a field change. Even some of the England players thought that their captain had overstepped the mark, but Hutton was unrepentant. In a press conference at Adelaide, he rejected any criticism, pointing out that he was merely giving his young bowlers advice with the field placing, something that Bradman himself had done.

Although the 1956 Ashes series, won by England 2–1, was dominated by crumbling wickets ideally suited to their top-flight spinners Jim Laker and Tony Lock, the emphasis on raw pace continued throughout the 1950s. England had been given a taste of the South African opening pair, Peter Heine and Neil Adcock, in 1955, and they proved even more formidable on their own patch in 1956/57. According to Peter May, England's captain between 1955 and 1961, they were the most hostile pair of bowlers he ever faced. Their aggression with the ball matched their combative personalities, especially Heine, who was one of the game's great vocal abusers. 'I want to hit you, Bailey, I want to hit you over the heart,' he informed the England batsman during a battle of wills. On another occasion he said to Bailey's opening partner, Peter Richardson, 'Get up. I want to knock you down again,' after he'd flattened him. Having struck Laker a stinging blow on the shoulder, he trenchantly inquired, 'Have I hurt you?' to which Laker replied, 'I'll hit you over the head with the bloody bat if you do that again,' a crude choice of words which he always regretted.

Although South African hospitality proved generous in the extreme, the animosity of some of the home team and some indifferent umpiring contributed to the ill-feeling, in the worst series that Laker ever played in.

Brighter skies dawned the following year when Ian Craig's Australians toured South Africa, partly because of the gentlemanly restraint of South African captain Clive van Ryneveld. He refused an opportunity to run out Neil Harvey in the Durban Test after off-spinner Hugh Tayfield had given the impression that a ball that Harvey had glanced had run over the boundary; and he limited his quick bowlers to one bouncer an over, much to their consternation. With South Africa two down in the series, Heine and Adcock approached the final Test at Port Elizabeth in more aggressive vein. Having hit three Australian batsmen in the first innings, they were at their most intimidating in the second innings, when Australia needed a mere 68 to win. Adcock's first over contained three successive vicious bumpers to opener Colin McDonald, and, after a warning from the umpires to ease up, he then produced another unplayable delivery to have him caught. The onslaught continued until van Ryneveld, after consulting with the umpires, told his bowlers to curtail the short stuff. Later, after Australia had won by eight wickets, he apologised to his opponents.

Exceeding all these fast bowlers in ferocity was Roy Gilchrist, a temperamental Jamaican from humble stock who played 13 Tests for the West Indies. According to Sobers, he hated batsmen and delighted in knocking them down. In the fourth Test against England at Headingley in 1957, he greeted Trueman with a terrifying bouncer that whistled past his nose and rendered him speechless. Even more lethal than his bouncer was the beamer he bowled on occasions, and, having terrorised the Indians on tour there in 1958/59, he was sent home in disgrace by his captain, Gerry Alexander, for bowling beamers at Swaranjit Singh, a team-mate of Alexander's at Cambridge. Gilchrist, aged only 24, never played for his country again. It was the beginning of a more turbulent period for cricket as throwing became a running sore within the game.

Chapter 3

The Throwing Controversy

'**C**HUCKING is cricket's most controversial word, a synonym for unfair play,' wrote Bobby Simpson, the Australian captain between 1963 and 1967 and from 1977 to 1978, in his autobiography. 'To brand a bowler a chucker is to cast a shadow of doubt on the man's sense of sportsmanship.'[48]

Throwing had reared its head intermittently through cricket's long history ever since the professional Tom Walker was criticised by Hambledon for his illegal action in the 1780s. Kent farmer John Willes left Lord's in a huff in 1822 after being called. The problem re-emerged in the 1880s because umpires and county captains turned a blind eye to those who threw, including C.B. Fry, England's greatest all-round sportsman. In 1897, former Australian fast bowler Fred Spofforth wrote to the *Sporting Life* to assert that throwing was widespread. Drastic action was needed. His clarion call was taken up by *Wisden* editor Sidney Pardon, who pledged his support to any umpire brave enough to take a stand.

One such umpire was Jim Phillips, the Australian-born former Victoria and Middlesex fast bowler, who no-balled Australian fast bowler Ernie Jones during the second Test on MCC's 1897/98 tour – the first time a bowler had been called in a Test. On returning to England in 1898, Phillips also no-balled Fry. His bravery encouraged his English colleagues to be bolder, and Fry was no-balled by three other umpires. Two years later, in 1900, Phillips called Fry again, along with several other offenders including Lancashire's Arthur Mold, the deadliest fast bowler of his generation. That December, a meeting of the county captains at Lord's overwhelmingly declared that Mold's action was illegal, but Lancashire continued to play him the following season. He emerged unscathed until the Somerset match at Old Trafford, in which Phillips was officiating. The umpire promptly no-balled him 16 times, effectively ending his career. Weeks later, MCC decreed that once a bowler had been no-balled for throwing, he couldn't bowl again in the match, and that persistent offenders should be banned at least for a season. That did the trick, for, apart from a couple of isolated cases, throwing disappeared, only to gradually re-emerge in the 1950s as bowlers dragged the back foot to become more accurate, thereby causing the elbow to collapse a little and the arm to crinkle.

Frank Chester had allegedly been instructed by Pelham Warner not to call South Africa's fast bowler Cuan McCarthy for throwing during his country's tour of England in 1951, to prevent any discord between the two nations, although he was called the next year when playing for Cambridge University. Two of England's leading bowlers, Peter Loader and Tony Lock, were known for their suspect actions – the former with his bouncer and yorker, the latter with his quicker ball, which was lethal on soft-turning wickets. Lock was called three times in Surrey's match against the Indians at the Oval in 1952 by former England wicketkeeper Fred Price, and twice during MCC's tour to the West Indies in 1953/54, including once in the first Test. Even in the Surrey dressing room, there were doubts about the legality of Lock's quicker ball, but aside from a touch of leg-pulling about how well he could throw the javelin, his team-mates were careful not to undermine his confidence. According to Laker, 'So many bowlers over the years had got away with throwing or jerking the ball that we decided that we were not going to act as the jury. It was up to the umpires to decide.'[49]

In theory, this was true – but the brave ones, such as Fred Price and Syd Buller, were abused for their pains, and, with little support emanating from the game's authorities, most opted for a quiet life. Besides, they had no wish to deprive a professional of his living, especially if the bowler posed no physical threat or merely threw the occasional ball. Soon after Hutton became captain of England in 1952, he was asked whether he thought Lock's action was 'a little strange'. 'It is,' he warily replied, 'but I think I will beat the Aussies next year with him.'

Hutton knew what he was talking about. England regained the Ashes in the final Test at the Oval very much on the back of Lock's 5–45 in the second innings. Complimented on his gracious concession speech, Australian captain Lindsay Hassett agreed 'considering Lockie threw us out'. 'We all reckoned he threw his express delivery,' recalled Neil Harvey, one of Australia's finest batsman. 'It was like a 90 mph yorker and he used to knock the county blokes left, right and centre.'[50]

It wasn't just MCC that failed to confront throwing. Australian Board chairman Bill Dowling claimed there was no problem in Australia, despite plenty of evidence to the contrary on MCC's disastrous tour there in 1958/59. 'I knew there were illegal bowlers around but like everyone else I left it to everybody else,'[51] admitted Colin Egar, one of Australia's top umpires, while, according to Fingleton, leading officials from Bradman downwards had sat on their hands for far too long.

During MCC's opening first-class match against Western Australia, there were murmurs about the action of Keith Slater, who dismissed captain Peter May twice, the second time for nought with a vicious break-back. The murmurs grew ever louder when the tourists played Victoria and confronted Jim Burke, the Australian opener and occasional off-spinner, and fast bowler Ian Meckiff, who'd made his debut for Australia the previous year. Meckiff's lack of rhythm, the sudden jerk and the inaccuracy all convinced the shocked players that he threw. Godfrey Evans, adamant that something had to be done, approached manager Freddie Brown after the game and suggested that they contact the

Australian Board to apprise them of their views. Brown agreed and promised to have a word with the captain, but May, figuring that Meckiff posed no great threat as a bowler and reluctant to create a diplomatic scene, chose to let sleeping dogs lie, a decision that Evans called the crime of the century.

It was in the New South Wales match that MCC had their first encounter with Gordon Rorke, the giant fast bowler with a dubious action – although he was never called for throwing. Dragging his rear foot several feet over the bowling crease, he bowled the ball from such a height and at such a pace that even the tallest batsmen had trouble playing him. According to Evans, it was 'another example of blatant cheating, which, to our cost, we chose to ignore'.[52] By the time the tourists reached Queensland, Ray Lindwall introduced himself as the 'last of the straight-armers'.

Reputed to be one of the strongest sides ever to have left England for Australia, May's side went into the first Test relatively confident, but, batting first, they were soon in for a shock. Vice-captain Colin Cowdrey recalled that the first ball from Meckiff to England opener Arthur Milton went for four byes down the leg side. The next went straight at first slip. The third knocked his stumps over. 'For the batsmen facing the throwers in that series there were about two balls an over to play at. You never felt that you were building an innings simply because you never saw enough of the ball.'[53] Taxing the patience of the batsmen, Meckiff turned in valuable figures of 3–33 and 2–30 as England, in one of the dullest Tests of all time, struggled in both innings and lost by eight wickets.

In the second Test at Melbourne, England batted first and suffered the worst of all starts until rescued by a fighting century from May. On the second day, he was batting beautifully until, out of the blue, he had his middle stump removed by a thunderbolt from Meckiff that he completely lost from the moment it left his hand. All out for 259, England kept Australia's lead down to 49 thanks to superb bowling from Statham. Within several hours, he was bowling again, after May's team were shot out for 87 by Meckiff, who, urged on by his home crowd, took 6–38. *Daily*

Telegraph cricket correspondent E.W. Swanton said he had never seen anything as blatant as Meckiff's action that afternoon. 'Yet fifty thousand or so Australians roaring away round the ring appeared to have no scruples about it. Hence, perhaps, the phrase "blind patriotism".'[54] Former England players Johnny Wardle, Ian Peebles and Alf Gover were among those in the England press corps who accused Meckiff of throwing, and although the Australian media accused Fleet Street of bleating – they had Lock and Loader after all – Fingleton thought that Meckiff should have been called.

Defeated again by eight wickets, the mood darkened in the England camp as they bemoaned their fate and rued their failure to speak out against Meckiff. In private, May compared the Tests to a 'local darts match', but the nearest the management came to speaking out was a private warning to the Australian Board before the Adelaide Test that Australia was awash with suspect actions and that they intended to deal with the problem on their return home. When Bradman asked Brown whether he thought that the law on throwing should be changed, he said that it should.

Other fast bowlers, such as New Zealand's Gary Bartlett, were suspected of throwing, and MCC, determined to banish all throwers before the Australians toured England in 1961, instructed all umpires to do their duty.

In 1960, the South African tour party to England included Geoff Griffin, a young fast bowler who broke his elbow in an accident at school and was unable to straighten his arm naturally. Fortunate to be selected for the tour, since he had been no-balled for throwing twice at home the previous season, Griffin was called 17 times in three matches by six umpires prior to the second Test at Lord's. During England's first innings, he not only became the first South African to take a hat-trick in a Test and the first cricketer to take a Test hat-trick at Lord's, he was also no-balled 11 times by umpire Frank Lee. Worse was to come in an exhibition match following the early conclusion of the Test. This time Griffin was no-balled persistently by umpire Buller, which spelt the end of his Test career. He moved to Rhodesia, but, after being repeatedly no-balled against North Eastern Transvaal in a Currie Cup match two years later, he was forced to retire.

Griffin's humiliation at the hands of England's umpires, and the likely fate that awaited Meckiff in England the next year, gave added significance to the meeting of the Imperial Cricket Conference in 1960. The previous year, Bradman had been elected chairman of the Australian selectors, and so seriously did he view the situation that he and Dowling attended in person (they were normally represented by local proxies). After endless discussion and films of dubious actions, the delegates agreed to reword Law 26 to provide a more precise definition of throwing, forbidding the straightening of the arm at the instant of the ball's delivery, and to change the no-ball rule to eliminate dragging. On returning to Australia, Bradman was elected unopposed as chairman of the Australian Board and he agreed with the chairman of the England selectors, Gubby Allen, that any bowler with a suspect action wouldn't be called publicly during the first five weeks of Australia's 1961 tour to England, but would be reported to MCC. In the event, with both Meckiff and Rorke absent, the former owing to loss of form after injury, the latter owing to a debilitating attack of hepatitis contracted on Australia's tour to India in 1959/60, the tour passed off without controversy.

Meckiff returned to form in the 1961/62 season and the following year took 47 wickets in the Sheffield Shield, more than any other bowler, but didn't represent Australia against England because his action was still under critical scrutiny. Although he continued to be among the wickets at the beginning of the 1963/64 season, his selection for the first Test against South Africa at Brisbane astounded many. The previous season, Bradman had entertained the Sheffield Shield captains at his home during the Adelaide Test and had shown them some incriminating films he had gathered of bowlers with suspect actions. Afterwards, Australian captain Richie Benaud resolved that in future he wouldn't bowl anyone called for throwing by an umpire or whom he considered to have a suspect action. Given that the Australian Board had instructed all its umpires to clamp down on potential throwers that year, it seemed bizarre to Benaud and to many others that Meckiff should be picked for the first Test.

Having scored 435 in their first innings, Australia took the field on the second afternoon, and Meckiff bowled the second over, filmed by the South African manager. Four times he was no-balled by Colin Egar, an umpire who had cleared him on five previous occasions. Benaud immediately took off Meckiff and refused to bowl him at umpire Lou Rowan's end, much to the disapproval of the crowd, who continued to chant unavailingly for Meckiff's return. At the end of the day's play, they chaired him off the field and booed the umpires, who needed police protection for the rest of the match. Finding a shattered Meckiff in the bar, Egar, a good friend of his, offered brief but heartfelt condolences on the day's events before turning the conversation to other matters. Later in the match, Meckiff met up with Bradman, who advised him to retire immediately, advice that he reluctantly accepted.

Whether Meckiff was set up by Bradman, Benaud and Egar remains a matter of some conjecture, but his retirement signalled the end of throwing as a major problem in Australia. Attention now switched to the West Indies and their fast bowler Charlie Griffith.

Griffith hailed from the northern tip of Barbados, where his family worked on the sugar plantation. With his big, strapping physique and natural ability, he looked to cricket as a means of escaping a life of rural poverty, but his rise to prominence as a hostile fast bowler was accompanied by doubts about his action, especially his bouncer and yorker, delivered chest-on and from wide of the crease. These doubts were compounded when Barbados played the Indians in 1962. Having inflicted a near-fatal injury on their captain, Nari Contractor, as he ducked into a short ball that didn't get up as he'd imagined, Griffith was later no-balled in the match for throwing by Barbadian umpire Cortez Jordan. Although Jordan called him only that once, the damage had been done. Before the West Indies party to tour England in 1963 was announced, their Board of Control had Griffith's action filmed, since the captain, Frank Worrell, among others, appeared to have doubts about its legitimacy.

West Indian doubts were soon shared by many in England. During the first Test at Old Trafford, England captain Ted Dexter informed MCC president-elect Gubby Allen that Griffith threw and said that something should be done. Allen said that it was up to the umpires, but he assured Dexter that he would use his influence to stop Griffith. What precisely occurred behind closed doors remains unclear. Trueman later alleged that he overheard a conversation during the second Test at Lord's between chairman of selectors Walter Robins and the umpires, in which the former advised the latter not to call Griffith because of the explosive effect this would have on race relations in London. While no umpire did call Griffith that summer, the mutterings grew ever louder, especially after the fourth Test at Headingley, where Griffith took nine wickets.

In the final Test at the Oval, Griffith took another nine wickets, helping the West Indies to a 3–1 series win. In the second innings, he clean bowled Ken Barrington with a fast swinging yorker that he barely saw. Back in the pavilion, the batsman let out his frustration, convinced that he had been thrown out.

The following year, the private protests went public when Barrington refused to play against Griffith in three exhibition matches, staged for the benefit of Frank Worrell. After officiating in one of these games, Australian-born umpire Cec Pepper informed Lord's that had the matches been first-class, he would have called Griffith for throwing. His confidential remarks met with approval from MCC assistant secretary Donald Carr, but any talk of Lord's confronting the problem head-on failed to materialise. Consequently, the West Indies Board of Control and their new captain, Gary Sobers, were unaware of Pepper's doubts as they prepared to host Australia in a series billed as the unofficial world championship. Compared with the epic series in Australia four years earlier, this one was tainted by allegations over Griffith's action by Australian players past and present. Bobby Simpson, the captain, was hit four or five times on the elbow by Griffith because he hadn't had time to pick up the flight of the ball, and many other front-line batsmen took a fearful pounding, fuelling their sense of persecution. On the final day of the first Test at Kingston, Richie Benaud, now working for *The Sun* (Sydney), published photographic evidence which convinced him that Griffith threw. Ignoring Swanton's advice that he raise the matter in private with the West Indian authorities, Benaud, left traumatised by Meckiff's public humiliation, was determined to bring the whole Griffith controversy into the open. Not surprisingly, the West Indians rallied behind their man, professing his arm to be straight at the point of delivery and accusing the Australians of being bad losers. The controversy continued unabated throughout the series, which the West Indies won 2–1; and at the end of it, Australian batsman Norman O'Neill, who missed the final Test because of a broken hand, accused Griffith of throwing. He was followed into print by Simpson and wicketkeeper Wally Grout, while Dexter used his column in *The Observer* to make similar claims.

The matter remained unresolved when the West Indies returned to England in 1966. The media kept up a merciless campaign against Griffith at every stage, and he clearly felt the strain, since he wasn't the threat he had been three years earlier. Although he was called once for throwing by Test umpire Arthur Fagg in the dying stages of their match against Lancashire early in the tour, the occasion passed off almost unnoticed, compared with a series of controversies in the Tests. In the closing stages of the third Test at Trent Bridge, which the West Indies won, Griffith caused outrage by hitting England number eleven Derek Underwood with a bouncer.

'I have never known such a feeling of shock and anger to be common to so many players as when that happened,' recalled England batsman Tom Graveney. 'For minutes the England dressing room seethed.'[55]

As the crowd rounded on Griffith, the media went for him with their pens. Brian Chapman in the *Daily Mirror* described the incident as vicious, uncouth and utterly uncalled for, and Swanton wrote in the *Daily Telegraph*: 'This ball so offended the convention whereby tail end batsmen are not threatened by bouncers.'[56] A flustered Sobers, knowing the hostile press reaction that awaited them, reproached Griffith after the match and told him that he should never bowl bouncers at the tail.

The bad feeling occasioned by Trent Bridge carried over into the next Test at Headingley, which, according to Graveney, was the nastiest match in which he'd ever played. The incident that sparked the friction occurred on the third morning, when England, in reply to the West Indies' first innings of 500/9 declared, were floundering at 18/2. Having seen Griffith bowl a vicious bouncer to Graveney that the batsman never saw, umpire Charlie Elliott at square leg conferred with his colleague, Syd Buller, and then approached Griffith. 'You can bowl, Charlie, but any more like that and I will have to call you,' he cautioned him. 'That delivery to Graveney was illegal.' Upset by the warning and his belief that the umpire had been influenced by the batsman, Griffith consulted his captain, who sought clarification with Elliott. Elliott assured him that it was his decision and his alone.

Following this altercation, controversy soon engulfed Basil D'Oliveira, England's Cape-Coloured all-rounder. The trouble arose when D'Oliveira, leading something of a fightback, clipped Lance Gibbs low to Conrad Hunte at midwicket and refused to walk for what the West Indians thought was a certain catch. The fact that it was Hunte, a committed Christian and a man, like Australia's Brian Booth, deemed incapable of cheating, who claimed the catch only added to their indignation. 'From that moment on, the whole team bristled,' wrote Sobers. 'An ugly feeling entered the match, a nasty needle that we hadn't known before, for this, we all felt, was not the sort of spirit normally found in first-class cricket.'[57]

The failure of the West Indian team, Hunte aside, to applaud D'Oliveira on his dismissal for a gallant 88 made for further bad publicity. Even the post-match socialising following the West Indies' innings victory to give them the series was soured by Griffith's curt response to Cowdrey when the England captain tendered his congratulations, a gesture that contributed to the loss of Griffith's tour bonus. It transpired that the Barbadian was still upset by Cowdrey's failure to rebuke Graveney for supposedly influencing the umpire over his illegal delivery.

Cowdrey's poor form that summer led to him being dropped for the final Test at the Oval. Brian Close became England's third captain of the summer, and led them to an innings victory by playing a form of attacking cricket not seen for some time. When Griffith was rapped on the knuckles by John Snow while batting, he threatened revenge on the England batsmen. 'Get on with the bloody game, Charlie,' Close told him. 'You're ready enough to dish it out, but when it comes to taking it it's another tale altogether.'

Griffith continued to play Test cricket for another couple of years, but, because he was something of a fading force, he no longer attracted the kind of controversy that had dogged him during his pomp.

One unfortunate aspect of the throwing controversy was the fate of Derbyshire fast bowler Harold Rhodes, suspected of throwing his quicker ball. Selected twice for England against India in 1959, he was no-balled six times against the South Africans in 1960 by umpire Paul Gibb at Derby, much to the fury of the crowd. He was again no-balled by Gibb in a county match the following year, and by Syd Buller against the South Africans at Chesterfield in 1965, Buller requiring a police escort from the field.

Filmed several times by the Test and County Cricket Board (TCCB), Rhodes was officially cleared in 1968, closing a chapter on a controversy that didn't re-emerge until Sri Lankan off-spinner Muttiah Muralitharan was called for throwing in Australia in 1995.

Chapter 4

The Sedate Sixties?

C ARIBBEAN sparkle aside, the 1960s was a depressing decade for the game of cricket, with rows over South Africa, throwing and time-wasting. In England, the proprieties of the game seemed safe in the hands of amateur captains such as Peter May, Ted Dexter and Mike Smith, but elsewhere the winds of change began to blow, fuelled by youthful unrest, the collapse of deference and strident nationalism. Out of the 11 matches featured in Ray Robinson's book *The Wildest Tests*, written in 1972, seven of them took place in the 1960s – four in India, two in the West Indies and one in Pakistan – and, while some of the crowd disturbances were due to non-cricketing reasons, it was a sign of more turbulent times. Although contentious umpiring decisions had always been part of the game, a greater willingness to show dissent was becoming more commonplace, especially during the South Africa–Australia series of 1966/67 and 1969/70. Robinson found it distasteful that four men captaining their countries had been guilty of various acts of dissent: Gary Sobers at Kingston in 1965, Bobby Simpson at Durban in 1967, Colin Cowdrey at Kingston in 1968 and Bill Lawry at the Oval in 1968. By the time Ray Illingworth locked horns with umpire Lou Rowan at Sydney in 1971, a trend had been well and truly set.

After the turgidity of the late 1950s, the new decade began in thrilling style with arguably the greatest series ever played. Under their urbane new captain, Frank Worrell, the West Indies arrived in Australia in October 1960 committed to an attacking form of cricket that caught the imagination of the Australian public. With his opposite number, Richie Benaud, cut from the same cloth, an epic series was in the offing.

From the moment Sobers enthralled Brisbane with a scintillating 132, the first Test turned out to be a classic. In a game of fluctuating fortune, Australia, chasing 233 to win, were faltering at 107/6 at tea on the final day, but the not-out batsmen, Benaud and fellow all-rounder Alan Davidson, remained set on victory. Their enterprising approach appeared to have paid off as Australia advanced to 226/6, until Davidson was run out with eight minutes left.

At the beginning of the final (eight-ball) over bowled by fast bowler Wes Hall, Australia needed six for victory, but the tension proved too much as three wickets fell. With two balls left and one run needed, Meckiff was thrown out by Joe Solomon from square leg going for glory. As the press box stood in tribute to what they had witnessed, Benaud emerged from the pavilion to greet Worrell and draped his arm around his shoulder as they trudged off together. The crowd surged in front of the pavilion and cheered the two teams, who then mingled together in the dressing room well into the night, drinking champagne and singing calypsos.

The tie in Brisbane, described by Bradman as the greatest Test of all time, set the scene for the rest of the series. 'Good fellowship between the teams had been transparent from the very beginning,' wrote Australian cricket writer Gideon Haigh. 'Batsmen had walked, umpires had been heeded without question, catches on the bounce had been promptly disclaimed.'[58] Nothing better illustrated the sporting rivalry than the confrontation between Wes Hall and Australia's opener Colin McDonald, who, despite receiving a series of painful blows from the paceman, presented his Australian sweater to him at the end of the summer. Even the crowd entered into the spirit of the contest by placing the cause of good cricket above their partisan interests. When Benaud successfully appealed against West Indian opener Joe Solomon after his cap fell on the wicket in the second Test, the 65,000

Melbourne crowd roundly booed the Australian captain for the rest of the day.

Australia won comfortably in Melbourne, and the West Indies triumphed in the third Test at Sydney. In the fourth Test at Adelaide, the visitors looked set to go one up in the series as Australia, chasing 460 to win, sank to 207/9 with nearly two hours remaining. Several overs later, it appeared all over when all-rounder 'Slasher' Mackay pushed Worrell to Sobers at silly mid-off. Sobers, like the rest of his team, thought it a clean catch, but umpire Egar adjudged that the ball had bounced. So horrified was Peter Lashley by the decision that he threw himself forward to the ground. On the way down, he saw Worrell shaking his head and immediately got to his feet again. He couldn't have his captain disapproving of him, he later told Australian cricket journalist Mike Coward. For the final 110 minutes, Mackay and last man Lindsay Kline resisted everything the West Indies threw at them – not one bumper was aimed at the latter – and emerged, amid mounting excitement, unbeaten. Although his players had been cruelly denied, Worrell absolved the umpires of any blame, and vice-captain Gerry Alexander led the team into the Australian dressing room to congratulate their opponents on their resilience.

Another titanic struggle took place at Melbourne in the fifth and deciding Test – a record-breaking crowd of 90,000 watched the second day – eventually won by Australia by two wickets, helped by a modicum of luck. With four still required, Wally Grout appeared to play on to West Indian spinner Alf Valentine, the ball dislodging the bail, but neither umpire had noticed the bail fall off and two runs resulted. (Knowing that he was out, Grout contrived to get out next ball by spooning a simple catch to cover.) In line with his pre-series resolution, Worrell refused to criticise the umpires, and, at the presentation ceremony, presided over by Bradman in his capacity as chairman of the Australian Board, he gave Benaud his cap, tie and blazer. His magnanimity earned him a rousing chorus of 'For He's a Jolly Good Fellow', and two days later, tens of thousands of well-wishers turned out in Melbourne to bid farewell to the tourists. 'They Lost the Series,' proclaimed one Sydney newspaper, 'But They Won Australia.'

'Benaud and Worrell have proved this truism,' commented *Wisden*. 'You can vary the Laws and do what you like, but without the goodwill of the captains all is in vain.'[59]

Having raised the standard of sportsmanship, Benaud kept it flying aloft in England during the Australian tour of 1961, a tour which many of his team ranked the happiest of all. At a meeting on board ship on the journey over, they resolved to walk if they hit the ball. Such was Benaud's determination to adhere to his principles that he even walked against Sussex on a pair despite having not hit the ball. 'The presence of Richie Benaud and the Australian team contributed to a rekindling of all that is best in cricket,' wrote the editor of *Wisden* after a series which Australia won 2–1. 'On all controversial issues he and his players intended to leave matters entirely in the hands of the umpires. Benaud proved as good as his word.

'Good fellowship and friendliness pervaded the tour and for once the importance of winning a game or a series was not allowed to impinge upon the true spirit of cricket. I have been watching Test cricket for forty years and I cannot recall a more pleasant atmosphere. I am sure that all cricket-lovers will say: Long may it continue.'[60]

Although Benaud's Australia never quite recaptured the flair of 1960/61, they continued to play hard but fair. During the 1962/63 series, the two captains, Benaud and Ted Dexter, forged a healthy regard for each other, ensuring that their teams played in the right spirit. England wicketkeeper John Murray recalls batting in the third Test with a severely damaged shoulder and being indebted to Davidson and McKenzie for keeping the ball up to him at all times during his second-innings vigil.

Nobody better exemplified the sportsmanship of that era than Wally Grout, Australia's wicketkeeper between 1958 and 1966. At Trent Bridge, on the opening day of the 1964 series, England's makeshift opener Fred Titmus was accidentally knocked over by bowler Neil Hawke as he ran a quick single, and was some way short of his ground when Grout received the ball, but he refused to remove the bails. When one of his team-mates reminded him that this was a Test match, Grout responded that 'It would not have been cricket, old boy.' The umpires, Syd Buller and Charlie Elliott, reckoned it was the nicest gesture they had seen on an English ground.

Grout's influence pervaded the return series in Australia in 1965/66. Following a confident appeal for a caught-behind against Geoff Boycott in England's first innings in the first Test at Brisbane that the umpire ruled not out, much to the crowd's consternation, the Australian wicketkeeper apologised to the batsman.

In England's second innings, Boycott played a ball from leg-spinner Peter Philpott that spun back off the pitch and towards the stumps, at which point Boycott intervened with his hand to deflect the ball clear of the stumps. It only needed one Australian to appeal and he would have been out handled the ball. ('Just as well he wasn't playing against Victoria,' remarked Bill Lawry to the square-leg umpire.) Instead, Grout warned Boycott about repeating such an offence, and Boycott, undefeated with 63 at the end of the match, later apologised to Australia's stand-in captain, Brian Booth.

Grout again showed his colours during the second Test at Melbourne, where, in an incident comparable to Trent Bridge 1964, he gave Titmus another reprieve. Having square-driven Graham McKenzie towards third man, Titmus set off on a third run only to be sent back by his partner, Jim Parks. The return from Doug Walters struck the wicket with Titmus well short of his ground, but in his excitement Grout, unbeknown to everyone else, had broken the wicket with his pad. As umpire Egar was about to raise his finger, Grout explained to him what had happened, and Titmus survived to make an unbeaten half-century.

After two drawn Tests, Australia lost their captain, Simpson, to chickenpox for the third Test at Sydney, and Booth once again took charge. In what proved to be his last Test, everything went wrong for Booth, a committed Christian and one of the most honourable men ever to play for Australia. His side lost by an innings and he failed twice with the bat but, in keeping with his character, he stood by the English dressing room and shook the hand of every player as they filed past before congratulating his opposite number, Mike Smith. Dropped after the match because of his poor form, he received a consoling letter from Bradman, the chairman of the selectors – the first of its kind – assuring him of the high personal regard in which the selectors held him and their appreciation of the way in which he had always upheld the good name of Australian cricket.

Booth's gesture was emulated by Smith in the fourth Test at Adelaide, which England lost by an innings. Bowled out cheaply in their first innings, England began their second innings 275 runs behind and were in some bother at 129/4 when Smith went to sweep leg-spinner Keith Stackpole. The ball brushed his pad and glove before popping to McKenzie at short leg, who threw himself forward to catch it. As the Australians hesitated, wondering whether Smith had hit the ball, the England captain walked.

One of the most popular captains ever to lead his country, Smith failed in his mission to recapture the Ashes, since the series was drawn one each, but few England sides generated such goodwill as the one he led in the mid-1960s. On tour to India in 1963/64, he'd found a fellow Corinthian in his opposite number, the Nawab of Pataudi, and goodwill prevailed throughout, so that when the tourists could only field ten fit men for much of the second Test, the Indians willingly lent them their twelfth man.

With captains such as Smith, Pataudi, Trevor Goddard, Hanif Mohammad and John Reid in charge during the mid-1960s, most Tests continued to be played in a cordial atmosphere. Reid even kept the New Zealanders on the field in heavy rain during the final stages of the fourth Test against India at New Delhi in 1965, enabling the home side, chasing 70 in 50 minutes, to win by seven wickets and take the series. 'Never forget it is only a game,' he told Pataudi.

While few would dissent from such sentiments, the line between gamesmanship and cheating became ever murkier as the old certainties no longer held good. After the ill-tempered series between England and the West Indies in 1966 because of the furore surrounding Griffith's action, MCC were concerned that England captain Brian Close might lack the necessary tact and sensitivity for the tour to the Caribbean in 1967/68. Those who doubted his credentials felt vindicated when his county, Yorkshire, was severely censured for unfair play to deprive Warwickshire of victory at Edgbaston in August 1967. The fact that Close as captain refused to apologise for this lapse in sportsmanship hardly endeared him to his critics, and Lord's stripped him of the captaincy, replacing him with Cowdrey, the master diplomat who surprised friend and foe alike with his steeliness in the Caribbean.

For the most part, the series was played in a good spirit, exemplified by the sportsmanship of West Indian batsman Rohan Kanhai in the first Test at Port of Spain. Having led the resistance to England's first innings of 568, he edged a ball to Cowdrey, who took a tumbling catch at slip. Unable to see whether the ball had carried, Kanhai asked Cowdrey whether he had caught it cleanly, and, being assured that he had, he walked smartly off. As far as the large crowd was concerned, he had fallen victim to a touch of chicanery on Cowdrey's part, and they heckled every time he fielded the ball thereafter. When the Jamaican crowd rioted during the second Test at Kingston following the dismissal of Basil Butcher in the West Indies' second innings, Cowdrey viewed the incident as only the outward show of a most vehement spirit against his team and their successful cricket.

The riot turned the game on its head as England, so dominant until then, lost their cutting edge; and, with Sobers in prime form, the West Indies gradually assumed the ascendancy. Set 159 for victory, England were soon in desperate trouble on a treacherous pitch. On the final morning, in time added to compensate for the riot, as they battled to save the match, a rattled Graveney berated the local drinks waiter for racing on to the pitch compared with his normal sluggish demeanour. Amid mounting tension, which even saw one of the umpires pick the ball up at one stage and return it to the bowler, much to batsman Fred Titmus's consternation, England just managed to salvage a draw.

For the critical fourth Test at Port of Spain, England fought hard to stay in the match, replying to the West Indies' 526/7 declared with 404. They then slowed the over rate down to 11 an hour, rather less than Yorkshire's over rate at Edgbaston, on the final morning, as the West Indies dawdled to 86/2 at lunch. On an unblemished wicket, a draw seemed a near-certainty until Sobers surprised one and all by suddenly declaring, setting England 215 to win in 165 minutes at 78 runs an hour.

Even if Sobers's declaration wasn't quite as sporting as it appeared, thinking that England wouldn't take the bait and his leg-spinners might cause them trouble, it soon appeared a gross miscalculation. Deprived of their one quick bowler, Griffith, because of a thigh injury, and let down by the inaccuracy of their spinners, the West Indies were soon in trouble as Boycott and Cowdrey led the victory charge, yet there was no question of Sobers resorting to time-wasting. (The mandatory 20 overs in the last hour only came in later that year.) Instead his side continued to bowl 18 overs an hour, enabling England to win by seven wickets with three minutes to spare.

The outrage across the Caribbean caused by Sobers's reckless declaration placed added pressure on him for the final Test at Georgetown. He responded to the manor born by scoring 152 and 95 not out as the West Indies took control. Needing 308 to win, England subsided to 41/5 before Cowdrey and his Kent colleague Alan Knott came to the rescue with a stand of 127 that helped them to escape with a draw with nine wickets down and win the series. During the final stages, the tail-enders incurred the displeasure of the opposition and the crowd with their time-wasting. 'I asked myself why this should happen when you are playing a game,' Sobers later wrote. 'It is not our lives at stake and it should be played in the right spirit, winning if you are good enough and losing if not.'[61]

Sobers invariably practised what he preached. At one stage, he appeared to have caught Knott at leg slip off Gibbs, only to indicate to the umpire that he had caught it on the half-volley and that the batsman was not out. Grateful for such small mercies, Cowdrey strolled up to Sobers a few minutes later and commended him for his sportsmanship. 'Ah man, I did not catch it,' the latter replied. 'If I do not catch the ball, no fun in that. That's not cricket!'

Sobers later wrote that he always walked when he knew he was out, but, according to Clive Lloyd, later a renowned captain of the West Indies, this code of sportsmanship wasn't always practised by the England team. 'Until then, I had always been under the mistaken impression that cricket was a "gentleman's game" and that *walking* was part of its great tradition. However, when I watched players who had been gods to me in my youth stand there and await an umpire's verdict when they had hit the ball hard, my mind and attitude changed.'[62]

For most of their history, the South Africans had been regarded as the most chivalrous of opponents, who retained a healthy perspective about the game, win or lose. This began to change during the 1950s when Heine and Adcock's aggression was taken to excess, perhaps a reflection of the growing international antagonism towards the apartheid society that had come to pass when the National Party gained power in 1948. The MCC tour to South Africa in 1964/65, won 1–0 by England, passed off amicably enough except for one unpleasant incident in the third Test when South African opening batsman Eddie Barlow failed to walk for a bat-pad catch off Titmus. Words were exchanged, and Titmus was ordered to apologise to Barlow by his captain Mike Smith, but, according to MCC manager Donald Carr, this was but one sharp squall in an otherwise temperate climate.

The return series between the two sides in England later that year, won by South Africa under the captaincy of Peter van der Merwe, was full of harmony, with opposing players exchanging pleasantries on the field, a contrast with the South Africa–Australia series of 1966/67.

Van der Merwe seemed less enchanted with the Australians – Grout had admonished him on the South African tour of Australia in 1963/64 for not walking – and he seemed determined to beat them at all costs. Simpson, the Australian captain, in turn became obsessed by the home umpires, especially their leading official,

Hayward Kidson, an honourable man increasingly prone to error. The trouble began during the first Test at Johannesburg when Kidson adjudged Australian opener Bill Lawry caught behind on 98 in their first innings, and his partner, Les Baxter, failed to uphold a confident appeal against van der Merwe in South Africa's second innings.

As the Australians, led by Simpson, made their feelings clear, they then compounded their frustration by dropping van der Merwe three times in 11 balls. The errors proved crucial since van der Merwe and partner Denis Lindsay added 221 for the sixth wicket, a stand that went a long way towards setting up an improbable South African victory, their first ever against Australia on home soil.

Australia won the second Test at Cape Town by six wickets, but Simpson again took exception to the umpiring, not least his second innings dismissal for 18, caught low at slip by Trevor Goddard, a scrupulously honest player. He lodged a confidential objection to Kidson, which later became public, and was assailed by the press for his poor sportsmanship. To add to Simpson's woes, Kidson was reappointed for the third Test at Durban and gave him out in both innings: lbw in the first innings, when Simpson turned his back on him before he gave the decision, and caught behind for 94 in the second, when he left shaking his head. 'I'm sick of this failure to accept umpiring decisions,' Keith Miller told fellow columnist R.S. Whitington. 'Bobby should set an example in this respect, not be the worst offender.'

'The Australian team must change its whole approach and the change must initiate from its captain if it is to make a fight of this series, let alone win it,' Whitington cabled back to Australia. 'Simpson and some of his players are playing like angry men, resenting and questioning umpires' decisions, objecting to South Africa's best umpire, refusing to face up to the obvious fact that they are opposing a team which, on individual talent, is definitely their superior ...'[63]

Soundly beaten at Durban, Australia were fortunate to escape with a draw in the fourth Test before losing the fifth at Port

Elizabeth by seven wickets to give South Africa the rubber for a 3–1 series win.

'Your team hasn't created exactly the best of impressions here, you know, on the score of sportsmanship. The image isn't good,'[64] a leading South African official and great lover of Australia confided to Whitington at the end of the tour – sentiments which he shared. He admitted that he hadn't seen Australians behave like this before.

Simpson led Australia in the first two home Tests against India later that year, before giving up the captaincy and retiring at the end of that series. His successor, Bill Lawry, was cast in the same mould, his affability off the field in direct contrast to his dour, unyielding attitude on it. During his first two matches in charge, he twice tried unsuccessfully to stop Indian batsman Chandu Borde having a runner, and the following summer he refused West Indian batsman Basil Butcher a drink outside the regular drinks interval. More acrimonious was his niggling of umpire Arthur Fagg during Australia's first innings in the final Test at the Oval in 1968, by drawing his attention to the number of no-balls Fagg was missing. As a result, Fagg sent Lawry a note before the next day's play, warning that unless he stopped criticising him he wouldn't continue to officiate. Lawry reluctantly agreed, only then to show dissent when Fagg immediately gave him out caught behind down the leg side. It should be said in Lawry's favour that, as England battled the clock on the final evening to bowl Australia out, none of the Australian batsmen resorted to time-wasting, a ruse that could have saved them the game, since England only won with six minutes remaining.

At a time of growing crowd unrest on the subcontinent, the Australian tour to India in 1969/70, while resulting in a creditable 3–1 victory on pitches conducive to the home spinners, was marred by serious disturbances at Bombay and Calcutta. The tension caused by these events added to what was already an arduous tour. Aside from serious breaches of security, the shoddy standards of accommodation and travel, much of it due to the Australian Board's parsimony, so disillusioned the team that Lawry later wrote a blistering report to the Board outlining their grievances. The fact that they were now expected to travel on to South Africa to confront the best team in the world in a four-match Test series only added to their travails.

Arriving exhausted and malnourished, the team never played to their potential and displayed a churlish attitude to their hosts. Starved of Test cricket since the last Australian series three years earlier, the South Africans, boasting the most talented team in their history, were champing at the bit to show off their pedigree to their home supporters. In their determination to win, the South Africans sometimes trod a fine line between the letter of the law and the spirit of the game. 'The Springboks are socially pleasant, but utterly ruthless once they step on to a cricket field,' wrote Australian batsman Keith Stackpole, who toured South Africa under both Simpson and Lawry. 'As far as decisions are concerned, they tend to think that near enough is close enough.'[65] He thought the South African players were largely to blame for the defects of their umpires. 'They appeal for practically everything and will diddle anyone if they can get away with it. The umpires, who are not very capable anyway, are unsettled by so much pressure.'[66]

Once again, the umpiring was a bitter source of contention, beginning with the first Test at Cape Town, when umpire Billy Wade turned down a confident caught-behind against South Africa's Eddie Barlow in their first innings. Barlow, on 66 at the time, went on to score 132 as the home team compiled an imposing 382. According to South African opener Barry Richards, Wade was incapable of cheating and 'the Australians, who never walk themselves, could hardly expect Eddie to do the same, when Billy, in complete honesty, gave him not out.'[67]

With the Australians taking exception to several other contentious decisions, most notably an early reprieve for Graeme Pollock in the second innings, the atmosphere turned increasingly unpleasant. *The Times* cricket correspondent, John Woodcock, compared it to the trouble with the officials on Simpson's tour. 'But he never showed his feelings quite as plainly as Lawry did yesterday.'[68] Subjected to repeated taunts by the visitors, Wade, a former Test wicketkeeper, announced that he was finished with umpiring at the end of the Test.

At the beginning of the second Test at Durban, South African captain Ali Bacher resorted to a subtle bit of gamesmanship. After he had secured Lawry's agreement to toss early, the Australians were flabbergasted to find the pitch being rolled and cut to get rid of the green tinge, helping South Africa compile a match-winning 622/9 declared. Because this rolling took place outside the 30 minutes before the start of play, it was perfectly legal, but it was contrary to the spirit of the game. It was perhaps because of this that Lawry resorted to blatant time-wasting to deny Richards the honour of becoming the only batsman to score a century before lunch in South Africa.

Well beaten in the first two Tests, the Australians tried to get umpire Carl Coetzee replaced after his indifferent performance in the second Test, but they were overruled by the South Africa Cricket Association. They continued to react badly to his decisions, and, at the end of a series in which the Australians were thrashed 4–0, Lawry refused either to address the crowds or to accept a souvenir gift from Coetzee. It was an unfortunate end to an acrimonious tour in which sledging, short-pitched bowling and gamesmanship became commonplace. In Australia's second innings of the third Test at Johannesburg, their vice-captain, Ian Chappell, in the middle of a very lean run, square-drove Trevor Goddard to backward point and was caught low down by Tiger Lance. On being assured by Lance that he had caught the ball, Chappell strode off, only to be later informed that Lance had caught the ball on the bounce. When he later confronted Lance about his dismissal, Lance replied: 'You asked me if I caught it – not if it bounced!' It was this incident that confirmed Chappell in his view that all decisions should be left to the umpire, a view that became paramount within the game as it became increasingly competitive.

Chapter 5

The Subversive Seventies

ALTHOUGH the world of cricket wasn't immune to the wider social changes of the 1960s, it wasn't until the following decade that the game entered its modern guise. While the abolition of the distinction between amateurs and professionals in England in 1962 was in many ways a recognition that the cricketer with independent financial means was an anachronism, it deprived the game of a certain style and magnanimity. Increasingly exposed to the professional ethos, cricket lost much of its sense of adventure, and spectators continued to desert it in alarming numbers.

Confronted with the growing threat of insolvency, many English counties grasped the lifeline that limited-over cricket and commercial sponsorship offered. The impact of the Gillette Cup in 1963 may have been limited at first, but the introduction of the John Player League in 1969 and the Benson and Hedges Cup in 1972 were to have far-reaching ramifications. Not only did they place the game on a sounder financial footing – the spectacular hitting and exciting finishes also revived popular interest. Few Lord's finals were complete without the raucous chants of Lancashire and Somerset supporters willing on their idols, and, with ever more hinging on these games in terms of prize money and prestige, winning became everything.

This growing emphasis on success, combined with the new post-war generation raised in a more permissive, self-expressive era, placed added pressure on umpires and administrators. The change was perhaps greatest in Australia, where for too long the players had been held to ransom by hidebound officials. The derisory pay, the stringent restrictions such as no wives on tour and lack of representation, had come to a head on the arduous tour of India and South Africa in 1969/70. At the end of it, the captain, Lawry, wrote a stinging letter to the Australian Board, listing the main complaints, an act that helped precipitate his removal as captain a year later; while his successor, Ian Chappell, proved equally uncompromising, insisting that the players be better remunerated. With a brash, attacking style of cricket that appealed to the newly liberated youth of Australia, Chappell's side, containing personalities such as Rodney Marsh, a rumbustious wicketkeeper-batsman, and Dennis Lillee, an outstanding fast bowler, not only overcame all comers, they also revived the game's popularity. Yet this resurgence came at a price, as behaviour on and off the field took a distinct turn for the worse.

Since time immemorial, the integrity of the game had rested on the fundamental principle that the umpire's decision was final, although officials could come under pressure from volatile home crowds on the subcontinent and in the Caribbean. Pakistani fast bowler Fazal Mahmood recalled playing the West Indies at Kingston in 1957/58, when the umpires didn't give a couple of decisions in favour of his team. On raising the matter with one of the umpires afterwards, Fazal was reminded by the umpire that he had to live there. Four years earlier the Kingston crowd had attacked two members of umpire Perry Burke's family after he had given out local hero J.K. Holt in the first Test against England. All three Test match riots on successive MCC tours of the West Indies in 1953/54, 1959/60 and 1967/68 had the umpires in their sights, and Badge Menzies, one of the umpires in the Georgetown Test riot of 1953/54, was given a temporary police guard at his home.

Given the inconsistency of the umpiring and the frequency with which some touring sides suffered, it wasn't surprising that sometimes dissent was shown. Even Gary Sobers, that most noble of sportsmen, threatened to quit the West Indies' tour to Pakistan in 1958/59 after receiving two highly questionable lbws in the first Test, only to be talked out of it by manager Berkeley Gaskin. In general, strong leadership stamped out the first signs of dissent. Wally Grout was reprimanded by his manager, Sam Loxton, on Australia's tour to Pakistan in 1959/60 after hurling his bat in reaction to an lbw decision against his team-mate Ray Lindwall in the Dacca Test – a lesson learned, given his later chivalry. Months later, England's Ken Barrington was ordered to apologise to the umpire by manager Walter Robins after objecting to his caught-behind decision against the West Indies in the first Test at Bridgetown. One of the hallmarks of Richie Benaud's captaincy was the immediate steps he would take to stop any of his fielders from disputing an umpire's decision.

Australian cricket writer Ray Robinson saw most of Bradman, Hassett and Harvey's 286 Test innings between 1928 and 1963. They were no more exempt than anyone else from the risk of umpiring error, and yet in their 260-odd dismissals he never saw them linger at the wicket once the umpire had raised his finger. 'No meaningful stare, no scanning the skies, no tapping the pitch, no reluctant departure, no looking back. I did not even detect a momentary start of surprise if they felt sure an umpire was mistaken.'[69] Robinson went on to say that, as a witness to most of Hutton and May's innings against Australia and every one of Worrell's, he couldn't recall a single instance of dissent to decisions against them. He thought May's demeanour was particularly admirable during the difficult days of the throwing controversy (1958/59), when he must have felt several times that he was out to illegal deliveries.

No man better respected the proprieties of the game than Australia's Brian Booth. Alan Davidson recalls him receiving a bad decision when playing for New South Wales and saying to him on his return, 'You didn't hit that one, Sam [his nickname],' to which Booth replied cheerfully, 'I must have. The umpire gave me out.'

It wasn't only batsmen who respected umpires. Barry Jarman, the South Australia wicketkeeper, taught the young Ian Chappell to appeal only when the batsman was out, and fast bowler Alan Davidson used to appeal for lbw only when he genuinely thought it was out.

Although English umpires were by no means perfect, they were deemed the best in the world because of the frequency with which they practised their craft and the fact that nearly all of them were former players. Given the fellowship of the county circuit, there developed a bond of trust, with players trying to help umpires by taking as many decisions as possible out of their hands. 'In my early days as a player, the umpire's job was probably the easiest job in the world,' recalled David Shepherd, a Gloucestershire player between 1965 and 1979 and later a leading international umpire. 'All he had to do was to count to six and call "over". If a batsman thought he was out, he left the crease and often the umpire would not be called on to make a decision.'[70] Players who were victims of bad decisions mainly accepted them, and those who didn't were given short shrift by their captain. Former Kent all-rounder Alan Dixon recalls dropping his jaw in amazement when given out lbw by Frank Chester to a ball that he had hit, only to be reprimanded by his captain, Colin Cowdrey, and ordered to apologise to the umpire. Jack Birkenshaw, the Yorkshire and Leicestershire all-rounder who made his debut in 1958, recounted his captain Ronnie Burnet telling him that if he ever tried to 'do' the umpire he would never play for Yorkshire again. 'We never argued,' wrote Yorkshire slow bowler Don Wilson. 'If you were given out, you were out.'[71]

By the 1970s, attitudes were beginning to change as a new generation of players, unacquainted with the discipline of war and national service, became more questioning of authority and partial to the monetary rewards entering the game. With captains and county committees adopting a more competitive approach, a blind eye was turned to the growing gamesmanship and dissent if it was all in the cause of winning. Confronted with the ethics of this new professionalism, many umpires seemed to lose confidence as their performance came increasingly under scrutiny from television replays and a more critical media.

This was certainly the case in Australia, where the game changed out of all recognition. The retirement of strong, experienced umpires like Colin Egar and Lou Rowan led to a demise in authority, which was fully exploited by the players. Having officiated an unruly match between South Australia and Western Australia in December 1972, Test umpire Max O'Connell informed the Australian Board that he had witnessed an increase in foul language and bad sportsmanship during the season. The following month, his colleague Tom Brooks, another Test umpire and former Sheffield Shield fast bowler, wrote to the New South Wales Cricket Association to complain about the prevalence of offensive language increasingly used by the players. On Australia's tour to New Zealand the following year, there were complaints about the tourists' behaviour. During the second Test at Christchurch, Ian Chappell became embroiled in a bitter confrontation with New Zealand opening batsman Glenn Turner as New Zealand closed in on their first ever victory against Australia. After a lofted on-drive by Brian Hastings was mistakenly signalled six by umpire Bob Monteith, Chappell ran up to the umpire to query his decision. Turner, at the non-striker's end, informed Chappell that he had already explained the situation to Monteith, whereupon Chappell angrily told Turner to mind his own business. After a second subsequent confrontation, during which Chappell used some ripe language towards Turner, the New Zealand management demanded an apology from the Australian captain at the end of the match. Chappell's refusal to give one, contending that what occurred on the field stayed there, helped intensify the ill-feeling between the two sides and give rise to the image of the 'Ugly Australians'.

Similar ructions were apparent in South Africa, where domestic cricket was played with a greater intensity than in the county championship. In 1972/73 a team of English professionals touring South Africa under the banner of Derrick Robins' XI were disconcerted by the gamesmanship of the home players, whereby spurious catches were claimed and batsmen failed to walk. On the eve of the match against Natal, their captain, former England fast bowler David Brown, informed Barry Richards that they would like to play the game in the right spirit, and Richards, used to the county ethos with Hampshire, agreed to relay the request to his team-mates. After some coaxing, he managed to persuade them to abandon their abrasive approach, but not for long. The new spirit lasted until the second over of the tourists' first innings, when Clive Radley edged Pat Trimborn to short leg, whereupon he stayed put, thinking he hadn't hit it. The umpire ruled in his favour, much to the disgust of the fielding side, who immediately resumed normal service.

According to Bob Taylor, the Derbyshire and England wicketkeeper who played first-class cricket between 1960 and 1984, the game became less enjoyable with the general erosion of etiquette. He recalled watching a film of the 1960/61 tied Test with some England players in Australia in 1982/83, and noting their disapproval when Richie Benaud complimented Wes Hall on the ball that dismissed him as the game neared its thrilling climax.

More serious to Taylor was the decline in the game's ethics as teams increasingly looked to win by any means. 'Cheating proliferates in all areas of play nowadays. The appeals from bowlers seem to get more ridiculous as well as the dumb insolence shown to the umpire when they are turned down. Fielders shout "catch it!" every time the ball lobs up off the pad and too often the umpire gets worn down by the persistence of the appeals and makes mistakes!'[72]

As a traditionalist, Taylor admitted that he stood his ground three times on his last two tours to Australia in 1979/80 and 1982/83 to conform to this new ethic of gamesmanship. 'You find it very hard to play the game in the right manner when you know that the opposition will beat you by unfair means. We have had to adapt to the ways in which other countries interpret the rules and, as a result, I have seen England captains on tour criticise a batsman on our side for walking when he knew he was out.'[73]

As a new era dawned, the choice to captain MCC in Australia in 1970/71 came down to two very different personalities: Colin Cowdrey, the gentleman amateur who had previously captained England until a ruptured Achilles tendon in May 1969 forced him to miss that summer's Tests, and Ray Illingworth, the canny Leicestershire all-rounder who had ably deputised for Cowdrey. Because of his seniority – three times he had been vice-captain in Australia – Cowdrey was deemed to be the favourite but, much to his distress, the honour went to Illingworth, leaving him with the vice-captaincy once again. It proved a fateful decision, because Cowdrey and his friend David Clark, the manager and former captain of Kent, appeared out of kilter with the uncompromising professional ethos which Illingworth instilled in the team.

Although the series was notable for its friendly relations between the teams off the field, the cricket was hard and attritional, with a surfeit of bouncers on both sides, some of them directed towards tail-enders, and histrionic appealing. After two dull draws in the first two Tests, the England manager upset his players with his public comments that he would rather lose the series than see all the Tests drawn.

Thanks to the assured batting of Geoff Boycott and the devastating bowling of John Snow, England easily won the fourth Test at Sydney before playing out a dull draw in the rescheduled Test at Melbourne. Two days later, the teams met again at Adelaide, a match marred by Boycott's petulant reaction to being adjudged run out on the first day by local umpire Max O'Connell. Devastated by a decision that he thought to be flawed, Boycott, on 58 at the time, threw his bat to the ground and stood there, hands on hips, glaring at the umpire. As an eerie silence gave way to a chorus of boos, Greg Chappell retrieved Boycott's bat and several Australians told him unceremoniously to leave. Although Boycott later accepted that his reaction to his dismissal had been out of order, his grudging apology failed to appease local sensitivities, and the England opener remained a target for the crowd's anger, until his second-innings century won them over.

England left Adelaide with the better of a draw, and returned to Sydney for the final Test one up in the series but without Boycott, who had broken his arm in an inconsequential one-day match against Western Australia. Inserted by Ian Chappell, captaining Australia for the first time following the controversial ousting of Lawry, they could only muster 184. They fought back, but, by the second evening, Australia had established a narrow lead when tail-ender Terry Jenner, having survived two short balls from Snow with difficulty, was hit on the head by a ball that failed to rise. His collapse drove many of the 29,000 crowd to fury, and when he was eventually led off with blood pouring from his ear, Rowan saw fit to warn Snow for persistent intimidatory bowling, a caution that ignited a slow-burning fuse of resentment felt by Snow towards Rowan.

Never the most malleable of characters, Snow had clashed with Rowan on previous occasions during the series, most notably at Perth when he refuted claims that he was bowling bouncers, insisting that they were balls pitched just short of a length and only chest-high. As umpire and bowler quibbled over the interpretation of 'persistent' intimidatory bowling, Illingworth came up to lend Snow his support. According to the England captain, not only had Rowan exceeded his legitimate powers by ruling that Snow had no right to bowl a bouncer at Jenner, but also a warning could only be issued for excessive bouncers. Intemperate language was used during the unedifying exchange before Snow returned to his mark to bowl the last ball of the over.

After a drinks break which saw some beer cans thrown on to the outfield by rowdier elements of the crowd, Snow made his way down to long leg, where he was greeted with a volley of abuse (and some cheers) by the crowd. One inebriated onlooker tried to grab him before he was restrained by the others, but as Snow moved away from the boundary he was pelted by a second wave of cans.

Confronted by this disorder, Illingworth, in the interests of safety, called his team together and, without consulting the umpires, led them off the field – the first time this had happened in 209 Tests. His decision, although supported by four former Australian captains, brought him into conflict with David Clark. He ordered him to return, but Illingworth was having none of it. When the umpires asked him whether he was coming back or forfeiting the match, the England captain replied that he would return when the ground had been cleared, and seven minutes later his team reappeared to a mixed reception.

At the close of play, Snow visited Jenner in the Australian dressing room to see how he was, but expressed no regret for the injury. The next day, Jenner resumed his innings and added 22 runs to his score as Australia gained a first-innings lead of 80. England fared better in their second innings, scoring 302. By bowling Australia out for 160, they won by 62 runs, enabling them to regain the Ashes after an absence of 12 years.

Their achievement in becoming the first side to regain the Ashes in Australia since Jardine in 1932/33 was a cause of national celebration, but to many at Lord's the manner of their victory had been troubling. According to Swanton, there had been a lowering of standards, and later, in conversation with Illingworth on BBC Radio Four's *It's Your Line*, he expressed his regret at the way the England captain had argued with an Australian umpire in front of 29,000 spectators. When Illingworth asked Swanton whether he thought the umpire was right, Swanton replied that the umpire must always be right and he must always be respected by the players.

Swanton repeated his comments at the official dinner at Lord's shortly afterwards, and the Cricket Council, cricket's new governing body in the UK, officially warned all players that dissent towards umpiring decisions would not be tolerated. A decade later, Bob Willis, the junior member of the touring party and a future England captain, noted that, compared with the conduct of certain sides at the end of the 1970s, Illingworth's team was a paragon of virtue. Certainly, there were no complaints from the Australians.

England's image remained tarnished the following summer, when Snow barged India's Sunil Gavaskar to the ground during the Lord's Test while the diminutive opening batsman completed a quick single. As Gavaskar picked himself up, an unrepentant-looking Snow casually tossed him his bat, which earned him a quiet word of reproach from umpire David Constant and a dressing-down from an irate Billy Griffith, the MCC secretary, shortly afterwards. Although Snow apologised to Gavaskar that evening and the Indians responded graciously, Snow was dropped from the next Test for disciplinary reasons.

MCC's tour of India a year later brought evidence of changing attitudes, but also a smack of firm leadership, all too rare thereafter. Central to this new hard-nosed approach was Tony Greig, England's charismatic all-rounder, who'd made his debut against Australia earlier that year. Born and raised in South Africa, Greig was a street fighter par excellence who loved to needle his opponents through blatant displays of aggression. 'He was the first England player I remember actively indulging in gamesmanship,' wrote Bob Taylor. 'The England lads who played under him thought Greigy great value and I am afraid that his gamesmanship rubbed off on some of them.'[74]

Such tactics were deployed in India, where the volatile crowds, and the vociferous appealing of the close-in fielders clustered around the bat to the spinners, placed additional pressure on the inexperienced umpires. Adopting a similar approach to the Indians, Greig appeared in a class of his own as he crouched at silly point appealing for everything. Gavaskar recalls being given out caught off his pads by Greig after he and Alan Knott applauded the bowler with great gusto, and Greig laughing about it when they met in the Indian dressing room at close of play.

During the third Test at Madras, as India chased 86 to win, their captain, Ajit Wadekar, edged English seamer Chris Old to Greig at slip, only to be given not out. Incensed by the decision, Greig charged down the wicket with the ball raised high in his hand to make his case, and Knott threw one of his wicketkeeping gloves up in the air, an act of dissent he later regretted. Once the captain, Tony Lewis, had intervened to calm down his players, the umpire consulted his colleague and gave Wadekar out.

Convinced that this incident was the inevitable result of both teams trying to con the umpire, Lewis went to the Indian dressing room at the end of the match and said to Wadekar, 'Shall we play cricket for the next two Tests, or shall we cheat?'

'Let's play cricket,' he replied.

The whole Indian team insisted that Greig curb his acting near the bat, a guarantee Lewis gave provided the Indian close-in fielders followed suit. Before the fourth Test, Lewis called a team meeting to say that under his captaincy there would be no pressure on the umpires to get decisions. Few applauded other than manager Donald Carr, who had reprimanded Greig for his antics in the previous Test. 'Are we both left over from a different age?' he asked Lewis, but both sides adhered to the agreement, and for the rest of the series, won 2–1 by India, harmony prevailed.

Greig's personality was again to the fore the following winter when England toured the Caribbean under a new captain, Mike Denness. Traditionally the most chivalrous of opponents under the genial Sobers, the West Indies developed a harder edge under his successor, Kanhai. Touring England during the summer of 1973, their convincing 2–0 win was somewhat overshadowed by an ugly spat during the Edgbaston Test, when umpire Fagg gave Boycott not out to a confident caught-behind appeal off opening bowler Keith Boyce. The West Indians, led by Kanhai, fielding at first slip, reacted with indignation and proceeded to heap abuse on Boycott and Fagg for the rest of the day. It was, according to Boycott, the worst conduct he had ever seen in a Test match team, and even Sobers admitted that Kanhai had gone too far in showing his displeasure.

As for Fagg, he felt so upset by Kanhai's behaviour that he told several newspapers he was quitting the match. 'If they won't accept decisions, there is no point carrying on. Why should I? I am nearly sixty. I don't have to live with this kind of pressure. ... I don't enjoy umpiring Test matches any more, nor Sunday League matches. There is so much at stake. The players shout for things and when they don't get the decision, they react in the way Kanhai reacted today. The game has changed, and not for the better. Umpires are under terrific pressure. The players have to learn to accept decisions, otherwise there is no point continuing.'[75]

When play began the next morning, there was no sign of Fagg and it was Warwickshire coach Alan Oakman who accompanied Dickie Bird, Fagg's partner, to the middle. It needed a public statement of support from West Indian manager Esmond Kentish to patch things up and enable Fagg to resume after one over and officiate for the rest of the match.

The editor of *Wisden* chided Fagg for having gone public with his reservations about Kanhai, but at least it brought the matter to a head. 'For too long, and not only in this country, players from junior to senior standing have been reflecting their dislike at umpire's decisions with disdain. ... Captains more than anyone hold the key to clearing up a bad habit which has no place in the game of cricket.'[76]

The bad blood continued when MCC toured the West Indies that winter. Willis noted that his four Warwickshire team-mates in the opposition made little effort to befriend him, and England off-spinner Pat Pocock recalls the atmosphere between the two teams as horrendous, 'the worst I have ever known between two cricket teams'. The England close-in fielders, led by Greig, embraced sledging, the Australian term for vocal abuse towards an opponent, believing that West Indian batsmen such as Kanhai and Alvin Kallicharran could be cajoled into playing impetuous shots. The one exception would be Sobers. He would walk to the middle with a friendly word to the fielders, and players would get on with the game in respectful silence. 'Nobody would dream of swearing at Gary, for the gods of the game are far above and beyond such petty abuse,' wrote Pocock.[77]

Part of the acrimony stemmed from a notorious incident at the end of the second day of the first Test at Port of Spain, when an undefeated 142 by Kallicharran had placed the West Indies in a commanding position. On the last ball of the day, his partner, Bernard Julien, played Derek Underwood past Greig at silly point. As Greig ran after it, Knott uprooted the stumps, and Kallicharran, at the non-striker's end, started walking down the wicket towards the pavilion.

Greig by now had retrieved the ball, and, seeing Kallicharran out of his ground, he threw down the wicket at the non-striker's end. He appealed, and umpire Douglas Sang Hue, because he had not called 'over', had no option but to give Kallicharran out. While Greig raised his hands in celebration, Kallicharran hesitated for a minute before stomping furiously back to the pavilion, smashing his bat on the pavilion steps, the signal for the crowd to turn hostile.

With tensions running high, Sobers drove a bewildered Greig back to his hotel to avoid any reprisals, and an emergency meeting was convened in the pavilion between the respective officials, captains and umpires to try to resolve the situation. While everyone accepted that Greig had acted within the laws of the game – it was Kallicharran's responsibility to maintain his ground – an injustice had been done, especially as Knott had removed the stumps, and to ignore that injustice ran the risk of fuelling popular unrest, thereby endangering the future of the tour. Consequently, England manager Donald Carr asked the umpires to accept the withdrawal of their appeal and Kallicharran was reinstated. A statement was issued by the West Indies Board of Control, which expressed Greig's regret for the incident, and when play resumed after the rest day, he shook hands with Kallicharran, who was out soon afterwards.

The decision to reinstate Kallicharran didn't meet with the approval of all the England team – even Sobers thought he deserved to be out – and Ted Dexter accused Carr of placing the cause of diplomacy above the support of his player. Yet given the controversial nature of the dismissal, which appeared to breach the spirit of cricket, and the potential for further trouble, Carr had little option but to act in the way he did. The climbdown brought the best out of Greig, as he went on to have an outstanding series, culminating in a memorable 13-wicket haul in the final Test at Port of Spain, which gave England a narrow victory and an undeserved share of the rubber.

After a summer in which they comprehensively beat India and had the better of a rain-affected series against Pakistan, England arrived in Australia in October 1974 confident of retaining the Ashes. Dennis Lillee, Australia's talismanic fast bowler, was recovering from a career-threatening back injury, and Jeff Thomson, his unknown opening partner, raised few concerns despite his much-quoted comments about the pleasure he derived from hitting batsmen.

Without Snow, their most hostile bowler, who unaccountably wasn't picked for the tour, England fielded first in the first Test at Brisbane and dismissed Australia for 309 – five of their batsmen, including Lillee, falling to bouncers. Had England known what lay in store for them, they surely would have limited the use of the short ball, because it gave their opponents carte blanche to return fire with interest. On an increasingly uneven pitch, Lillee and Thomson, with his slinging action – he was a skilled javelin thrower – and ability to get the ball to rear off a length, worked up a terrifying pace. Unable to cope with the rising ball, England were 57/4 in no time, and it needed a superb hundred by Greig to keep them in the game.

In their second innings, Australia extended their lead to 333 before declaring near the end of the fourth day. It proved no contest. Subjected once again to the raw pace of Thomson on a treacherous surface, England capitulated for 166, with two of their leading batsmen, Dennis Amiss and John Edrich, nursing broken bones. Keith Miller later wrote that Thomson frightened him sitting 200 yards away.

In these difficult circumstances, England took the momentous step of recalling Cowdrey, a veteran of five Australian tours, to the colours a month short of his 42nd birthday. Thrust straight into the second Test at Perth, he found there was little room for sentiment, since despite two dogged innings, he encountered the same treatment meted out to his team-mates. Unfazed by his rough baptism, he took the opportunity to introduce himself to Thomson at a drinks break during the first innings. 'How do you do, I'm Colin Cowdrey,' he said, stretching out his hand. 'G'day, I'm Jeff Thomson,' came the gruff reply. With Australia's close-to-the-wicket fielding in the arc between first slip and gully near infallible, England's inability to withstand the sustained pace and bounce cost them dear. All out for 208, they conceded a first-innings lead of 273, and on a beautiful batting wicket they once again offered inadequate resistance, losing by nine wickets.

Exposed to increasing partisanship by raucous crowds keen to inflict maximum humiliation on the mother country – they recalled Headingley 1972 and the doctored wicket to help Underwood – England performed better at Melbourne, earning a hard-fought draw as Australia kept up their barrage of bouncers and harsh invective. According to Willis, there were too many verbal exchanges in the series and only Greig enjoyed them. Even the traditional socialising between the two teams at the end of the day's play seemed somewhat contrived in the circumstances. 'I could not see the point of drinking with a bloke who had just tried to knock your head off and called you every name under the sun,' recalled Willis. 'So I would stand there, feeling rather embarrassed and trying to think of things to say.'[78]

Any encouragement England took from Melbourne soon vanished over the New Year period in Sydney, where, in front of their largest crowds for years, England were once again pummelled by Lillee and Thomson. 'Stork' Hendry, who batted against Larwood and Voce in 1932/33, thought the Australian bowling worse than bodyline.

The simmering tensions between the two teams erupted on the morning of the second day, when Lillee was struck on the left elbow by a ball from Greig. Objecting to the lack of sympathy he received from Keith Fletcher as the Englishman retrieved his bat, he let fly at him, vowing revenge, while umpire Tom Brooks warned Greig about bowling short at tail-enders. It was a bizarre ruling, given that Lillee's indiscriminate use of bouncers against the English tail had gone unchecked.

Spurred on by the frenzied chants of 'LILL-EE, LILL-EE, LILL-EE' from the Hill, the Western Australian bowled like a man possessed as England, in reply to Australia's 405, once again struggled against the lifting ball. On 106/3 overnight, they briefly rallied the next day, until the innings ended when

Lillee struck Underwood on the shoulder and bowled Willis an unintentional beamer.

Their second innings was more of the same. Set 400 to win, their opening batsman Amiss received a brute of a ball from Lillee that kept coming at him and was caught behind. He left, body quivering and shell-shocked. The very next ball, Edrich, captaining instead of the out-of-form Denness, ducked into a short one from Lillee and sustained cracked ribs. As he doubled up in pain and was helped off the field, the crowd chanted. His replacement, Fletcher, survived for an hour before a venomous lifter from Thomson nearly decapitated him. Shaken by this experience, he was out the next ball and departed in a ghostly trance. It said much for Geoff Arnold, England's last man, that he survived a lethal introductory bouncer from Lillee to provide solid support to Edrich, who had gallantly returned to the fray at the fall of the sixth wicket. Together they defended stoutly until Arnold was caught with 43 balls left, giving Australia the series and the return of the Ashes.

Adelaide resulted in another Australian victory, before England, taking advantage of the absence of Thomson at Melbourne – and Lillee for most of the match – recorded their sole win. This, however, couldn't undo the nightmare of the previous three months. 'Many of the players, including myself, were extremely concerned about their safety,' recalled Denness. 'Never in my career have I witnessed so much protective gear applied to individuals before they went out to bat.'[79]

After all the brutality of Australia, it was ironic that a near fatality occurred in the tranquil setting of New Zealand, when the home team's young seam bowler, Ewen Chatfield, deflected a bouncer from Peter Lever on to his temple during the dying embers of the first Test at Auckland. Amid mounting horror from England's fielders, Chatfield sank to the ground and began to have convulsions. His heart momentarily stopped beating, but prompt action from MCC physiotherapist Bernard Thomas revived him and he later made a complete recovery, much to everyone's relief – especially that of Lever, whose distress was all too visible.

Although New Zealand exonerated Lever of any blame, the accident did highlight the growing preponderance of intimidatory bowling, not least against tail-enders. Those with the game at heart should regard the use of the bumper as a menace, commented John Woodcock. 'Action should be taken before someone is hurt,' declared *Wisden*.[80]

When England hosted Ian Chappell's Australians during the summer of 1975, a combination of slow wickets and home umpires kept the hostile bowling in check, but standards on the field continued to decline. According to the Australian-born Bill Alley, umpiring his second Test, at Lord's, the first two hours of the match were the most unpleasant of his career. Never had he been subjected to such a barrage of hostile appealing, and at no other time had he felt like walking off the field in disgust. 'Every time the ball touched the pads, even via the bat, or every time a batsman played and missed, the entire team leapt and screamed as one.'[81]

Alley took exception to the way that the Australians 'swore and gesticulated' whenever he rejected an appeal, especially since he gave three lbws in their favour during that pre-lunch session – but the England players, now under the captaincy of Greig, weren't blameless. A fierce sporting rivalry dating back nearly 100 years had become coloured by personal antipathy between the two captains and Greig's habit of halting his quick bowlers in their approach to make field changes. When Kent's Bob Woolmer scored a painstaking century to save the final Test at the Oval, he was the victim of non-stop verbal abuse by a team who appeared to have lost all respect for their opponents.

Back home, the Australians, now under Greg Chappell, overwhelmed Clive Lloyd's West Indians 5–1 in a series blighted by blatant gamesmanship and flawed umpiring that favoured the home team. West Indian opener Gordon Greenidge later recalled that as a schoolboy he was taught that the umpire's word was law, and that if one was out, one walked. During his early years at Hampshire, that ethic still held good, but after Australia 1975/76 he never walked again. 'It was the experience of Australia which taught me I had to change because I saw that in opponents it was successful to cheat. ... I know it's sad but it is just a question of survival.'[82]

His team-mate Viv Richards remembered it as the hardest, meanest tour he ever experienced, and described how it changed his whole outlook on Test cricket. 'Until then I had believed, however naively, that Test cricket was the ultimate sport of gentlemen. The Australians smashed that view wide open. ... It was a kind of nastiness that I had never encountered previously, not just in cricket but in life in general.'[83] Aside from their propensity to engage in sledging, with even third man and long leg joining in, they took every opportunity to humiliate the tourists.

With Lillee and Thomson heading a four-man pace attack that also included Gary Gilmour and Max Walker, again in prime form, the West Indians had no answer to their pace and bounce. Several batsmen were badly hurt, 16 were dismissed hooking, and well before the end of the series they were a divided and demoralised team. Exposed to the brutal reality of modern Test cricket, the West Indians vowed never to roll over again. In future, they would discard their sunny calypso style and become a more ruthless, professional outfit.

This new thinking was given added credence in the home series against India immediately following the Australian debacle. Having slumped to a shock defeat in the third Test at Port of Spain after India easily overcame a turning wicket and three spinners to score 406/4 to win and square the series, Lloyd terminated his faith in spin. From now on, beginning with the deciding Test at Sabina Park, Kingston, four pace bowlers would form the basis of their attack.

With an unpredictable pitch of varied bounce and a noisy partisan crowd to contend with, the Indians, batting first, were subjected to hostile bowling from Michael Holding and Wayne Daniel, the like of which they had never seen before. What particularly incensed them was Holding's tactic of bowling around the wicket and aiming at the body, since it increased the prospect of batsmen getting hit. According to West Indian cricket writer

Tony Cozier, Holding, playing his first Test on his home ground, was as fast and dangerous as anyone he had seen. After one over in which he faced four bouncers, Gavaskar marched down the wicket to protest to the umpire, but all to no avail. He later accused the West Indians of barbarism and called the Kingston crowd a mob, particularly objecting to the cries of 'Kill him' and their joyous celebrations when his opening partner, Anshuman Gaekwad, was hit a sickening blow behind the ear. Already suffering from cracked ribs, Gaekwad was helped off and taken to hospital with bleeding from the ears. 'It was a harrowing time,' he later recalled. 'The x-ray technician paid no heed to my cracked ribs and lifted me from under my shoulders and placed me on a hanger. I couldn't even scream because I was in so much pain.'[84] In time, he returned to India to have two operations on his ear and a lifelong legacy of poor hearing.

With two other batsmen, Gundappa Viswanath and Brijesh Patel, already retired with a broken hand and a blow in the mouth respectively, Bishan Bedi, India's captain, declared his first innings at 306/6 to spare his bowlers the risk of injury. Calling a press conference on the rest day, he accused the West Indians of conducting a war, a charge that drew little sympathy from his opposite number, Lloyd, especially in light of his team's travails in Australia. Fast bowling was a legitimate part of international cricket, he countered, and if the Indians couldn't play it, they shouldn't be playing at Test level.

Facing a first-innings deficit of 85, India knocked it off with two wickets down, but with three wickets falling on 97, Bedi closed their second innings because five of his batsmen were absent injured. Set 12 to win, the West Indies won by ten wickets to take the series 2–1, leaving the Indians to return home battle-weary and enveloped in plasters.

After seeing off India, the West Indies travelled to England and gave notice of their new-found resolution by winning 3–0. Although the relationship between the two teams was reasonably civil, there's no doubting the galvanising effect that the England captain Greig, a white South African, had on the West Indians with his inflammatory pre-series remark that he would make them 'grovel'.

After draws in the first two Tests, the third Test at Old Trafford took on a greater significance. The climax came at the end of the third day as England, bowled out for 71 in their first innings, set out on the forlorn task of scoring 552 for victory. On a cracked, unpredictable surface that caused the ball to fly dangerously, England's veteran openers, Edrich and Close, were subjected to what their team-mate Pocock called the most appalling 85 minutes he ever saw in first-class cricket. Assailed by a glut of bouncers and short-pitched bowling from Andy Roberts, Holding and Daniel, Close was hit three times and buckled on another occasion; then, five minutes before the close, Edrich was struck a nasty blow on the thigh. As he mouthed off some oaths about his opponents to the umpire, his anger and dismay was all too apparent.

While the England dressing room sat in stony silence – Greig admitted that it was the first time he felt frightened about going out to bat – umpires Bill Alley and Lloyd Budd looked on passively until the former finally warned Holding for intimidatory bowling. It was a near miracle that Edrich and Close survived to stumps, by which time the score had advanced to 21 for no wicket, 11 of them off the bat. Appalled by what they had witnessed, the English media to a man lacerated the West Indian tactics.

'That Clive Lloyd allowed this exhibition to go on when it achieved nothing for his side and so infringed the spirit of cricket was probably the most remarkable aspect of it,' declared Michael Melford of the *Daily Telegraph*.[85]

'In happier times the West Indies sang to the calypso of Cricket, Lovely Cricket,' wrote *Daily Mail* cricket correspondent Alex Bannister. 'Now it's Cricket, Ugly Cricket, a travesty of a duel between bat and ball, a bore and an affront to the paying spectator. Who wants to watch batsmen at the receiving end of a coconut shy at a fairground? There have always been bumpers, but I am sure there is a growing threat to the game at large from deliberate short pitchers at the batsman's rib cage.'[86]

Learning from their mistakes, the West Indian quicks kept the ball up when the match resumed after the weekend, and bowled England out for 125 to win by 425 runs. They went on to win the next two Tests with some classical fast bowling, most notably Holding's 14 wickets on a featherbed of a wicket at the Oval.

That winter, England, under Greig, toured India. Asked on arrival about the umpiring controversies that had marred New Zealand's recent tour there, Greig, a great favourite with the Indian crowds, was diplomacy itself, declaring that Indian umpires were among the best in the world and that his players wouldn't place undue pressure on them. His words worked a treat as England swept to an unassailable 3–0 lead after three Tests. It was only when Mohammad Ghouse, the object of New Zealand's ire, stood in the fourth Test that the wheel of fortune turned against them.

After India, England headed to Melbourne for the Centenary Test. As with any match between England and Australia, the match lacked nothing in intensity, but two acts of chivalry stood out. The first involved Bob Willis, who, having broken Australian opener Rick McCosker's jaw as he missed a hook, kept the ball up to him when he returned with his jaw wired up late in Australia's second innings. The second involved Rodney Marsh, who recalled Derek Randall after he had been given out caught behind off Greg Chappell for 161. Set 463 to win, England, led by Randall, were still in with a chance when Marsh owned up to the fact that the ball hadn't carried to him. (Chappell wondered whether Marsh had found religion.) Randall went on to make 174 as Australia emerged victors by 45 runs, the same margin of victory as in the first Test at Melbourne 100 years earlier.

On the Australian tour of England in the summer of 1977, the divisions among the tourists caused by the announcement of Kerry Packer's World Series Cricket (WSC) drained them of spirit and morale. As they entered the fourth Test at Headingley 2–0 down, their pent-up frustration finally broke when a confident appeal for a caught-behind against Boycott in England's first innings was rejected by umpire Alley. While bowler Ray Bright remonstrated with Alley, the whole team, led by David Hookes, abused both

Boycott and the umpire. When Hookes wouldn't shut up, Alley went over to him and told him that he wouldn't tolerate such a challenge to his authority; he then warned captain Greg Chappell that unless he controlled his players the game wouldn't restart. On retiring from umpiring in 1984, Alley wrote bitterly about the overall decline in standards: the ludicrous non-stop appealing, the sullen resentment of those given out lbw and the general lack of manners among the players. It was an opinion widely shared within the umpiring community as the Packer revolution enhanced player power and promoted greater insubordination, turning the world of cricket upside down.

Chapter 6

Kerry Packer's Legacy

UNTIL 9 May 1977, the name of Kerry Packer, the Australian media magnate, was virtually unknown outside his own country – but all that was about to change as he became the most important influence on the game of cricket since W.G. Grace.

Packer was the heir to an eminent media dynasty. His grandfather, Robert Clyde Packer, began as a reporter, moved into management, secured share holdings and became a press baron in his own right, possessing an uncanny ability to make newspapers appeal to the masses. He brought his only son, Frank, into the business even before he was 20, and taught him the basic principles of management of capital and people and how to secure a powerful base.

When Robert Clyde Packer died in 1934, Frank inherited his media interests. The following year, he bought the Sydney *Daily Telegraph*, and in 1936 he formed the Australian Consolidated Press, a parent company for all the various Packer publications, foremost of which was the *Australian Women's Weekly*. Frank Packer also took Consolidated Press into television, launching TCN 9 in Sydney, which became the nucleus of the commercial free-to-air Nine Network (often known as Channel Nine).

On Frank's death in 1974, his son Kerry assumed control of his media empire, and in 1976 he bought out his elder brother Clyde's share of the family business. An inveterate gambler and very keen sportsman, Kerry saw in cricket a lucrative product unexploited by the authorities and twice bid for the exclusive rights to televise the Tests in Australia, in 1975/76 and the following year.

Peremptorily rejected out of hand by the renamed Australian Cricket Board (ACB), Packer wasn't prepared to take his rebuff lying down. Discerning the defences of the cricket establishment to be fraying, he went for their jugular. The issue on which he took his stand was players' salaries, which, despite some recent improvement, remained a pittance compared with sports such as tennis, football and golf. Offering substantially better terms, he contracted 50 of the world's top cricketers for his WSC.

Repelled by this challenge to their authority, the TCCB, ACB and ICC (then the International Cricket Conference) were in no mood to compromise, banning all the Packer players from Test cricket from 1 October 1977; but, with the courts finding in favour of Packer on the vital question of breach of trade, WSC went ahead from that November. Although its early stages were inauspicious as the Australian public preferred watching traditional Test matches, Packer's fortunes began to look up the following year, when he was granted the right to stage floodlit cricket at Test grounds such as Sydney. These day-night matches proved a rollicking success. Large crowds marvelled at this new, dynamic form of cricket, and with an under-strength Australia no match for England in the Ashes, the wheel turned markedly in Packer's direction. With the ACB realising that he wasn't going away, they raised the white flag, and on 30 May 1979 granted Channel Nine exclusive rights to broadcast and promote cricket in Australia for ten years. It was to prove a defining moment as Packer's legacy became permanent.

It wasn't simply the night cricket, the coloured clothing and the celebrity lifestyles: the aggressive marketing gave cricket a more partisan feel. Even when consigned to play in front of sparse crowds in soulless football stadia, WSC lacked nothing in intensity as the world's cricketing elite competed against each other for substantial amounts of prize money. According to Wayne Daniel, the cricket was the most competitive he had ever played. 'The opposition were hard and mean. There was no friendship on the pitch. The verbals – especially from the Australians – would just fly.'[87]

Up against a battery of fast bowlers bowling persistently short on hard, bouncy pitches, batting became a hazardous business, with 14 players suffering head injuries during the first year. According to South African all-rounder Mike Procter, a one-day match between the West Indies and the World XI at VFL Park in Melbourne during the second year staged the biggest bouncer war he'd ever seen. Not even tail-enders were spared the ordeal of short-pitched bowling, as West Indian number eleven Joel Garner discovered on walking in to bat against the World XI with his side in a hopeless position. Greig, the opposing captain, aware that Garner had sustained a broken finger, instructed his bowlers to show him no mercy. Operating to orders, Clive Rice struck Garner first ball on his finger, causing him to wince with pain before knocking over his stumps in fury and stomping off back to the pavilion.

While purists may have abhorred such developments, the drama and controversy associated with hostile fast bowling made for compulsive viewing, along with the baying crowds and the contentious decisions, according to the moguls of Channel Nine. In a more nationalistic, market-driven age where the cult of wealth and success became ever more acceptable, WSC left a permanent mark on the game. To its supporters, it enhanced cricket as a spectacle, appealed to a new audience and boosted it financially in a way never previously imagined; to its detractors, it coarsened the game and accentuated declining standards of sportsmanship throughout the world.

On their 1977/78 tour to the West Indies, Bobby Simpson's Australians were subjected to a preponderance of short-pitched bowling by their opponents. After Colin Croft had injured two Australian batsmen in the Guyana match, Australia manager Fred Bennett issued a statement protesting about Croft's overuse of the bouncer, claiming it was in direct contravention of the law and the tour conditions.

Similar reservations emanated from the Indians on their tour to Pakistan in 1978, the first encounter between the two nations for nearly two decades. In the first Test at Faisalabad, Gavaskar called his captain, Bedi, on to the field to object to the barrage of bouncers that Imran Khan and Sarfraz Nawaz were firing at him. Only then did they cease, but in the third one-day international at Sahiwal, Bedi called off the match in protest, with India needing 23 to win off 20 balls, after Sarfraz bowled four successive bumpers in defiance of the law and with no intervention from the umpires.

Gavaskar, India's vice-captain, and Sarfraz were embroiled in further confrontation in the first Test when the former was reportedly verbally abused by the latter. Gavaskar complained to umpire Shakoor Rana about Sarfraz's bad language, but Shakoor just laughed. Later in the match, Gavaskar's growing impatience finally erupted when Mohinder Amarnath, India's opening bowler, was cautioned by Shakoor for running on the wicket, in contrast to Sarfraz and Mushtaq Mohammad, who had committed the same offence without even receiving a warning. Employing some ripe language towards Shakoor, Gavaskar so offended the umpire that he and his colleague refused to take the field on the final morning, delaying play by a few minutes, until an apology of sorts was made.

Any grievances that the Indians had about the Pakistani umpires were more than reciprocated when Pakistan toured India a year later, losing the series 2–0. Lbw decisions proved particularly contentious, and in the fourth Test at Kanpur, after Pakistan fast bowler Sikander Bakht had knocked down the stumps in frustration after having another lbw appeal turned down, his captain, Asif Iqbal, threatened to abort the tour.

Because of the greater respect that their umpires commanded, English crowds were spared the worst of the rancour and dissent that was becoming commonplace elsewhere; but, with the game becoming harder, there was no escaping the occasional controversy. In 1976, the ICC had agreed to outlaw fast short-pitched bowling against non-recognised batsmen, an agreement that was breached during England's tour to Pakistan and New Zealand in 1977/78. In the first Test between England and Pakistan at Edgbaston in 1978, Willis hit Pakistan nightwatchman

Iqbal Qasim with a bouncer and ignored the stricken batsman by striding back to his mark. Amid the criticism heaped upon Willis, his captain, Mike Brearley, defended him by claiming that a nightwatchman who had batted a long time should be treated like a normal batsman. The TCCB issued a statement deeply regretting the incident, reminded Brearley of his responsibilities, and encouraged captains to exchange lists of the non-recognised batsmen who would be protected from short-pitched bowling, none of which made a great impact.

In the second Test of England's tour to Australia that winter, Brearley rejected umpire Brooks's contention that his team shouldn't be bowling bouncers at Australian tail-ender Geoff Dymock on grounds of safety, asserting that anyone who walked to the crease accepted a risk. Weighed down by the constant appealing and dissent shown by both teams, Brooks, a respected umpire, decided to retire immediately after the Test. 'Such behaviour might not affect a younger man but it certainly had an effect on a fellow of my age,' he later wrote. 'I couldn't see why I should stand there and have players looking at me as if I were a leper.'[88]

Although the series contained much sledging and mass appealing, it was nothing compared with Australia's subsequent two-match series with Pakistan, fresh from a fractious tour to New Zealand. In the first Test at Melbourne, Australian fast bowler Rodney Hogg, having played a defensive stroke, was run out by Javed Miandad after leaving his crease to inspect the wicket, and when the umpires refused Pakistan captain Mushtaq Mohammad's offer to rescind the appeal, Hogg smashed his stumps. 'I thought Javed could have shown a bit more feeling for the spirit of cricket,' wrote Australian batsman Allan Border. 'Bit naïve of me probably, but I had just come into the Test scene.'[89]

'Where I came from nobody would have thought anything of it,' Javed countered, recalling the uncompromising code of street cricket of his youth in Pakistan, 'but down in Melbourne that run out seemed to get everyone worked up.'[90]

In the second Test at Perth, Australia's Alan Hurst ran out Sikander Bakht when he was backing up too far without a warning, to end a spirited last-wicket stand – much to the indignation of Sikander's partner, Asif Iqbal, who, out of character, broke his wicket. In retaliation, Pakistan appealed successfully against opener Andrew Hilditch during Australia's second innings when Hilditch, at the non-striker's end, picked up the ball and gave it to bowler Sarfraz Nawaz. All three incidents, according to *Wisden*, were much to be deprecated.

'The 1979–80 season was always going to be awkward and even more so for the disgraceful behaviour of some of the returning senior players,' wrote Chris Harte in his *A History of Australian Cricket*. 'No longer was cricket a gentleman's game in Australia: it was a tough, uncompromising battle with no quarter given in any direction.'[91] Twice during that season Ian Chappell was reported for abusing umpires, the first offence earning him a three-week suspension, the longest ban ever imposed on an Australian, and the New South Wales Cricket Association expressed such concern about declining standards at all levels of grade cricket that they issued a formal reminder to all clubs to behave. Yet for all their strictures, the browbeaten authorities struggled to hold the line in this new, turbulent climate.

During the first Test between Australia and England at Perth in December 1979, Lillee strode out to the middle with an aluminium bat that he was marketing, and held up play for ten minutes after the umpires told him to change it for a wooden one. Amid unedifying scenes in which Lillee threw a replacement bat 20 yards and challenged the authority of both the umpires and his captain, Greg Chappell, he was merely warned about his behaviour by the ACB. According to cricket writer and broadcaster Christopher Martin-Jenkins, the board had 'acted pusillanimously and irresponsibly ignoring the wider interest of the game, the conduct of which was still, officially, in their charge. Many young cricketers who saw Lillee go effectively unpunished for his open defiance might well have got the impression that rebellious behaviour is part of the game.'[92]

There was worse to come when New Zealand played host to Clive Lloyd's West Indies. After an arduous if successful tour of Australia, the West Indians found the weather and conditions in New Zealand totally alien to their style of cricket and reacted accordingly. During the first Test at Dunedin, a low-scoring affair, the bulk of the umpiring decisions went against the tourists, not least in New Zealand's second innings as they struggled to make the 104 they needed for victory. One such decision favoured their batsman John Parker after he appeared to glove a Michael Holding delivery to the wicketkeeper. The bowler was riled enough by this apparent injustice that he kicked two stumps straight out of the ground at the batsman's end.

After New Zealand won the first Test by one wicket, the West Indies didn't appear at the post-match presentation or share a drink with their opponents, and manager Willie Rodriguez criticised the umpires. Things were no better in the second Test at Christchurch, when, once again, the West Indies fell victim to poor umpiring. After being dismissed for 228 in their first innings, they fought back, quickly taking the first three New Zealand wickets, only to find that several confident appeals against home captain Geoff Howarth went against them. By tea on the third day, with Howarth on 99 and the match slipping away from them, the West Indians felt so aggrieved about their lot that they lingered in the dressing room for an additional 12 minutes at the end of the interval, and when they did appear they merely went through the motions. It later transpired that the team had threatened to abandon the tour and return home unless Fred Goodall, New Zealand's leading umpire, were replaced, but firm leadership by Jeff Stollmeyer, president of the West Indies Board of Control, put paid to such threats.

That wasn't the end of the trouble, however. When the match resumed after the rest day, another controversial not-out decision by Goodall, this time in favour of Richard Hadlee, so incensed bowler Colin Croft that he let fly with a barrage of bouncers and on one occasion cannoned into the back of Goodall as he entered his delivery stride. 'It was a calculated attack and one of the most shocking incidents ever to have occurred in cricket,' wrote Hadlee.[93] To compound matters, Goodall had to walk the entire length of the pitch to where Lloyd was standing in the slips to remonstrate with him about Croft's conduct. The Trinidad Umpires' Association came out with a statement highly critical of the West Indian team, and the New Zealand Cricket Council wanted Croft omitted for the third Test, but Lloyd took no action. After that Test had ended in a draw, giving New Zealand the series 1–0, Rodriguez refused to attend the traditional end-of-tour press conference, professing that it would achieve nothing, and Lloyd made a brief appearance only to defend his team. On his return home, the West Indies captain was made aware of his board's disapproval of his players' behaviour in New Zealand, and he, Holding and Croft wrote letters of apology to their hosts.

The following year, 1981, saw the game slip further into disrepute, beginning with the third and final Test of the Australia–India series at Melbourne. After a lean run with the bat, Indian captain Gavaskar was beginning to make amends with an opening partnership of 165 with Chetan Chauhan, whereupon he was given out lbw to Lillee for 70. Convinced that he had hit the ball, Gavaskar lingered at the crease, and when Lillee gave him a brusque send-off he lost his cool. He urged a reluctant Chauhan to leave the field with him in protest, only to be met at the pavilion gate by the Indian manager, Wing-Commander S.A.K. Durrani, who ordered Chauhan to return and get on with the match. 'Appalling though Gavaskar's action was,' wrote Richie Benaud, 'it was not, in my opinion, nearly as appalling as the lack of reaction he gained from it. In fact, he got away with it, with apologists for modern-day player behaviour murmuring that he was obviously under a lot of pressure.'[94]

Melbourne was the scene for further furore in the third of five one-day matches in the final of the Benson and Hedges World Series Cup between Australia and New Zealand. Australian captain Greg Chappell became engulfed in controversy when he appeared to have been caught at deep midwicket by Martin Snedden on 52. Television replays confirmed this, but both umpires' attention was fixed elsewhere, and Chappell, profiting from his escape, went on to score 90.

Needing 230 to win, New Zealand were competitive throughout, and even though they needed a six to win off the final ball of the match, Chappell was taking no chances. Ignoring the reservations of Rodney Marsh, his vice-captain, he instructed his younger brother Trevor to bowl an underarm grubber, which he duly did. New Zealand number ten Brian McKechnie blocked it and threw away his bat, while his captain, Geoff Howarth, came on to the pitch to check on the legality of the ball. The umpires confirmed it was legal. After the Australians had trooped off the field in silence, Greg Chappell was preparing to take a shower when Sam Loxton, the only national selector present, put his hand on his shoulder and said, 'You might have won the game, but you've lost a lot of friends.' Distraught by what had happened, Loxton cried all the way home, and within a couple of months he had severed all his links with Australian cricket as an administrator and selector.

While Greg Chappell defended his action at a press conference, stating that it was within the rules of the game, Benaud, in his post-match analysis, called his performance 'gutless'. New Zealand prime minister Robert Muldoon was equally scathing, and Malcolm Fraser, his Australian counterpart, and Sir Donald Bradman were among the other luminaries who condemned Chappell. 'Fair dinkum, Greg,' declared his brother Ian, 'how much pride do you sacrifice to win 35,000 dollars?'

Reeling from the fallout, Chappell changed tack the next day and admitted that in the cold light of day his decision wasn't within the spirit of the game. He regretted it and wouldn't do it again. 'Some say it is money that has caused this collapse in the ethics of the game, others that it is the reflection of a graceless age,' commented *Wisden* editor John Woodcock. 'In Australia, I am afraid, it is partly the result of weak government. For too long the Australian Cricket Board have been over-tolerant of indiscipline and actions of dubious intent. ... The latest precept, that Australian players shall penalise each other for misconduct, hardly seems a step in the right direction.'[95]

Woodcock's words were borne out the following season, 1981/82, by an unseemly confrontation between Dennis Lillee and Javed Miandad, two abrasive figures with a history of niggling each other. Set 543 to win in the first Test against Australia at Perth, Pakistan were 78/2 when Miandad pushed Lillee on to the leg side and was about to complete a run when he was obstructed by Lillee. Following a heated exchange between the two of them, Lillee launched a kick at Miandad, and Miandad raised his bat, before umpire Tony Crafter came between them. According to *Wisden*, the confrontation was one of the most undignified in Test cricket, but the initial A$200 fine imposed on Lillee by his team-mates (the Australian players sat in self-judgement on such matters then) was deemed so paltry that the umpires condemned it for its leniency. The ACB then intervened and suspended Lillee for Australia's two ensuing one-day internationals.

Yet the age of chivalry hadn't entirely vanished. In the Golden Jubilee Test between India and England in 1980, the Indian batsmen walked, and England wicketkeeper Bob Taylor was the beneficiary of an act of magnanimity by the Indian captain, Viswanath, when given out caught at the wicket. As Taylor lingered, flabbergasted by the decision, Viswanath, after consulting several of his colleagues, told the umpires that he wished to withdraw the appeal, to which the umpires consented. It proved a defining moment as England were struggling at 85/5; thereafter Taylor added 171 with Botham, helping England to a handy first-innings lead of 54; and, with Botham taking 7–49 in India's second innings of 149, they went on to win the match by ten wickets.

Less memorable was the fate of Keith Fletcher, captain of England on their 1981/82 tour to India. Frustrated by some dubious umpiring in the first Test, which England lost, and by a caught-behind decision against him in the second Test at Bangalore, Fletcher, in a momentary act of petulance, knocked off the bails as he departed, a lapse for which he later apologised. His apology and his otherwise impeccable conduct weren't enough to save him when the team arrived home. Peter May, the new chairman of the selectors and a stickler for propriety, took a dim view of such dissent and replaced him with Bob Willis, who was tasked with improving England's on-field demeanour. A sign of

Willis's intent came in the first Test against India at Lord's that summer when Phil Edmonds, England's left-arm spinner, was given a wigging for provoking Indian batsman Dilip Vengsarkar with some ill-advised comments as he fielded at short leg. He was soon omitted from the team and not selected for the tour to Australia that winter.

Willis fully lived up to May's expectations. Although a rather moody fast bowler, he had been brought up to respect the best of the game's traditions, and as captain he led by example. At Headingley in the third Test against Pakistan that summer, he publicly rebuked Surrey opening bowler Robin Jackman for giving Wasim Bari, Pakistan's wicketkeeper, a hostile send-off after dismissing him. Later, when selected for the 1982/83 tour of Australia, Jackman was warned by manager Doug Insole that any subsequent gestures would see him sent home immediately.

Following a series of unsavoury incidents in Australia over the previous several winters, the England players were asked not to appeal excessively and accept umpiring decisions, a request the players by and large complied with. This was particularly the case in the fifth Test at Sydney, when some crucial decisions went against them, the most critical of which involved Australia's John Dyson in the first over of the Test. As Dyson responded to a quick run by his opening partner, Kepler Wessels, Willis fielded well off his own bowling and threw down the stumps at the wicketkeeper's end. Although Dyson was well short of his ground, a fact confirmed by the television cameras, the umpire gave him not out. Dyson went on to score 79 in Australia's first innings, which went a long way towards giving them the draw they needed to regain the Ashes, but for all Willis's private reservations about the standard of umpiring in the series, he ensured that any dissent was kept to a minimum. He remained true to these principles in Pakistan the following winter, and when forced out of the final two Tests because of injury, he handed over to David Gower, whose outlook on the game drew comparisons with the Golden Age.

A batsman of effortless grace, Gower captained in similar vein, establishing a good rapport with his opposite number and treating his opponents with the respect they merited. Fully aware of the indifferent standard of umpiring in India, he implored his team in 1984/85 to respect their authority, and despite being a victim himself of a couple of wretched decisions, he practised what he preached. At the end of the series, which England won 2–1, the wife of Indian captain Gavaskar, while sympathetic to her husband's loss, admitted to feeling so much happier at seeing Gower smile. 'Whatever the critics may say about David Gower, he is every inch the perfect English gent in success and failure alike,' wrote sports journalist Frank Keating.[96] Ironic, then, that Gower's Corinthian ethos increasingly told against him. When he was discarded prematurely from a mediocre England team in 1992, it spelt the end of an era.

Chapter 7

Danger in Paradise

FEW images more aptly defined the cricket of the 1980s than that of a quartet of West Indian fast bowlers keeping up a relentless assault on opposing batsmen, as they struggled to survive over after over of hostile fast bowling aimed as much at the body as the wicket. The prowess of these bowlers was indisputable, but their sheer brutality upset those who viewed cricket primarily as a game of skill and chivalry, and led to some largely futile attempts to curb physical intimidation by tampering with the laws.

Intimidation has always been a vital part of a fast bowler's armoury, and captains possessing raw pace in their team weren't averse to using it to good effect. Warwick Armstrong did it with Gregory and McDonald, Jardine with Larwood and Voce, and Bradman with Lindwall and Miller – but most fast bowlers pre-1970 were less inclined to bowl short. When John Woodcock asked 'Hopper' Reid, the former Essex and England fast bowler of the 1930s, how often he bowled bouncers, Reid replied that he couldn't ever recall bowling one. 'I would have been afraid of hurting someone.' Les Ames, the Kent and England wicketkeeper during the 1930s, later told Alan Knott that he would have been shocked if he received more than five bouncers a season. It was a similar number to what Bob Gale, the Middlesex batsman of the 1950s and 1960s, received, although Gale acknowledged that those considered suspect against the short ball were targeted more frequently. Brian Statham used the bouncer sparingly, but, after bouncing the young Ken Barrington, he felt the full wrath of the umpire. 'Cut it out, Statham,' came the rebuke. 'He's only a youngster.'

One important convention at that time was the fast bowlers' union, whereby quick bowlers didn't bowl short at non-recognised batsmen, so that Trueman and Statham would bowl short at Keith Miller, knowing that Miller wouldn't retaliate against them. When Alec Bedser proved an obdurate nightwatchman at Headingley in 1948, going on to score 79, an exasperated Ray Lindwall struck him with a bouncer in the chest. That night Bill O'Reilly, Lindwall's club captain in Sydney, told him that he hoped he would never see him bowl another bouncer at a bowler. The message must have percolated through, because a few years later Lindwall berated his young New South Wales team-mate Alan Davidson for breaking this convention, and Arthur Morris, captain of New South Wales in the early 1950s, once forbade his bowlers from bowling quick against Victoria's Doug Ring, a useful lower-order batsman. By the time his bowlers asked Morris to reconsider, Ring was on 88.

Not all tail-enders were spared. Jim Laker received a nasty blow above the eye from West Indian fast bowler Frank King in the Port of Spain Test during MCC's 1953/54 tour to the West Indies, days after Fred Trueman had struck the Trinidad leg-spinner Wilf Ferguson with a bouncer. The New Zealand lower order was peppered by South Africa's quicks, Neil Adcock and Peter Pollock, in the fifth Test at Johannesburg in 1961/62, in what their captain, John Reid, called 'vicious and unwarranted stuff' – but Pollock wasn't to be deterred. Playing against Western Australia at Perth in 1963, he broke Tony Lock's arm with a bumper. Trueman was given a taste of his own medicine by Somerset's Fred Rumsey at Taunton in 1963. Finally, after being hit on the bicep, he walked purposefully down the pitch to Rumsey and asked him, 'Do you want to die?' Somerset declared before Rumsey batted in the first innings, and as he came out to bat in the second innings, Yorkshire captain Brian Close refrained from giving Trueman the ball, fearing the consequences of such a confrontation.

As cricket entered a more competitive phase, bowling short and hitting batsmen became a more accepted part of the game. Dennis Lillee recalls hitting a batsman in a grade match in Perth early in his career and his captain, Kevin Taylforth, ordering him back to his mark and to wait. 'If he carries on,' Taylforth told him, 'you run in and bowl to him as fast as you can.' Injuries to batsmen were all part of the game, and Lillee had to divorce himself from that.

Raw pace was nothing new in West Indian history. Peter May thought Wes Hall and Chester Watson, their opening pair in 1959/60, were two of the fastest bowlers he ever faced; and, with much of their attack directed at the body rather than the stumps, batting was a painful business. The hostility continued through the 1960s with Hall and Griffith, but there had never been anything to match the abundance of quicks that emerged in the Caribbean during the 1970s, and, after the pounding they took in Australia in 1975/76, the West Indies were intent on revenge. Under Clive Lloyd they became a more ruthless unit, using the ferocity of their pace attack as a means of demoralising the opposition. World Series Cricket further blooded them for battle and made them the all-conquering team they became in the 1980s.

Having emerged from their unfortunate fracas in New Zealand in March 1980, they quickly reasserted themselves with comfortable wins over England in back-to-back series. Their tactics of persistent short-pitched bowling and slow over rates, however, won them few friends. In one of his last assignments for the *Sunday Times*, Jack Fingleton wrote that watching them field was 'the most boring experience I have had in Test cricket'. He also took exception to Croft's failure to check on Boycott's welfare after hitting him, calling it 'unforgivable and contrary to everything good in the game'.[97]

Later in 1981, the West Indies went to Australia to play Greg Chappell's side. One down going into the third and final Test at Adelaide, they reduced their opponents to 17/4 in their first innings with some fearsome fast bowling. Chappell himself appeared to be their main target. After three overs of constant bombardment, the Australian captain called to umpire Robin Bailhache, 'I thought there was something in the rules about intimidatory bowling.' Twice Bailhache ignored Chappell's complaints, and, after another short-pitched ball smashed into his glove, he gave the umpire a piece of his mind.

Having easily disposed of India and Australia, the West Indies beat England 5–0 in the summer of 1984, the first time the latter had suffered such a humiliation since Johnny Douglas's tour of Australia in 1920/21. From the moment Malcolm Marshall and Joel Garner took the new ball on the opening day of the first Test at Edgbaston, they exuded menace. Two wickets fell in the first couple of overs, then, in the seventh over, England debutant Andy Lloyd was hit on the side of the head taking evasive action against Marshall and spent ten days in hospital with blurred vision. He never played for his country again.

After their drubbing at Edgbaston, England offered stiffer resistance in the next two Tests but were still comprehensively beaten, as they were in the fourth Test at Old Trafford, a match in which their young batsman Paul Terry sustained a broken arm. In the final Test at the Oval, they dismissed their opponents in their first innings for 190, only then to face the fury of Marshall, Garner and co on the fastest wicket of the series. Few suffered more than nightwatchman Pat Pocock, who hung on helplessly for 46 minutes without scoring. 'It was hard to watch the West Indian, Marshall, bowling to Pocock in last season's fifth Test match at the Oval without recoiling,' wrote Woodcock in *Wisden*. 'Pocock was the night-watchman from the previous day. As such, he could expect few favours. However, the Laws of Cricket make it abundantly clear that the "relative skill of the striker" must be taken into consideration by an umpire when deciding whether the bowling of fast, short-pitched balls amounts to "intimidation" and is therefore unfair. That Marshall, a superb bowler, should have kept bouncing the ball at so inept a batsman as Pocock was unwarrantable; that Lloyd should have condoned his doing was disconcerting; that Constant, the umpire at Marshall's end, should have stood passively by was unaccountable. It was a woeful piece of cricket, entirely lacking in chivalry. ... Perhaps, when the

International Cricket Conference do no more than pay lip service to the problem, it is not surprising that umpires are so compliant.'[98]

Dismissed for 162, England were eventually set 375 for victory, but once again they were all at sea against the quicks and were bowled out for 202. Pocock recalls opener Graeme Fowler returning to the pavilion after his dismissal and saying, 'It's over. I haven't got to bat against them again. ... Fowler's courage was beyond question, but after five Test matches against that viciously hostile attack, he was physically and emotionally drained.'[99]

The next team to face the music was New Zealand, a gritty side during the 1980s but mere journeymen compared with the artists on parade in the Caribbean. Ever since their defeat in New Zealand in 1979/80, the West Indies had been out for revenge, and now, on home soil, they had their chance. Two placid surfaces in the first two Tests enabled the tourists to escape with draws, but wicketkeeper Ian Smith was given a chilling foretaste of what awaited him in the middle of a prolific partnership with Martin Crowe. 'Smith, Smith, I'm going to kill you at Barbados,' cried Marshall. 'Wait till I get you in the next Test, Smith.'

He was as good as his word. Bowling fast and short round the wicket, he badly damaged Smith's left forearm with a nasty bouncer as the batsman protected his face. 'They were petrified and Smith himself was genuinely frightened while he batted,' Marshall later recalled. 'I can't say I have any regrets about resorting to psychological methods to sort out the New Zealanders. We were out for revenge ...'[100]

Well beaten in Barbados, New Zealand faced an even tougher grilling at Kingston, especially after Richard Hadlee had bowled five successive bouncers to Joel Garner in the West Indies' first innings. Sorely provoked by this breach of protocol, the West Indian quicks were in no mood to show mercy on a lightning-fast pitch. Egged on by the home crowd baying for blood, Marshall and Garner were at their most lethal as the tourists took some painful blows, one of which broke Jeremy Coney's arm. In the opinion of Geoff Howarth, the West Indian exhibition of fast bowling had little to do with his idea of cricket, while according to Coney, delivery after delivery was pitched short with the intention to injure. Law 42, which relates to the overuse of bouncers, might just as well have not existed for all the notice taken of it by the officials, though its wording was perfectly clear.

When these points were put to West Indies manager Wes Hall, he retorted that he didn't condone such tactics, but after Hadlee's aggression towards Garner, what did the New Zealanders expect? As for the media, he said they should suspend their judgement about intimidatory bowling and leave such matters to the umpires, which seemed a sure recipe for inaction given their repeated unwillingness to apply the law, as England discovered the following year.

Arriving in the Caribbean as very much the underdogs, the sight of vice-captain Mike Gatting having his nose broken by Marshall in the first one-day international at Kingston did little to raise morale ahead of the first Test on the same ground. On a lethal wicket, England were traumatised by bowling of extreme hostility, notably from Patrick Patterson, a strapping Jamaican whose recent life has been clouded in mystery. All out for 150, they tried to retaliate in kind, but they lacked the necessary pace and accuracy and ceded a first-innings lead of 223. In their second innings, batting became ever more torturous and even Botham looked apprehensive. 'The longer the match went on, the less like a civilised game of cricket it became,' reported Woodcock in *The Times*. 'Except on that evening of ill fame at Old Trafford in 1976, when Close and John Edrich were subjected to such a disgraceful barrage by the West Indian fast bowlers, I think I have never felt it more likely that we should see someone killed.'[101]

The climax to this intimidation came at the end of England's second innings when Patterson, having bowled five successive bouncers to Phil Edmonds, bowled him a beamer which thudded into his chest. As Edmonds staggered into his stumps, the West Indians seemed more intent on appealing for hit wicket than showing concern about his injury. Had he not been wearing a special form of protective body clothing, the consequences could have been dire. The umpire ruled not out, the first time in the match he had imposed any form of sanction because the delivery was unfair, only for Edmonds to be out quickly afterwards, leaving the West Indies victors by an innings.

Although none of the other Test wickets emulated Sabina Park in their venom, there was no respite from the quartet of Marshall, Garner, Holding and Patterson as they constantly ran through England's fragile batting. Demoralised by their inability to combat the West Indian attack and distracted by events off the field, England's limp performance earned them another 5–0 thrashing and a backlash from their own press corps. Yet, even allowing for their defects, the belligerence of their opponents' cricket once again became a matter of some concern. 'Under Clive Lloyd, the West Indies combined intimidatory bowling, expressly forbidden under laws drafted to prevent a repetition of bodyline, with a declining over rate designed to keep first five, and then four bowlers fresh throughout a six-hour day,' commented the *Sunday Times*'s Robin Marlar in his end-of-tour assessment. 'On this tour, the over rate was down to 11 an hour.'[102] Unless the West Indies were prepared to accept a two-an-over bouncer rule and an over rate of 15 an hour, he concluded they shouldn't be invited to tour England.

The clamour to change the laws to curb slow over rates and short-pitched bowling was vehemently dismissed by West Indians as a white imperialist plot now that they ruled supreme in the cricketing universe. They recalled their stoicism in Australia in 1975/76 as thunderbolts from Lillee and Thomson rained down on them ad nauseam. As far as they were concerned, the umpires were there to enforce the law, although interventions such as Dickie Bird's warning to Marshall at Edgbaston in 1984 hadn't been well received. 'The problem, however, lies not so much with the umpires or the old law but with the lack of technique of modern batsmen to contend with good, aggressive fast bowling,' claimed Michael Holding in his autobiography. 'More often than not, the batsman who is hit takes his eyes off the ball or plays too low.'[103]

It said much for Gower, Lamb and Botham that, despite their team's ignominious record against the West Indies, they remained on amicable terms with their opponents and matches rarely descended into acrimony. The 1988 series in England, won 4–0 by the West Indies and played in a good spirit, was the last time that the latter had it all their own way, as the first cracks in their imposing edifice became discernible. On their tour to the Caribbean in 1989/90, Graham Gooch's side provided stiffer resistance and were unlucky to lose the series 2–1. Having shocked their hosts by convincingly winning the first Test at Kingston by eight wickets, they had much the better of the third Test at Port of Spain. (The second Test in Guyana was abandoned owing to bad weather.) At lunch on the final day, they were 73/1 in pursuit of the 151 they needed to win. Gooch, it is true, had retired hurt with a broken hand, but with Lamb and Stewart well set, victory seemed a mere formality. It was then that a ferocious storm swept across the ground, causing a substantial delay. When play resumed in indifferent light at 4.05pm, England needed another 78 runs, but the West Indian bowlers, hampered by saturated run-ups, were in no mood to give up the ghost. Aware of the backlash that awaited them should they go two down in the series, they bowled their overs at a dilatory rate and kept the England batsmen in check with their nagging accuracy in deteriorating light. With dusk fast descending, the sixth-wicket pair of David Capel and Jack Russell eventually called off the chase with 31 still needed.

Although England refused to protest about West Indian gamesmanship in public, their press corps weren't so easily appeased. Perhaps the players better understood the reality of modern Test cricket, because in the fourth Test in Bridgetown they were the guilty party as they slowed down the over rate to just over 11 an hour on the fourth day as the West Indies chased quick runs for a second-innings declaration. This act of cynicism soon gave way to a right old rumpus when England, set 356 for victory, were rocked by the loss of three quick wickets that evening. The second of these was Rob Bailey, the Northamptonshire batsman on his first tour, given out caught behind to a ball that appeared to come off his pads. Lloyd Barker, the umpire, normally a fast decision-maker, had taken several steps towards square leg before raising his finger in the face of a vigorous appeal by the West Indian close fielders, who engaged in a scaled-down war dance.

Bailey's dismissal didn't impress Christopher Martin-Jenkins, who told BBC World Service listeners that a 'very good umpire had cracked under pressure' from a team intent on winning at all costs. His comments caused great offence on an island which prided itself on its sense of sportsmanship, and re-awoke ancient sensitivities about unreconstructed imperialism. Fully alive to the rumpus he had caused, Martin-Jenkins made an apology of sorts to Barker, who seemed determined to instigate libel proceedings against him and the BBC for defamation, a case which was eventually settled out of court.

Beaten by 164 runs with half an hour to spare, England faced a torrid time at St John's, Antigua, in the fifth and final Test, losing by an innings. On a lightning surface, the West Indian quicks Curtly Ambrose, Ian Bishop and Courtney Walsh were at their most combative as they pummelled England's middle order on the first day. Eleven of the first 13 balls bowled to Robin Smith, England's most accomplished batsman, were bouncers, and besides being hit in the face, he sustained a broken thumb which compelled him to retire hurt in the second innings. There were no complaints from England about the surfeit of short-pitched bowling, merely relief that they hadn't endured more of it earlier in the series, but it left Smith's mother distraught. 'If this is what Test cricket is all about, then I'm not very interested in it,' she told *Today* cricket correspondent Graham Otway. To rub salt into the wound, the umpires, having made no effort to curb the sustained physical intimidation in England's first innings, saw fit to warn David Capel for two consecutive short balls at Ambrose despite his military medium posing little threat compared with the West Indian quicks, a quirk that *Wisden* called nonsensically inconsistent.

In contrast to England, the West Indies' rivalry with Australia proved to be much more unpleasant, partly because they never forgot their humiliations there in 1975/76, and partly because of the verbal abuse they received from their players, which persuaded them to respond. (It may also have been due to the lack of Australians in county cricket at that time and hence fewer personal friendships such as those that Botham had with Richards and Garner at Somerset.) After a fractious tour to the Caribbean in 1983/84 in which Australia were well beaten, Greg Chappell called on umpires to restrict the West Indies' use of short-pitched bowling, comparing its danger to bodyline. His hopes proved wishful thinking when Australia hosted them six months later, since they were blown away in the first three Tests, losing captain Kim Hughes in the process. He was succeeded by Allan Border.

In the first Test at Perth, Larry Gomes and Jeff Dujon were hit on the head, and not one Australian went to see how they were; in the second Test at Brisbane, Desmond Haynes was severely reprimanded for an obscene gesture at Australian fast bowler Geoff Lawson after Lawson abused him on dismissal; in the fourth Test at Melbourne, Greenidge objected to the send-off Lawson gave him and continued the argument with the latter in the Australian dressing room; and in the fifth Test at Sydney, won by Australia, Border and wicketkeeper Steve Rixon were reported by the umpires for sledging after an unsuccessful appeal against Richards.

Border also crossed swords with Holding after the latter queried why he was walking down the pitch between overs in spiked boots. He snapped back with 'What's the matter? You can't take the heat now we're winning?' and continued his on-pitch strolling. Such flare-ups between the teams, Holding later wrote, became more and more commonplace.

The atmosphere was little better when the West Indies, under Richards, returned to Australia in 1988. After they had won the first Test at Brisbane by nine wickets, their fearsome pace quartet, led by Marshall and Curtly Ambrose, relished bowling on the fastest wicket in the world at Perth. Having endured something of a battering from Geoff Lawson and Merv Hughes in their first innings of 449, the West Indies repaid the favour in kind as Australia battled to stay in the game. They had reached 395/8 when Lawson, a stubborn tail-ender batting without a grille on his helmet, was felled by a rising ball from Ambrose that broke his jaw. He returned to the ground the next day, jaw all wired up, to be photographed alongside Ambrose, although not a word passed between the two of them.

Lawson's injury caused the Australian dressing room to see red. In a highly charged atmosphere, they took the field in defiant mood. Hughes dismissed Greenidge first ball and sent him on his way with some choice words, treatment that Greenidge didn't easily forgive. Despite Hughes's heroics in the second innings, the Australian batsmen were no match for the West Indian attack on a sporting wicket, losing by 169 runs.

The Australians lost again at Melbourne, where, on another notorious wicket, batsmen on both sides were repeatedly forced into evasive action. According to Woodcock, the West Indian attack in Melbourne was as 'relentlessly and ruthlessly hostile' as he had ever seen, and the failure of the team to register any concern or regret for batsmen who were hit he found thoroughly unedifying.

Set 400 to win, Australia experienced a traumatic final day as Patterson exacted revenge for the number of short balls he'd received from Steve Waugh the previous day. Bowling with terrifying pace, he pulverised the home team, not only by taking 5–39 but also causing multiple bruises and fractures. After hanging on grimly for the best part of three hours for 20, Border later said that he derived absolutely no pleasure or satisfaction from Test cricket as it had been in this match. 'I don't think I've ever seen so many blokes hit so much. It's just not enjoyable.' Feeling hard done by, the Australians chose to defy convention by shunning a post-match drink with the opposition, and, when they were criticised by the West Indians for this breach of protocol, Dean Jones explained: 'They talk about us not having a beer with them but it's a bit hard to come up to them afterwards and say: "Look, well bowled. I enjoyed that one in the stomach."'

Not surprisingly, the West Indies placed a different perspective on the bouncer war. When Richards was asked whether he could recall a match when so many batsmen had been hit, he referred to the Melbourne Test in 1975/76. Then the crowd were chanting 'kill, kill, kill' as the Australian bowlers ran in. He heard people complain about the surfeit of West Indian bouncers now, but he remembered how it was then.

Aside from the persistent short-pitched bowling and the numerous blows to the body suffered by the Australians, what appalled Woodcock was the failure of the umpires to act. 'Although entitled to protection under the law, the batsmen are not being given it, not even the tail-enders. They practically never are, either here or in the Caribbean, where short-pitched bowling is the staple diet. But can you be surprised at that, when all the umpires ever get from the International Cricket Conference is lip service, and from captains, when they do remonstrate, a flea in the ear?'[104]

Not everyone had it in for the tourists. 'It is outrageous to penalise the West Indies for their professionalism and their commitment to excellence,' said Mike Coward in the *Sydney Morning Herald*. 'They have taken the game to a new level. Rather than endeavour to match that new standard it would seem that England and Australia are more inclined to encourage action or legislation to bring them back to the field.'[105]

The fallout from short-pitched bowling added friction to a series marred by poor umpiring, slow over rates, verbal abuse and dissent. Having been a model of diplomacy on their recent tour of England, the West Indies adopted a more boorish attitude in Australia, not least the way they clashed with the umpires, some of whom were very inexperienced. This intimidation reached a climax in the fifth Test at Adelaide, where the umpires reported them for their misdemeanours. Particularly heinous was the case of Marshall who, having had an appeal against David Boon turned down by umpire Ric Evans, harangued him in unseemly fashion. In an article entitled 'Whatever happened to Calypso Cricket?', the Somerset captain and cricket columnist Peter Roebuck wrote that at times the intimidation of umpires appeared to be an acceptable tactic. 'During the series, senior West Indians could be seen smoking with rage at contrary decisions. Maybe it was the effect of 12 years at the top, or of the sharper politicisation of the Caribbean. In any event, grace had failed and things deteriorated so far that pressure was piled on in the hope of extracting a favourable verdict.'[106]

The festering animosity between the two teams reached new levels during the Australian tour of the West Indies in 1990/91, a tour which opener Mark Taylor called the hardest he ever encountered. Under Border's uncompromising leadership, Australia's rebuilding had begun to bear fruit. With comprehensive wins against England in successive series and with several West Indian greats past their pomp, the Australians arrived poised to snatch their crown.

The battle lines were drawn from the beginning when, in the match against Jamaica, Walsh was warned for intimidatory bowling after hitting Mark Waugh and Craig McDermott on the head with bouncers, much to the pleasure of crowd, a reaction which infuriated Border. To try to defuse the ill-feeling from previous encounters, the two teams arranged to share a drink at the end of each day's play, but this fraternisation lasted for only one Test, a match tarnished by excessive short-pitched bowling and plenty of harsh invective from both sides. Out to prove himself after his injury, McDermott sent three batsmen, Greenidge, Haynes and Gus Logie, to hospital during the West Indies' first innings. Logie's injury was particularly nasty, his blow requiring seven stiches above the eye, but he returned to much acclaim from the crowd to score a gritty undefeated 77 and steer his side to 264. Australia replied with 371, but, in a rain-affected match, the West Indies easily saved the game.

Led by a scintillating 182 from Richie Richardson, they won the second Test at Georgetown comfortably, but the match will always be remembered for the controversial run-out of Australia's Dean Jones in their second innings. Bowled off a no-ball by Marshall, Jones didn't hear the umpire's call and began walking off to the pavilion, whereupon Carl Hooper swooped in and broke the wicket. Despite Law 38 stipulating that if an illegal delivery is called the striker should be given not out unless attempting a run, umpire Clyde Cumberbatch upheld the appeal, and, with no one any the wiser, the decision stood. It was only later that the correct interpretation of the law was brought to the attention of the Australian dressing room, and, feeling highly aggrieved by the injustice meted out to Jones, Australian coach Bob Simpson confronted the umpires at the next interval. They sheepishly owned up to the error but insisted that bygones be bygones.

The refusal of the West Indians to show any remorse for the manner of Jones's dismissal brought condemnation from the Roman Catholic Archbishop of Trinidad and Tobago, Anthony Pantin, and widened the rift between the two sides. After a rain-ruined draw in the third Test at Port of Spain, the West Indies won the fourth Test at Bridgetown by 343 runs to take the series, their pace attack once again blowing away the brittle Australian batting. On an eventful opening day, the lingering feud between Desmond Haynes and Australian wicketkeeper Ian Healy, two volatile characters, was reignited when Haynes was given not out to a caught-behind down the leg side. Healy, objecting to Haynes's indication that the ball had come off his pad, told him to stop influencing the umpire, a rebuke that provoked Haynes into walking towards Healy, bat raised, to exchange insults.

Irked by Simpson's criticism of slow West Indian over rates, Richards launched a vitriolic assault on him after the match, accusing him of being a bad loser, a tirade that shocked the Australians as much as it offended them. The excoriation of their coach gave them an added incentive to perform well in the final Test at St John's, Antigua. They played their best cricket of the tour to win by 157 runs, but once again the match was marred by personal antipathy, Richards calling McDermott a coward as the Australian tail-ender backed away against the quicks, and Hughes clashing with Haynes after the latter was run out in the West Indies' second innings. Even at the end of the game, few of the traditional civilities were observed, with few West Indians congratulating the Australians on their victory. At the presentation ceremony, Clyde Walcott, president of the West Indies Board of Control, berated both sides for their churlish behaviour and urged a return to the game's traditional values. 'Above all else, what should have been a compelling advertisement for cricket was ruined by the obvious acrimony between the teams,' wrote Tony Cozier in *Wisden*. 'This manifested itself time and time again in verbal altercations on the field, and the rancour was accentuated by the television cameras which, for the first time, were transmitting live, ball-by-ball coverage back to Australia from the Caribbean.'[107]

The retirement of Richards that year and his replacement as captain by Richie Richardson, a more emollient personality, helped ease tension between the two sides, so that while future series weren't devoid of controversy, they lacked the deep-seated animosity of the 1980s and early 1990s. Relations were also helped by the ICC's decision in 1994 to clamp down on short-pitched bowling by limiting the number of bouncers to two an over, although non-recognised batsmen were afforded little protection compared with their predecessors of an earlier era.

Chapter 8

The Prowling Tiger

O F all the major Test-playing countries, Pakistan, with its tempestuous history and Islamic culture, was the most fascinating to visit – but touring there could be something of an ordeal. Teams from the affluent West didn't always appreciate the climate, the poverty and the political-religious sensitivities under which their hosts laboured. At the same time, the attitude of Pakistan's cricket authorities didn't always help. According to distinguished Pakistan cricket writer Omar Kureishi, 'Pakistan has a poor external image and cricket suffers from it. It is frequently seen as a dour, sad and corrupt place. This image rubs off on the cricket team. ... Frequently our team makes friends, plays exciting cricket, and has a pleasant demeanour, but the negative image of the country sticks to the team.'[108]

'Some of our bad reputation was well deserved,' wrote Arif Abbasi, a former chief executive of the Pakistan Cricket Board (PCB), the successor to the Board of Control for Cricket in Pakistan (BCCP). 'Cricket was frequently in the hands of small-minded men with chips on their shoulders and a certain paranoia that the whole world is against Pakistan ...'[109]

Nothing upset teams touring Pakistan more than the quality of its umpiring and the perceived bias in favour of the home team. MCC's 'A' tour there in 1955 caused ructions when a leading umpire, Idris Baig, responsible for a series of questionable decisions in the Peshawar 'Test', was splashed with water by the tourists after an official dinner. It proved an insensitive jape which upset their hosts and precipitated a major diplomatic furore. Only the friendship between Field Marshal Lord Alexander of Tunis, president of MCC, and General Iskander Mirza, governor-general of Pakistan and president of the BCCP, prevented the tour being cancelled.

During its first couple of decades, Pakistan's cricket culture, modelled on British values, tended to be deferential and defensive – but this began to change during the 1970s, when it threw off the shackles of its colonial past and forged its own identity, combining ingenuity and flair with a fervent desire to win. With television helping to give cricket a mass following, a host of new players emerged, untrained and self-taught and with little respect for the game's traditional proprieties. No one better encapsulated this new type of cricketer than Javed Miandad, one of Pakistan's most brilliant batsmen, whose introduction to the game on the back streets of Karachi instilled in him an ultra-competitive mentality. 'I have always had a militant approach to cricket,' he wrote in his autobiography. 'To me it is not so much a game as it is war.'[110]

With this new aggression defining their teams of the 1980s and 1990s, Pakistan proved formidable opponents, not least to the great West Indies side of that era; but, too often, this aggression was pushed too far, leading to charges of chicanery from their opponents. What fuelled these charges was the age-old problem of umpiring in Pakistan, while Pakistani teams on tour felt victimised by the home umpires and stigmatised by Western media stereotypes of them as fanatically partisan and morally suspect.

Under the captaincy of Imran Khan, Pakistan lost a hard-fought series in England in 1982, marred by their excessive appealing. Pakistan in turn felt aggrieved about a couple of decisions in the final Test at Headingley by David Constant, a fair-minded umpire possessed of a rather officious manner. Having taken exception to Constant as far back as 1974, Pakistan felt affronted that the TCCB declined their request to remove him from the Test umpires' panel, a request granted to India earlier that summer;

and, following their narrow defeat at Headingley, Imran went public with his criticism of Constant.

England's tour to Pakistan in 1983/84, sensitively led by Willis and his deputy, Gower, passed off without any major controversy, which is more than could be said of New Zealand's tour later that year. After losing the second Test at Hyderabad, the tourists spoke out against the umpires; then, in the third Test, their frustration boiled over when Javed Miandad was given two apparent reprieves. So strongly did captain Jeremy Coney feel about the umpiring of Shakoor Rana that he threatened to lead his team from the field. Only after consulting his manager was he persuaded to return.

In 1985 it was the turn of Sri Lanka to feel aggrieved about the Pakistani umpires, although some thought that their complaints acted as a convenient veneer for their own shortcomings. Their disaffection conveyed itself to the rest of their countrymen, so that when Pakistan arrived there for a return series three months later, they found a sullen people united by a blind hatred of the opposition. Even the umpires weren't immune from the general hostility. According to Imran, an appeal by one of his bowlers in the first Test was met by a response of 'Shut up. This isn't Pakistan.' After Sri Lankan batsman Arjuna Ranatunga had survived several confident appeals, the close-in Pakistani fielders accused him of being a cheat, whereupon Ranatunga left the field, taking the umpires with him. Despite the Pakistanis getting few concessions from the umpires, they won by an innings.

In the second Test, won by Sri Lanka, Imran called the umpiring a travesty. (In the first two Tests, 11 Pakistanis had been given out lbw compared with one Sri Lankan.) Javed Miandad just avoided a punch-up with the Sri Lankans after receiving a dubious decision, and was then attacked by a spectator on his return to the pavilion. With the morale of his players at rock bottom, Imran saw little point in continuing the tour. Only the intervention of the Pakistani president, General Zia, prevented an early return.

More contentious decisions in the drawn third Test accentuated Imran's belief in the need for neutral umpires, an idea he had first mooted back in 1978, as complaints about Pakistani umpiring grew ever more strident. While accepting that his country's umpires weren't always models of integrity – he recalled two of them approaching him before a Test against Australia in 1982/83 asking for instructions – he also thought that their counterparts the world over were vulnerable to domestic pressure. 'In the hothouse atmosphere of modern cricket it is not at all surprising that umpires tend to err in favour of the home side, which is also their own team,' he later wrote in his autobiography. 'The combined pressure of intense public emotion and personal affiliation proves too strong.'[111] If discipline were to be imposed on the players, he believed, the umpiring standards around the world needed to improve. Otherwise, efforts to improve discipline by fining players would prove futile.

On Imran's recommendation, the BCCP appointed Indian umpires for the final two Tests of Pakistan's three-match home series against the West Indies in 1986/87. The series proceeded amicably enough, and *Wisden* alluded to 'the welcome absence of bickering over decisions', not least the decision of the umpires to come off early for bad light in the final Test with Pakistan struggling to save the match and the series. The ICC were yet to be converted to the idea of neutral umpires, however, especially in countries like England which took great pride in the quality of their officials – a view which Imran didn't fully share, especially after Pakistan's victorious tour there in 1987.

Even before the Tests began, the legacy of Pakistan's previous tour returned to exacerbate past grievances. Once more, the Pakistanis expressed reservations about Constant and requested that he shouldn't officiate in the Tests; once again, the TCCB dug their heels in, professing to have the fullest confidence in their umpire. The fact that these private talks were leaked to the press prompted columns of bitter comment about Pakistan's irascible manager, Haseeb Ahsan, a former Test spinner sent home from the 1962 tour because of doubts about his action, and his impugning of England's umpires.

An unseemly fracas between rival groups of supporters during the third one-day international at Edgbaston, in which an English supporter was seriously injured, formed a sinister backdrop to an acrimonious Test series. Fresh from their Ashes triumph in Australia, Mike Gatting's side approached the summer with confidence, but Pakistan, captained once again by Imran, would prove no pushover. A rain-ruined first Test saw England coach Micky Stewart lash out at Pakistan's slow over rate and spurious use of substitutes, a broadside returned with interest by Haseeb Ahsan, who recalled England's time-wasting at Lahore in 1983/84.

After more rain in the second Test at Lord's, Pakistan won the third Test in style at Headingley, but their victory was overshadowed by the antics of wicketkeeper Salim Yousuf, who claimed a catch off Ian Botham when the ball had clearly dropped in front of him. His faux pas embroiled him in a furious altercation with Botham and earned him a reprimand from his captain. Tabloid suspicions that Pakistan didn't play the game were fuelled by Haseeb Ahsan's assertion that cheating had become part and parcel of international cricket, comments that left their mark on England in Pakistan the following winter.

Following an exciting draw in the fourth Test at Edgbaston, Pakistan had much the better of a draw in the final Test at the Oval, giving them a well-merited series win, their first in England. Their triumph was once again tainted by their indecorous behaviour on the field. As England, following on, battled to save the match on the final day, the histrionics of the tourists' close-in fielders brought them into conflict with umpire Constant. Having turned down a confident appeal against Botham when he had made 20, he told them to get on with the game, a rebuke which infuriated the manager, who called the umpire a disgrace in his post-match press conference.

After a summer of discontent, it was unfortunate to say the least that within less than three months the two sides resumed hostilities in Pakistan. With Pakistan having lost to Australia in a World Cup semi-final in front of their own supporters, and been beaten 3–0 in the one-day internationals by England, the sense of anti-climax was palpable. The team were summoned to meet their president, General Zia, who told them that national pride demanded an improvement in their performance.

With the Pakistanis still seething over their treatment by Constant, they were in no mood to accommodate England's wishes over choice of umpires. Nevertheless, the absence of all three of their World Cup umpires in favour of Shakeel Khan, a friend of Haseeb Ahsan, raised eyebrows. With the wicket at Lahore, the venue for the first Test, a spinner's paradise, Abdul Qadir, Pakistan's talismanic leg-spinner, exploited it to the full, taking 9–56 in England's first innings of 175. What galled England, however, was the dubious dismissal of several of their top-order batsmen, including Gatting himself. Their mood didn't lighten as the home side, availing themselves of better fortune from the umpires, compiled a near-unassailable lead of 217.

England's second innings began sedately with Chris Broad, top scorer in the first innings with 41, and Graham Gooch seeing off the new ball with few alarms. At 23/0, Broad played forward to left-arm spinner Iqbal Qasim and, despite missing it by some way, was given out by Shakeel Khan on a loud appeal. Clearly astounded by the decision, Broad remained rooted in his crease for the best part of a minute, vigorously proclaiming his innocence, until Gooch wandered down the pitch and persuaded him to go. 'Irrespective of whether Broad hit the ball or not, his behaviour was indefensible,' wrote Woodcock.[112] His refusal to leave the crease earned him a stern reprimand from the tour management but nothing more, as manager Peter Lush released a strongly worded statement that evening insinuating that the umpiring hadn't been entirely impartial. He went on to advocate neutral umpires, which was not TCCB policy.

After England slumped to an innings defeat the next day, Gatting gave vent to his feelings, claiming that nine of his batsmen had been the victims of bad umpiring during the match. 'I'd warned the team, but these things are a matter of degree, and none of us expected anything so blatant. You cannot play the game unless you do so on even terms. ... They obviously wanted to win this Test match very badly.'[113]

For all the provocation, England's behaviour in the first Test was inexcusable, according to an editorial in *The Times*. While accepting that the umpiring errors had been unusually frequent, the editorial opined that the players had to rise above them, or the game became meaningless.

> Mr Broad's angry refusal to 'walk', in contravention of the game's traditional standards, was regrettable. But the premeditated absence of the team from the prize-giving ceremony and the comments of the manager, Mr Peter Lush, made matters much worse. For Mr Lush, then the captain, Mr Mike Gatting, to become personally embroiled at a time when the occasion cried out for calm leadership reflects badly on their judgement.
>
> The England side was beaten not by bad umpiring but by leg-spin bowling, and it is hard to imagine how anyone could think differently. Had the players retreated with good grace to prepare for the second Test next week they would have saved their dignity at least. As it is, they have returned the moral ground to Pakistan who, it is fair to recall, themselves abandoned it last summer in this country.[114]

With England deflated and slumped on the canvas, their hosts had no intention of helping them to their feet. Without consulting them, the BCCP appointed Shakoor Rana for the second Test in Faisalabad. He was the country's most experienced umpire, but his abrasive style had embroiled him in several altercations with touring teams in the past, most notably with New Zealand in 1984/85.

Shakoor also had history as far as Gatting was concerned, since he had been one of the umpires in his debut match at Karachi in 1977/78, when he was twice lbw, and again in the Karachi Test of 1983/84, when he was lbw without offering a stroke. They had also clashed earlier on the tour, during a one-day international in which Gatting had refused Pakistan's request for a specialist wicketkeeper to replace the injured Salim Yousuf. Confronted with such a divisive personality, Gatting warned his team to keep their cool, but in the heat of battle he failed to follow his own instructions. His altercation with Shakoor came at the end of the second day, when England, despite some problems with the umpire, had reduced Pakistan to 106/5 in reply to their 292. During the penultimate over, bowled by off-spinner Eddie Hemmings, Gatting, fielding at backward short leg, informed batsman Salim Malik that he was bringing in David Capel to stop the single. As Hemmings turned to bowl, Gatting gestured to Capel that he had come in close enough, at which point Shakoor, from his position at square leg, halted play and accused Gatting of sharp practice. Gatting angrily denied the charge and told Shakoor to stop interfering, something he had been doing all innings. As he returned to his mark, Shakoor, employing some industrial language, called Gatting a cheat, prompting an infuriated Gatting to respond in kind as the two of them went head-to-head in an ugly finger-wagging confrontation.

For all the provocation meted out to him and his team, especially the implication that he had cheated – the England captain was one of the most honest players around – Gatting's behaviour was indefensible. His insulting language had offended Shakoor, who refused to resume his duties the next morning without receiving an unconditional written apology from Gatting – a request that the England captain was prepared to accede to, provided Shakoor did the same. A high-level meeting between the two sides the next morning appeared on the brink of resolving the impasse when Pakistan captain Javed Miandad, aware of his team's unpromising position in the match, persuaded Shakoor not to compromise. Consequently, the whole of the third day's play was lost as fruitless negotiations dragged on interminably. At one stage in the afternoon, manager Peter Lush drove 100 miles to meet the president of the BCCP, only to discover on arrival that he had gone out to dinner.

As footage of Gatting's confrontation with Shakoor was broadcast around the world, it divided opinion back home. Tom

Graveney, recounting his own experiences there in 1951, claimed that Pakistan had been cheating for 37 years and called for the team to come home, while Ray Illingworth said it was right that Gatting had stuck up for himself.

Others took a different view. Ted Dexter declared that the crisis was entirely England's fault. Cricket couldn't be played unless everything the umpire said and did was accepted. A further editorial in *The Times* opined that Gatting, by giving in to frustration, had destroyed the game's most precious code, and in doing so helped put cricket at risk from the same malaise plaguing football, tennis and boxing. In the same paper, their sportswriter Simon Barnes accused England of double standards.

> By open dissent, and by implicit support of open dissent from captain and tour management, England abandoned the principles of fair play they claimed they were defending. In effect, they said that if a Pakistani refused to walk, it is because he is a cheat; when an Englishman refuses to walk, it is because the umpire is a cheat.
>
> I dare say that umpire was in the wrong, but, with Gatting's rant, he and England have forfeited all claim to moral rightness.[115]

As England's manager worked frantically to find a compromise acceptable to all sides, the TCCB came under growing pressure from the Foreign Office to mend fences with a trusted ally, even if that meant the England captain eating humble pie. Consequently, an aggrieved Gatting was ordered to apologise unconditionally to Shakoor, something he acceded to with the tersest of notes. Incensed that management and captain had been badly let down by the TCCB, the mutinous England team vowed to return home, before opting for a compromise proposed by Gooch: their agreement to continue the tour was conditional on issuing a contract-breaching statement of their own defending Gatting, and criticising the TCCB for insisting on a written apology to Shakoor after the umpire had called him a cheat.

Gatting's enforced climbdown was slated by most of the British press and public. The *Daily Mail's* headline was 'Betrayal', *The Sun* lashed out at Mrs Thatcher for not backing the team, and the *Mirror* evoked memories of the notorious Munich agreement permitting Nazi Germany's carve-up of Czechoslovakia. Even the Lahore newspaper *The Nation* admitted that the umpiring had been deplorable. Once Shakoor had received his apology, the match resumed on the fourth morning, but the loss of more than a full day's play and bad weather prevented any hopes of a positive result.

Although the replacement of Shakoor by Mahboob Shah, Pakistan's best umpire, for the third Test didn't entirely eradicate the controversial decisions, with even the *Daily Mail* berating England for their dissent, the match ended in stalemate. More significant, perhaps, was the arrival of the heads of the TCCB, Raman Subba Row and Alan Smith, on a goodwill mission to repair some of the damage of the previous month. Somewhat out of the blue, Subba Row awarded each player a £1,000 hardship bonus, a gesture that suggested to the outside world that touring Pakistan was a real trial. That the tour should have ended with the traditional BCCP dinner being cancelled because England couldn't be persuaded to attend was 'dismally fitting', according to Woodcock, the retiring cricket correspondent of *The Times*. During his 34 years in that position, he had never felt the game to be in greater need of firm, honest and generous leadership both on and off the field. 'As the years go by the old values become harder to maintain, but there is no mistaking them, and, win or lose, they are still the most rewarding.'[116] 'Yet, at the end of the most acrimonious cricket tour of modern times,' wrote Alan Lee, Woodcock's successor, 'the hard truth was that, whatever the extraordinary nature of the provocation, England had performed poorly and behaved reprehensibly.'[117]

Their behaviour barely improved on their tour of Australia and New Zealand after Christmas. In the Bicentennial Test against Australia at Sydney, Broad was fined £500 for smashing his stumps in anger after his dismissal, and in New Zealand there were several disciplinary lapses involving dissent and bad language. 'The most alarming aspect of all was that the players themselves, and even their team manager, Mr Micky Stewart, seemed unwilling to acknowledge the poor impression which was created by such conduct,' wrote Lee in *Wisden*. 'Their oft-repeated reasoning was that other Test teams behaved similarly. True or not, this was no justification.'[118] It was a view endorsed by TCCB cricket committee chairman Ossie Wheatley, who vetoed Gatting's return to the captaincy in 1989: he thought England had a duty to set the right standards for others to follow.

Following England's shambolic tour of Pakistan, it was the Australians' turn to go there the following year. Before their departure, ACB chairman Malcolm Gray had impressed upon the players the need to show forbearance when up against the volatility of local conditions and the umpiring. Yet forbearance was soon in short supply as a familiar scene greeted them in Karachi, the venue for the first Test. On an underprepared wicket ideal for spin, Pakistan batted first, and Javed Miandad, fortunate to escape two marginal lbw decisions early in his innings, went on to score 211 out of Pakistan's 469. By the end of the third day, with Australia in deep trouble, manager Colin Egar and coach Bob Simpson called a press conference to castigate the Pakistanis for tampering with the wicket and for their incompetent umpires, most notably Mahboob Shah, an umpire Egar had specifically requested on their previous tour. They professed that they were at the end of their tether and had decided 'to let the outside world know we are battling against great odds'.

Not surprisingly, their protestations affronted their hosts, who accused them of bungling diplomacy, a line that met with some sympathy in the Australian press corps. 'There is no doubt that they [the Australians] have grounds for an emphatic protest,' wrote Mike Coward in the *Sydney Morning Herald*. 'But the lack of diplomacy is to be regretted. The Australians' cavalier treatment of Mahboob Shah smacks of the elitism of a representative of a developed country.'[119]

When the match resumed after the rest day, Australia continued to struggle with the Pakistan spinners and the umpiring.

Bowled out for 165 in their first innings, they followed on and were dismissed for 116, losing by an innings and 188 runs. When it was announced that Mahboob Shah had been reappointed for the second Test, the Australians perceived that as the final insult. At the post-match press conference, captain Allan Border described the match as 'a conspiracy from the word go' and raised the possibility of their going home, an option overwhelmingly supported by his players. The ACB soon quashed such mutinous talk, and the next day in Faisalabad Egar informed the tour party that they were obliged to stay put. They did, however, issue a statement, supported by the ACB, that was highly critical of the ICC for their unwillingness to censure the Pakistan authorities for what they claimed were flagrant breaches of the laws and conventions of the game there in recent years. After they had made their stand, the tour proceeded relatively uneventfully, the final two Tests being drawn, leaving Australia without a win on three tours of Pakistan in the 1980s.

Pakistan's troubled decade concluded with a bad-tempered tour to New Zealand. The tourists complained about biased umpires, while their aggressive behaviour, especially during the final Test at Auckland, in turn upset their hosts. 'But the Pakistan way of approaching the umpires almost *en masse* and the filthy language that was used, caused great concern among the umpires and the New Zealand public,' wrote veteran New Zealand cricket writer Dick Brittenden.[120]

When Pakistan returned to England in 1992 as recently crowned world champions, they once again had to run the gauntlet of the jingoistic British press, in no mood to forgive past clashes between the two countries. According to Peter Oborne, the author of *Wounded Tiger: A History of Cricket in Pakistan*, 'By 1992, British tabloid media especially had established the idea that Pakistan cricketers were representatives of an alien and barely civilised country. None of England's other cricket opponents have ever been so constantly vilified.'[121] Such was the depth of antipathy that Intikhab Alam, Pakistan's team manager and a former all-rounder for Surrey, told Jonathan Agnew, the BBC's cricket correspondent, that he would rather go home victorious than help restore relations between the two countries.

England began the summer on an encouraging note by winning the first three one-day internationals, despite their conviction that their opponents were illegally interfering with the ball. It was a conviction that lingered throughout the summer as opening bowlers Wasim Akram and Waqar Younis caused mayhem to their middle and lower order with their late swing and pace.

The first Test at Edgbaston, a high-scoring draw, was marred by crowd disturbances between rival sets of supporters; the second, at Lord's, was a low-scoring classic, with Pakistan winning by two wickets after an undefeated ninth-wicket stand of 46 between Wasim and Waqar, who between them had taken 13 England wickets in the match.

Before the third Test, the tourists played Hampshire in a vicious game which did no credit to either side. The seething antagonism reached its apogee when Hampshire captain Mark Nicholas, disillusioned to be given out to a bump ball on appeal and by the general spirit of the occasion, refused to walk – a refusal which led to the decision being reversed, much to the indignation of the Pakistanis, who continued to abuse him at every opportunity.

Nicholas's brazenness won him no favours from John Woodcock in *The Times* the next day. Having digested his criticism, he sought him out in the press tent and explained the facts behind his defiance.

> He had no sympathy. In fact, he fired everything back, saying the greater the provocation, the greater my responsibility to the game. John reminded me of more innocent days when the manners that were once an integral part of cricket's charm were taken for granted. He said it was the chippy English pros and the sly remarks they passed off as banter that were to blame for the attitudes so prevalent on the modern-day field of play. Banter all too soon turned into sledging, he insisted, and the arrogance of the English game was inexcusable. He said that if I honestly thought that cricketers

from the subcontinent were the root cause of such crass and aggressive behaviour, I was deluding myself. In summary, he said that anything that came out of the mouths of the Pakistan players could be traced back to the haughty English and the hostility of the Australians. Anyway, he said, you should know better.

I left with my tail between my legs.[122]

The third Test at Old Trafford was ruined by the weather, but the near-certainty of a draw did nothing to curb the poisonous atmosphere, the worst that Wasim ever encountered in a Test match. Pakistan were a highly talented side, capable of playing the most dazzling cricket, but under Javed Miandad, their sledging – far worse than Border's Australians according to Robin Smith – histrionic appealing and dissent gained them few friends. At Old Trafford, they rounded on Roy Palmer, officiating in his first Test, and the brother of Ken Palmer, whose umpiring they had objected to on their previous tour. Having already made a couple of contentious decisions, Palmer became embroiled in an unseemly confrontation with Pakistan's young fast bowler Aqib Javed, after warning him for bowling bouncers at England number eleven Devon Malcolm. Pakistan were aggrieved that Malcolm had escaped censure for bowling bouncers at their tail in their first innings, but Palmer was well within his rights to warn Aqib Javed under Law 42.8 if he thought he was attempting to intimidate the striker. At the end of that over, the umpire further irked Aqib Javed by appearing to return his sweater, which had got caught in the belt of his white coat, in a dismissive fashion. Suddenly the umpire was surrounded by a group of angry Pakistani players, led by their finger-wagging captain, who objected to his interpretation of Law 42.8, a sight that brought instant condemnation by the British media.

The match referee was also unimpressed. Conrad Hunte, the former West Indies opening batsman standing in for Clyde Walcott, who was on ICC duty, for the final two days of the Test, fined Aqib Javed half his match fee for intimidatory bowling. He also reprimanded Intikhab for his post-match criticism of the umpires, which was in breach of the ICC Code of Conduct, fined him for repeating the offence, and called on both captains to ensure that their teams played in the right spirit, remarks that infuriated England captain Graham Gooch. He objected to his team being implicated in the general criticism of the on-field misdemeanours and won an apology from Hunte for the wording of his press release.

The events of Old Trafford left a legacy of antipathy between the two sides. A peace summit between the respective managers and captains, together with the two umpires for the Headingley Test, ICC chairman Colin Cowdrey and match referee Clyde Walcott, resolved little. On a typical Headingley wicket, Pakistan struggled in both innings, whereas England, thanks to a Gooch century, reached 270/1 in their first innings before losing their last eight wickets for 28 runs to Wasim and Waqar with a ball that was 85 overs old. Before the collapse, on-field umpires Mervyn Kitchen and Ken Palmer asked third umpire Don Oslear to show the ball to Walcott during the lunch interval on the third day, because of its damaged condition on one side. Walcott examined it but decided to take no action.

Throughout the match, Pakistan experienced misfortune with umpiring decisions, not least on the final day, when England needed 99 for victory. Television replays showed Gooch, on 14, well short of his ground when adjudged not out by Ken Palmer; and when Gower was on 7, he survived a confident appeal for caught behind off leg-spinner Mushtaq Ahmed. At 65/4, it proved a crucial decision, since Gower remained, amid much tension, to guide England home to a six-wicket victory. After the match, twelfth man Rashid Latif was fined for hurling his cap to the ground in reaction to the Gower decision and wicketkeeper Moin Khan was reprimanded for his frenzied appealing.

At the Oval, firm but sensitive umpiring by England's two best officials, Dickie Bird and David Shepherd, greatly improved the atmosphere. Pakistan won the fifth Test by ten wickets to take the series 2–1 thanks to magnificent swing bowling by Wasim and

Waqar. Their success was subsequently questioned by England team manager Micky Stewart, who hinted that it was due to underhand methods, unleashing further media hostility against Pakistan. Both *Today* and *The Sun*, with the aid of a murky photo, alleged that Waqar was scuffing the seam with his finger and thumbnail to make it swing. He vigorously denied the allegation and was exonerated by Walcott, but it was one that was to surface again and again over the coming weeks and years.

Chapter 9

The Headmaster's Study

WHILE Colin Cowdrey prided himself on being a traditionalist, well-versed in social and sporting proprieties, he was no blind reactionary. In retirement, he continued to follow the game with unabated passion, never short of encouragement and praise to a new generation of players. He did, however, decry the decline of sportsmanship which was disfiguring the game. During his final years as a player, he saw for himself the proliferation of short-pitched bowling, the increase in sledging and an erosion of respect for the umpire. 'Less and less can an umpire look to the good nature of the players in the tight decision. More and more he has to walk a tightrope, striking a balance between the aloofness of decision on the one hand and the warmth of consideration on the other,' he wrote in his 1976 autobiography, published just after his retirement.[123] For all his wise words, Cowdrey found himself swimming against the current as increased player power and on-field aggression placed ever more pressure on the umpire. A sign of this hostile new milieu came in 1988 when David Constant, one of England's most senior umpires, chose to withdraw from the Test match panel. 'I did 36 Tests in all as well as 29 one-day internationals, but in the end I decided I had had enough, and it was not worth carrying on. I always did my job to the best of my ability, and I must have got most things right to get so many Tests, but the attitude of the players changed so much, it took a lot of pleasure out of the game.'[124]

His view that the game had become more difficult to officiate was supported by John Holder, who stood in 11 Tests during his 27 years as a first-class umpire between 1983 and 2009. 'The game has degenerated alarmingly in terms of acceptance of decisions and general behaviour. The right spirit is not there anymore, which is a shame because we are all in the same game, trying to earn a living and give the public something to watch.'[125]

Following his year as president of MCC in 1986/87, Cowdrey was appointed chairman of the International Cricket Council, as it became known in 1989. Originally founded in 1909 by England, Australia and South Africa, the ICC developed into cricket's international governing body, composed of representatives from all the Test-playing countries and, since 1965, Associate members. Traditionally it met annually at Lord's, presided over by the president and secretary of MCC, to discuss topical matters and suggest amendments to the laws of the game. For the most part, the deliberations had been leisurely and informal until the advent of political boycotts, the World Cup and WSC took them into rougher, uncharted waters. Faced with a profusion of unwelcome developments, as well as growing commercial opportunities, the ramshackle ICC proved unequal to the task. It was to help equip it for a more professional era that, following the review of its machinery and methods between 1986 and 1989, a new constitution was established. At the heart of it was the proposal that the new ICC chairman would be an elected four-year appointee, with time at his disposal to deal with the increasingly complex issues.

Conscious of the growing rift between players and authorities and the diminishing control that captains wielded over their teams, Cowdrey earmarked discipline on the field as his greatest priority. He thought an international code of conduct was needed to reinforce the traditional accepted standards of behaviour, and a match referee to enforce the authority of the umpire. Having travelled the globe throughout the winter of 1989/90 to convey his vision to the various boards of control, he managed to win unanimous consent at a special meeting of the ICC at Melbourne,

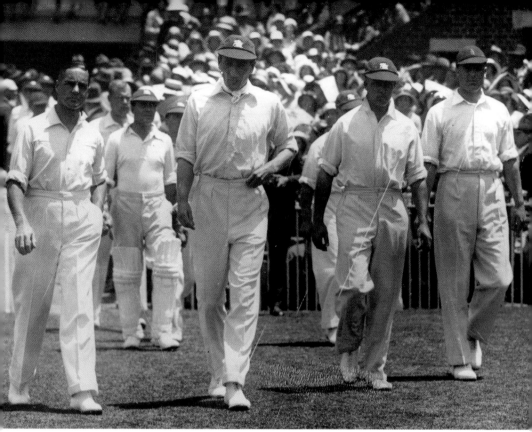

Douglas Jardine, the instigator of bodyline, leads the England team at Melbourne in the second Test, January 1933.

Harold Larwood, England's fearsome fast bowler, forces Australian captain Bill Woodfull to take evasive action in the fourth Test at Brisbane in 1933.

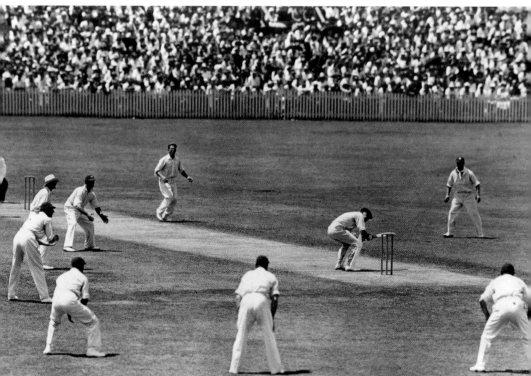

'The enemy'. Don Bradman going out to bat for Australia in the fourth Test against England at Headingley, 1938.

Walter Hammond, the England captain, goes out to toss with Bradman, his Australian counterpart, Trent Bridge 1938. Their personal *froideur* added a frisson to Ashes cricket in the 1930s and in 1946/47.

Frank Tyson, the man of the series in Australia in 1954/55, is escorted from the field after being hit on the head by fast bowler Ray Lindwall. His injury helped galvanise his match-winning bowling in Australia's second innings.

Richie Benaud, Australia's captain in the epic 1960-61 series against the West Indies.

Charlie Griffith, West Indies' controversial fast bowler, under the watchful eye of England umpire Syd Buller in the first Test at Old Trafford in 1966.

Frank Worrell, at the beginning of the West Indies' tour of England, 1963.

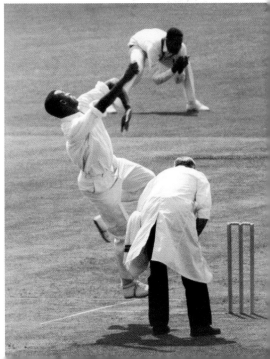

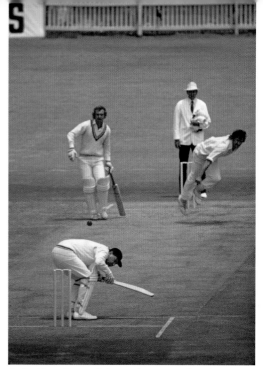

Colin Cowdrey and David Lloyd open England's second innings at Perth on their ill-fated 1974/75 tour of Australia.

Colin Cowdrey, a late replacement for the tour just short of his 42th birthday, getting the treatment from Dennis Lillee.

A formidable West Indian pace quartet at Port of Spain, Trinidad, 1981. From front to back: Andy Roberts, Michael Holding, Colin Croft and Joel Garner.

Dennis Lillee and Javed Miandad square up to each other in the first Test between Australia and Pakistan at Perth in 1981. Umpire Tony Crafter steps in to keep the peace.

Shakoor Rana [left] in dispute with Mike Gatting [middle] during England's acrimonious tour of Pakistan 1987-88. On the right is the manager Peter Lush.

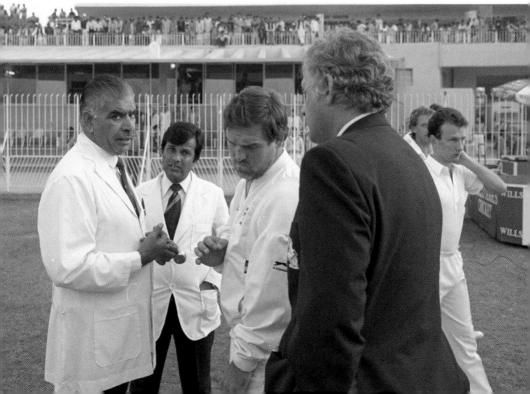

England captain Michael Atherton is interviewed by the BBC's Jonathan Agnew after he'd been accused of ball-tampering in the first Test between England and South Africa at Lord's in 1994. Chairman of selectors Ray Illingworth looks on uneasily.

Darrell Hair inspects the ball in England's second innings against Pakistan at the Oval, 2006. Confronted with a charge of ball-tampering, Pakistan refused to take the field.

Following their refusal to take the field, Hair removes the bails to signify the end of the match, the first time that a side had forfeited a Test match.

Australia's Andrew Symonds and India's Harbhajan Singh during the second Test at Sydney, 2008, a match in which the former was allegedly abused by the latter, an offence which brought Harbhajan a a three-Test ban.

Harbhajan's ban provoked widespread protests in India and the threat of the tour's cancellation led to the ban being overturned.

The Australians appeal in vain for the dismissal of England's Stuart Broad in the Trent Bridge Test in 2013 after Broad edged Ashton Agar to slip and was given not out.

Cameron Bancroft, the young Australian opening batsman, discusses ball-tampering with the umpires in the third Test between South Africa and Australia at Cape Town, 2018.

Cameron Bancroft and Australian captain Steve Smith later that evening admit to altering the condition of the ball, an admission that saw both of them, and vice-captain David Warner, receiving lengthy bans from international cricket.

in January 1991, to the introduction of an international code and match referees for Tests and one-day internationals. The referees would wield wide disciplinary powers, including the fining and suspension of players, from either their own observance or what had been reported to them by the umpires.

Yet for the code to be effective, it needed umpires and referees of stature to apply it without fear or favour. Unfortunately, this wasn't always the case. Umpires either proved unduly tolerant of misconduct or lacked support from match referees when they did report it. The introduction of one independent umpire per match, from an umpiring panel comprising two members from each Test-playing country, in 1992 didn't help, since inevitably some of the less experienced umpires from the newer countries proved out of their depth in the heat of battle. 'Both the ICC and its members pay lip service to the idea of cutting out bad sportsmanship on the field,' wrote esteemed Australian cricket writer Peter McFarline in January 1998, 'but in practice the situation now is as bad as it was five years ago.'[126]

Not that match referees were much better. Most of the original panel were household names from the 1950s and 1960s – but, while some of them, such as Peter Burge, John Reid and Jackie Hendriks, proved adept at maintaining standards, the majority were found wanting. Consequently, behaviour failed to improve and justice was dispersed indiscriminately, fuelling the suspicion that those from the founding members of the ICC were treated more sympathetically than everyone else. Several cases illustrate this.

In the first Test between Australia and the West Indies at Brisbane in 1992/93, Australian captain Allan Border was cited for dissent towards umpire Steve Randell and was fined half his match fee by match referee Raman Subba Row. More important was Border's refusal to attend the disciplinary hearing, a breach of protocol that, he later conceded, should have earned him a suspension, something that Subba Row was considering until talked out of it by Cowdrey.

Border's fortunate escape was emulated by his team-mates Shane Warne and Merv Hughes at Johannesburg just over a year later. Warne's verbal harangue of departing South African batsman Andrew Hudson shocked even some of his own team, but he was fined only 10 per cent of his match fee by match referee Donald Carr. With Hughes receiving a similar 10 per cent fine for verbal abuse, despite it being his third offence in 15 months, the ACB chose to come down hard on both players and impose a much more stringent punishment.

Various South Africans also managed to escape sanctions. On India's 1991/92 tour to South Africa, home captain Kepler Wessels collided with Indian bowler Kapil Dev, some alleged deliberately, as he turned for a second run following Kapil's run-out of Peter Kirsten when backing up. In the triangular series final at Durban in 1997, Allan Donald abused India's Rahul Dravid, and, most bizarrely of all, South African captain Hansie Cronje hurled a stump at the umpires' dressing room door at the end of the final Test against Australia in January 1998, to register his disgust at a crucial umpiring decision.

The Indians felt particularly hard done by. During the first Test against Australia at Madras in 1998, their wicketkeeper, Nayan Mongia, on being adjudged lbw, was fined for dissent, but match referee Peter van der Merwe took no action against Australian batsman Ricky Ponting, who stood his ground and left cursing after being given out. Two years later, in the second Test between Australia and India at Melbourne, Indian fast bowler Venkatesh Prasad was given a heavy fine by match referee Ranjan Madugalle for his exuberant reaction on dismissing Michael Slater. His punishment contrasted with Madugalle's inaction against Australian fast bowler Glenn McGrath for his indecorous send-off of Sachin Tendulkar in the third Test at Sydney, and Ponting for verbally abusing Prasad's opening partner, Javagal Srinath. 'The Indians have been receiving sentences most unjustified from the time the concept of match referee was introduced,' said *The Hindu*. 'It may not yet dawn on the cricketing fraternity that two teams, Australia and South Africa, have been spared the fines and humiliation by a bunch of incompetent umpires the world over.'[127]

According to Mike Coleman of the *Courier-Mail*, both the Pakistani and Indian sides touring Australia in 1999/2000 had every reason to complain of double standards, suspect umpiring and victimisation. For years Australians had complained of being stitched up on the subcontinent. Touring teams to Australia would soon be able to enforce the same disclaimer. Alluding to McGrath's treatment of Tendulkar, he said: 'If ICC match referees consider this sort of behaviour acceptable, so be it. But surely, if it is acceptable for McGrath it should be acceptable for Venkatesh Prasad and anyone else...'[128]

With umpires still under pressure, and captains failing in their responsibilities, Cowdrey, as chairman of the MCC cricket committee, in conjunction with Ted Dexter, sought to make players aware of their responsibilities to the game. Consequently, for the first time since the laws were devised in 1788, MCC agreed to include in their revision in 2000 a preamble which outlined and defined the Spirit of Cricket. Upholding the spirit meant no physical or verbal abuse; no sharp practice such as dangerous bowling, ball-tampering and unnecessary appealing; above all, it meant respecting the authority of the umpire and tasking the captain with the responsibility of ensuring that sportsmanship prevailed. 'It's a noble attempt to urge the players to reclaim the game's ethos, if only it was clear what that ethos was,' declared Simon Hughes, the former Middlesex bowler turned columnist, in *The Independent*.[129] That elusive definition has remained the central weakness in the preamble over time as modern players have marched to a different drumbeat.

Chapter 10

'Ugly Australians'

A S West Indian cricket plummeted into steep decline, Australia's rose in ascendancy, as they won an unprecedented eight successive Ashes series between 1989 and 2002/03. Figuring that they played their best cricket by adopting a combative approach, they unsettled their opponents at every conceivable opportunity. Such ruthlessness won them few friends, but their growing ascendancy encouraged them to keep pushing the boundaries of acceptable conduct, an approach that others in time sought to emulate.

Although Ashes cricket throughout the 1980s lacked nothing in passion, the matches were generally played in a reasonable spirit, helped by harmonious relations off the field among many of the leading players. As England battled to save the third Test at Headingley in 1981, Ian Botham entertained the whole Australian team to a barbecue at his home. His generosity was reciprocated by Australian captain Kim Hughes and other senior members of his side when they appeared at a dinner dance for Bob Willis's benefit on the night of their shock defeat in the fourth Test at Edgbaston.

During the Ashes series of 1985, which England won 3–1, Australian captain Allan Border established a close rapport with his opposite number, David Gower, and many of his team. One memorable picture of Gower fiddling with Border's bat and chatting amicably with him during a break in play during the Old Trafford Test neatly encapsulated the spirit of that series. 'Some, believe it or not, contended that this show of mutual affection illustrated a lamentable dearth of the requisite aggressive spirit expected of Ashes combatants,' commented Gower.[130]

The goodwill prevailed through England's triumphant tour to Australia in 1986/87, but as Border's side began to emerge from the travails of that era, they presented a very different face to their opponents. Stung by criticism from Ian Chappell regarding his cordiality towards the England players, Border returned to England in 1989 a harder, meaner leader. Not only did he end the social pleasantries off the field, he actively encouraged a more intimidating atmosphere on the field of play, a trait that was to continue throughout his time as captain.

Whether referred to as banter, gamesmanship or mental disintegration, aggressive or insulting talk between opponents on the cricket field was nothing new; it could be traced back to W.G. Grace and beyond. Gubby Allen, so often depicted as the gentleman cricketer because of his refusal to bowl bodyline, accused his England colleague R.E.S. Wyatt of being yellow after knocking him senseless in a county match, and Bill Voce threatened Australian opener Vic Richardson with physical intimidation at the beginning of the bodyline tour. Bill O'Reilly, the great Australian leg-spinner of the 1930s, used to loudly curse opposing batsmen when the luck went their way, and Bradman's relentless run-making made him the object of some barbed comments from frustrated opponents, most notably in the Sheffield Shield.

The renowned Australian cricket commentator Alan McGilvray, when bowling for New South Wales, taunted Bradman, then playing for South Australia, after Bradman had told him he was going to get a big score against him. Having had him caught at leg slip for nought, McGilvray shouted to Bradman, 'Well, we can dream about that 300' as he left the crease. When he later apologised for his comment in the dressing room, Bradman allowed himself a little smile: 'There's always a second innings, you know,' he replied.

Another to berate Bradman was the temperamental New South Wales all-rounder Cec Pepper, one of the finest post-Second World War cricketers to be denied Test status. Playing for the Australian

Services XI against South Australia in 1946, he was so enraged when umpire Jack Scott rejected a confident lbw appeal against Bradman that Pepper swore at the Australian captain. An apology was sought, but his letter was mislaid, and Bradman helped ensure that he never did represent his country.

Perhaps the most famous comment directed at Bradman was Walter Hammond's, 'Well, that's a bloody fine way to start a series,' after the Australian captain's refusal to walk in the 1946 Test at Brisbane. During the following Test at Sydney, Hammond berated Australia's Sid Barnes for time-wasting as Barnes continually appealed against the light, while in the fourth Test at Adelaide, Godfrey Evans briefly lost his cool with his friend Keith Miller after the latter gave him a couple of fast bouncers.

Miller, in turn, liked to have his say in the middle, although his comments were invariably humorous and often flattering to his opponents. An exception to this rule occurred when he was batting against Sonny Ramadhin, the Trinidadian leg-spinner, during the 1951/52 Australia–West Indies Test series. 'You're a nice little chap, but you haven't improved your bowling much since the last match, have you?' he said – a patronising put-down that hurt and angered Ramadhin in equal measure as his effectiveness against Miller rapidly declined. It is worth stressing that for all the ferocious exchanges that Hutton had with Lindwall and Miller, not once did he recall any harsh words being directed at him.

What comments there were seem relatively mild, certainly by modern standards. 'You play and miss too many balls,' Hutton informed the young Neil Harvey. 'Here comes the festival cricketer,' was the Englishman's greeting for Richie Benaud in 1954/55, alluding to his cavalier batting, and 'You must really enjoy batting, Slasher,' was the nearest Peter May came to damning his opponents after watching Australia's Slasher Mackay stonewall the England attack.

During MCC's troubled tour to the West Indies in 1953/54, the language on occasions became rather saltier, especially from Trueman and Tony Lock, a highly aggressive left-arm spinner with no love for his opponents. When Benaud patted the pitch during Australia's second innings of the Old Trafford Test in 1956, Lock bowled him a bouncer and swore at him, an outburst which prompted his team-mate, David Sheppard, an Anglican cleric, to head to the Australian dressing room at the tea interval to apologise to Benaud. Farokh Engineer, the Indian wicketkeeper-batsman, recalls meeting Lock at a reception before his Test debut against England at Kanpur in 1961/62 and finding him very friendly. The next day a nervous Engineer went out to bat, only to be met with a string of profanities from Lock, who happened to be bowling. At another reception later in the match, Lock sidled up to him and complimented him on his innings, whereupon Engineer asked him why he had been so abusive to him, especially given his nerves on Test debut. 'I sure knew that and I was making you even more nervous,' Lock replied, 'because I wanted your wicket and you almost gave it to me. You were swiping from mid-stump.'[131]

Lock's captain at Surrey during the golden years was Stuart Surridge, one of several county captains of that era, such as Freddie Brown and Wilf Wooller, who were inclined to abuse opponents when the winds of fortune weren't blowing their way. Surridge retired in 1956, but Surrey's tendency for strong invective survived his passing, most notoriously the following year when they played the West Indians at the Oval. Having set their opponents 270 to win, the Surrey players felt aggrieved when a couple of bat-pad decisions weren't upheld, and they took their frustration out on the batsmen with non-stop appealing and constant abuse. According to Frank Worrell, who batted throughout the second innings, it was the unhappiest match he ever played in. 'If we had behaved half as badly as Surrey behaved on that last day we would have been dubbed as a lot of savages – and deservedly so. No wonder then I left the Oval that August a very sad man.'[132]

Compared with the more sedate atmosphere of the county championship, Australian state and grade cricket was rather more adversarial in its approach and contained some colourful language on occasions. This was particularly the case in Victoria–New South Wales games, where the rivalry was most acute. Bill Lawry remembers being sledged during his debut season for Victoria in

1955, and young South Australian batsman Ken Cunningham was given similar treatment against New South Wales in 1960, until the opposing captain, Benaud, put a halt to it. When Cunningham asked his captain and fellow opener, Les Favell, whether he had heard Benaud's command, Favell replied, 'Son, that is how Richie Benaud plays the game.'

Brian Booth, who played under Miller, Benaud and Simpson, recalled that sledging as a premeditated practice didn't exist in his day. When Booth made his Sydney grade debut in 1952, the former Australian opener Sid Barnes shook his hand and said, 'So you're young Booth from Bathurst. I've read about you in the paper. Welcome to grade cricket, son, and all the best.' In 1955 Booth walked out to bat in his first Sheffield Shield match for New South Wales against Queensland to be greeted with 'Good luck, Brian,' from Peter Burge. 'Four balls later, when I scored a duck he said, "bad luck Brian". He wasn't being smart. He meant it.'[133]

With sledging becoming more commonplace in Australia – according to Ross Duncan, the Queensland fast bowler, it was in the 1971/72 season that it really took off – few of Border's side that toured England in 1989 would have winced at the tactics employed against the opposition. The unfriendliness and abuse surprised and depressed Robin Smith, playing in his first Ashes series, especially since Border had been one of his heroes, but despite his sensitivities he still averaged over 60 in the Tests. England wicketkeeper Jack Russell recalled that his Gloucestershire team-mate Terry Alderman barely said a word to him, and the compliments offered to him by some of the Australians as he walked off at Lord's undefeated with 64 were the only civilised words he heard from them all summer. According to Gower, the atmosphere on the field was as unpleasant as many of his players could remember. At the end of the series, won 4–0 by Australia, Border confessed to him that, after all the previous defeats his team had endured, he was prepared to be as ruthless as necessary to win and win well.

The fractiousness continued when England toured Australia in 1990/91, losing 3–0. Allan Lamb and Robin Smith went to the Australian dressing room during the first Test to socialise, but such was the frosty reception accorded them that they quickly left and vowed not to return. 'Australian cricket is facing a crisis which, in its current euphoric state, it is utterly failing to acknowledge,' wrote Peter Roebuck during the third Test at Sydney, which had featured some unseemly antics from Border's side in the field. 'Codes of conduct, founded upon respect between players and umpires, and players and players, have broken down to such a degree that sooner or later violence will occur.' No such decline had taken place during the Chappell era because his team rarely influenced umpire and challenge decisions. 'What is mystifying is Bob Simpson's failure to stop these habits creeping in to a fundamentally honest team which has worked enormously hard to reach its current status.'[134]

Little had changed when Border returned to England for the third time as captain in 1993, this time winning 4–1. While his leading fast bowler, Merv Hughes, won a personal battle over Graeme Hick with his verbal and physical intimidation, Australia's new spinning sensation, Shane Warne, wasn't slow in baring his teeth. According to England batsman Matthew Maynard, he had never been spoken to in the way that the Australian addressed him. 'However, his incessant niggling of umpires and truculent questioning of unfavourable decisions made it obvious that the sunny exterior hid a graceless streak, which stopped him earning the unqualified respect of his opponents,' wrote cricket journalist John Thicknesse in *Wisden*.[135]

He wrote in similar vein about Border. 'That he will be remembered in England with respect rather than affection stemmed from his condoning, not infrequently his participation in, the sledging of opponents and umpires during play, in open violation of the International Cricket Council's code of conduct.' He accepted that the umpiring had been indifferent. 'But Border, who usually fielded within earshot of his bowlers, may also have contributed indirectly to the more obvious misjudgements of lbws and bat-pad catches, estimated by some at more than a dozen in the series, by failing to stamp out the questioning of decisions that sapped the umpires' confidence.'[136]

While such criticism could be portrayed as a loser's lament, since England weren't exactly angels, the worst was yet to come as Border's leadership entered the twilight zone. The reintroduction of South Africa to international cricket in 1991 resulted in closely fought contests with Australia in back-to-back series in 1993/94. The first series in Australia, which featured many a verbal spat between Warne and South African batsman Daryll Cullinan, ended in acrimony as the host team, one down after the second Test at Sydney, won the third Test at Adelaide on the back of some controversial umpiring. This in turn led to South Africa's veteran batsman Peter Kirsten being fined 65 per cent of his match fee for twice displaying dissent, and the visitors' dressing room being damaged.

The bad blood continued when the two sides renewed combat in South Africa weeks later, with Allan Border responding to taunts about his age with a few jibes of his own. During the first Test at Johannesburg, convincingly won by South Africa, the Australians were abused by rowdier sections of the large crowd, none more so than Warne on the third day. Frustrated by his treatment and his belated entry into the attack as South Africa built a commanding lead in their second innings, Warne totally lost his cool after bowling Andrew Hudson, the most placid of men, in his opening over. Rushing up to him as he left the middle, Warne gave him a verbal lashing that offended all canons of good taste and which made even him cringe when he later viewed it on television. He was reported by the umpires to the match referee Donald Carr, as was Hughes for consistently abusing Gary Kirsten, his third offence in his previous 15 Tests. They were both fined 1,000 rand (A$450), about one-tenth of their match fees, a derisory amount that provoked strong criticism in the Australian media about the repeated failure of international referees to support umpires. According to an editorial in The Age, both Warne and Hughes had continually transgressed the area between sportsmanship and mindless aggression. 'There are few more pathetic sights in sport than grown men throwing temper tantrums on the cricket field. The Australian cricketers seem to be making a habit of this sort of boorish behaviour, and it is no coincidence that it reaches a crescendo whenever Australia is being beaten.'[137] In the opinion of Peter Roebuck, Warne and Hughes were merely reflecting the mood of a team determined to blast their opponents off the field with word and deed. When Simpson declared that the team management would be taking no further action, the ACB, meeting in Sydney, considered his statement to be inadequate.

Concerned for some time about the declining standards of the Australian team, the board had recently announced a crackdown against verbal abuse and send-offs of dismissed batsmen, which its chairman, Alan Crompton, called 'cowardly and un-Australian'. Now, with its team once again in the dock, the ACB felt compelled to read the riot act. Empowered to act independently of the ICC under the terms of its Code of Conduct, it imposed further fines of A$4,000 each on Warne and Hughes. Hughes was also given a suspended A$2,000 fine for remonstrating with an abusive spectator on the final day of the first Test.

While the Australian team thought that their board had overreacted – Test cricket, after all, was a tough sport, they argued – the Australian media begged to differ. Trevor Grant in the *Herald Sun* contended that the two players should have been suspended, and Patrick Smith in *The Age* saw the present crisis as the result of the ACB's repeated failure to rein in its players and team management.

Following Border's retirement, his vice-captain, Mark Taylor, took over and promised a fresh start, not least in improving his players' on-field behaviour. An affable personality and a natural leader with a mind of his own, Taylor passed his first test with flying colours by restoring Australia's reputation in Pakistan, since, despite losing the series 1–0, his team won a citation for sportsmanship from ICC match referee John Reid. Playing a more attacking form of cricket than under Border, Taylor's Australia remained the most formidable of opponents and easily disposed of England in 1994/95. A greater challenge now awaited them on their tour to the West Indies, given the recent antagonism between the two teams. The retirement of Viv Richards and his replacement by Richie Richardson had helped soothe tensions during the 1992/93 West Indian tour of Australia. Although not quite the force of yesteryear, the West Indians still had their awesome fast bowling partnership of Curtly Ambrose and Courtney Walsh in tow, and it was primarily down to them that they had won that series 2–1. Knowing what awaited them in the Caribbean, the Australians elected to fight fire with fire by bouncing the West Indian tail, something their hosts didn't appreciate, especially Walsh when facing Glenn McGrath in the first Test. 'The instant he broke into an ungainly jig around the crease, smiling nervously, eyes wide open, after a searing bouncer narrowly missed the grille of his helmet, we sensed the mood of the battle had changed,' recalled Steve Waugh. 'Suddenly, we were in the driver's seat. The roles had been reversed. We liked our new position of authority.'[138]

Their audacity paid off with a comfortable win in the first Test, but Australian opener Michael Slater's contention that the West Indian pace bowlers held no fear for his team riled Ambrose enough for him to warn Slater there would be 19 ambulances waiting for him in Antigua for the second Test. True to his word, he and Walsh peppered the Australian openers with bouncers on the second evening, so much so that Taylor expressed his concern about his opponents' methods. 'It wasn't cricket. Honestly, I don't think the people over here know what cricket is half the time. All they want to see is short balls and blokes either ducking or hooking – or getting hit. ... And it's a damned shame because there's a hell of a lot more to cricket than that.'[139] With the umpires unwilling to police the experimental two-bouncers-an-over rule, the bombardment continued the next day, Mark Waugh asserting that he had never experienced so many short balls. Yet he and his team-mates stood firm, Australia emerging with a comfortable draw.

On a damp, seaming pitch for the third Test at Port of Spain, Australia were confronted with Ambrose in full flight, but, consistent with their aggressive approach, they refused to buckle. On one occasion, as Ambrose advanced down the pitch, Steve Waugh told him to clear off in language so undiplomatic that

Ambrose was roused to fury; but Waugh stood firm, and although Australia were soundly defeated, their defiance helped quell the aura of West Indian intimidation, their secret weapon for so long.

For the fourth and final Test at Kingston, the Waugh brothers withstood the full force of the West Indian attack in an epic fourth-wicket stand of 231, setting up an innings victory and their first series triumph over their opponents since 1976. Although the West Indies were weaker than at any time in the last 20 years, the Australians had won by playing positive cricket, devoid of the coarseness that had defined the Border era.

Taylor's diplomacy was on full view the following summer at home, in the wake of allegations of bribes to Shane Warne and Mark Waugh to fix matches by Pakistan's Salim Malik during Australia's 1994 tour to Pakistan. Despite the animosity directed towards the latter, Taylor and his opposite number, Wasim Akram, successfully ensured that the tension didn't spill over on to the field.

Yet Australia's Damascene conversion was by no means complete. Taylor's side hadn't abandoned sledging, and, following a fractious series against Sri Lanka (see Chapter 12), the issue resurfaced when the West Indies returned to Australia in 1996/97. Although the relations didn't revert to the feuding of the Border–Richards era, there were several incidents featuring Brian Lara, one of the world's great batsmen but a mercurial personality, especially in the company of Australians. Already the recipient of several dubious decisions in past clashes between the two teams, Lara fell victim to another one in the second Test at Sydney. Convinced that Healy had caught him on the half-volley, he stormed into the Australian dressing room on his dismissal and told their coach, Geoff Marsh, that Healy wasn't welcome in the West Indian dressing room, a breach of protocol which brought an apology from West Indies manager Clive Lloyd. The animosity boiled over in the final Test at Perth, which the West Indies, having already lost the series, won by ten wickets. The trouble began in their first innings during a third-wicket stand of 208 between Lara and his inexperienced partner, Robert Samuels, in which the former took exception to the sledging of the latter by the opposition. Irritated with Lara for going public about their on-field comments, the Australians objected to his reappearance the next day as runner for West Indian captain Walsh, and, following a fracas in which Lara collided with Australia's Matthew Hayden, the umpires called the two captains together to restore calm. After the match, Taylor defended his side's tactics and accused Lara of being the raw catalyst for any tension between the two sides that summer.

His statement failed to satisfy Clive Lloyd or large elements of the home media. 'It is a sad end to a series played with passion but good spirit,' wrote Australian sports journalist Patrick Smith. 'The West Indians were not blameless and the boiling heat and a wretched pitch combined to burn the coolest nerves. ... Australia does not always react well when opponents do not bend to its will. It pouts, it bullies, it loses the plot. There were more dummies on the WACA than in the local crèche. The Australians can dish it out but it seems they cannot take it.'[140]

That was the high-water mark of controversy under Taylor's captaincy. Australia's verbal aggression never deserted them, but it became less offensive, while dissent towards umpires and unacceptable gamesmanship became the exception rather than the rule. (In the Lord's Test of 1997, wicketkeeper Healy won acclaim from umpire David Shepherd for disclaiming a possible catch he might have taken on the half-volley.) When Taylor retired after retaining the Ashes in January 1999, he left to universal plaudits, well respected by friend and foe alike. 'His moral authority has been absolute, as Woodfull's was, his desire to win as sharp as Bradman's,' wrote David Hopps in *The Guardian*. 'These can occasionally lie in conflict, which might explain why he retained a practical approach in tempering Australia's on-field aggression, notably the sledging of his chief fast bowler Glenn McGrath.'[141] Under Taylor's successors, Australia continued to play their highly attacking form of cricket while trying to adhere to the ethos of fair play, a balance they were ultimately unable to achieve.

Chapter 11

Conning the Umpire

EVER since the 1970s, umpiring had become increasingly taxing, as gamesmanship became rife and their decisions became subject to critical scrutiny by candid commentators. The growing commercialisation of the game in the 1980s, following the burgeoning popularity of one-day cricket, enhanced the need for correct decision-making just at a time when umpiring standards appeared on the wane. Consequently, after much stalling, the ICC agreed in 1992 to the introduction of a third umpire with access to television replays to advise the umpires on the field over run-outs, stumpings and boundaries. It was the beginning of a major technological revolution that saw television cameras play a much greater role in decision-making, but, in the short term at least, it didn't make the task of officiating cricket matches any easier, as umpires appeared less willing to exert their authority.

Few countries had pushed harder for the readmission of South Africa to international cricket than England, but there was little room for sentiment once the latter had returned as a keen rivalry took hold between the two sides. On England's tour of South Africa in 1995/96, the series was all square going into the fifth and final Test at Cape Town. In a low-scoring match, the visitors were struggling in their second innings until a fifth-wicket stand of 72 between Graham Thorpe and Graeme Hick gave them a semblance of hope. In his best innings of the series, Thorpe had advanced to 57 when he pushed slow bowler Paul Adams to short fine leg and was called for a quick single by his partner. He was slow to set off and a direct throw by Andrew Hudson found him short of his ground, but South African umpire Dave Orchard, standing in only his second Test, was negligent in rejecting the available replay and ruled him in. Thorpe's reprieve, shown immediately by the broadcasters on the giant screen, incurred the displeasure of the large crowd, and their heated reaction convinced South African captain Hansie Cronje that Thorpe was out. He immediately badgered Orchard into referring the decision to the third umpire, a breach of ICC regulations that cost him half his match fee, and Orchard meekly submitted to the pressure, much to Thorpe's irritation. He accepted that he was out, but objected to the umpire's ruling being overridden by the reaction of the crowd and South African players. It proved the game's defining moment, because England lost their last six wickets for 19 runs and South Africa swept to victory by ten wickets. 'Just a few faltering steps have so far been taken towards scientific decision-making in cricket,' reported Robin Marlar in the *Sunday Times*. 'The players want more of it and who can blame them? Not a series passes without a hatful of bad umpiring decisions which inevitably stultify the enjoyment. Cricket has to be pushed firmly and willingly towards a life without the men in white coats.'[142]

The umpiring remained a source of rancour during South Africa's tour of England in 1998, a closely contested series marred by much ill-feeling on both sides. Following a draw in the first Test, South Africa won by ten wickets at Lord's, helped by some umpiring decisions that went their way, one of which was Mark Ramprakash's caught-behind in England's first innings. He was fined for telling the Australian Darrell Hair that he was 'messing with his career' on his departure, a comment picked up by the stump microphones.

Before the fourth Test at Trent Bridge, the National Grid international umpires' panel conference voiced resentment regarding the growing tendency of players to cheat. 'It's like a cauldron in Test cricket – it is calculated to make the job of umpiring harder,' commented Mervyn Kitchen, one of England's leading umpires. His words came back to haunt him as he and his colleague Steve Dunne of New Zealand had matches they would rather forget at Trent Bridge, as they wilted under the orchestrated appealing of both sides. The errors began to mount, including the dismissal of Jonty Rhodes, caught behind off his thigh for 2 in South Africa's second innings. Later, when Kitchen apologised for his error, Rhodes smiled and said, 'Don't worry. It's only a game.'

Not everyone was quite so gracious about their lot. After South Africa had been dismissed for 208 in their second innings, England were set 247 to win the match. They had progressed to 87/1 when Allan Donald came around the wicket to bowl to Michael Atherton in what was widely acknowledged as being a crucial stage in the match. In his second over, Atherton gloved a rising ball to the wicketkeeper, but, despite a clear touch, England's opener stood his ground and was given not out by umpire Dunne, much to Donald's fury. Having told Atherton precisely what he thought of him, he proceeded to spray him with bouncers in a torrid spell of bowling that made for compulsive viewing. Atherton didn't give an inch, and survived to stumps before guiding his team to an eight-wicket victory the following day with an undefeated 98. It was the perfect end to a memorable match from an England perspective, but the blatant gamesmanship and raw antagonism between the two sides had disturbed many cricket lovers. According to Peter Johnson of the *Daily Mail,* Trent Bridge showed that Test cricket couldn't go on tolerating the law of the jungle. 'Frankly, the game is slithering into a muddy hole that will leave it with a stain on its good name.' The line of fair play was being moved all the time. 'What began as a trickle of unpleasant incidents is now an avalanche.'[143]

Although Atherton soon made his peace with Donald, he resolutely defended his decision to stay put, declaring in an interview with Julia Llewellyn-Smith of *The Times* that not walking wasn't cheating – that modern-day batsmen don't walk, but instead wait for the umpire to give his decision. His view was overwhelmingly supported by a poll of *Daily Mirror* readers and by John Etheridge, *The Sun*'s cricket correspondent, who cited the pressures of international cricket. 'Batsmen get enough bad decisions, so it is unrealistic to expect them to take the rough with the even rougher.'[144]

Atherton's argument, however, failed to convince the *Daily Mail*'s acclaimed sports journalist Ian Wooldridge. 'What Atherton told the world through a lady conduit was that cheating is now an acknowledged part of the game. Ghastly, isn't it? Of course you'd be wet behind the ears to pretend you didn't know it already, but the sadness is that cricket, so long the exemplar of fair play, has embraced the morality of other sports.'[145]

Although walking was regarded as the epitome of fair play in cricket, it had a more chequered history than sometimes met the eye. W.G. Grace never walked, and luminaries such as Don Bradman, Walter Hammond and Les Ames did so only intermittently, while even a paragon such as Jack Hobbs was known to have remained at the crease. Gubby Allen said that most of his contemporaries in the 1930s didn't walk, although Charlie Elliott, the Derbyshire wicketkeeper of that vintage and later a renowned Test umpire, thought otherwise. According to Derek Birley, walking evolved in the English county game through the gentlemen captains, who set their honour code above the authority of the humble umpire, and certainly in the post-Second World War era it became the fashion. As far as Ray Illingworth was concerned, 98 per cent of batsmen walked in the 1950s, a view endorsed by Warwickshire all-rounder Raymond Hitchcock. David Sheppard, a non-walker at school and university, was converted to walking by his opening partner at Sussex, John Langridge. 'I was brought up to believe that umpires give you out when you are in and in when you are out. So if you stood there and got away with it, these decisions balanced out. But when I started to go out to bat with John Langridge for Sussex, I never saw John not walk if he knew he'd touched a ball to the wicketkeeper. I remember the last time I continued to stand there, against Middlesex at Lord's when I was 21. I felt badly about it afterwards and decided that thereafter I'd do what I'd seen John do.'[146]

Peter Parfitt recalls getting a lesson in sporting etiquette from his captain, Bill Edrich, at Middlesex. Playing against Glamorgan in the mid-1950s, Parfitt gloved a ball to the wicketkeeper and was given not out. His reprieve didn't escape the notice of his captain, who asked him at the interval whether he had hit the ball. When Parfitt confessed that he had, Edrich told him that 'in this side, if anyone touches the ball to the wicketkeeper, they don't require the umpire to make the decision. You are just as much out as if you had lobbed it to cover point. Now then, Peter, while you are in my team, if you hit the ball, you walk.'[147] Edrich's words struck home, and from that moment on Parfitt was a committed walker.

Another player to feel the wrath of his county captain was Leicestershire's Tony Diment, who was given not out against Sussex for a catch to short leg off Robin Marlar in the late 1950s. When he later confessed to not walking, he was ordered by his captain, Charles Palmer, to go into the Sussex dressing room and apologise to Marlar, an experience he found to be truly humbling. Glamorgan and England all-rounder Peter Walker recalled his regret for failing to walk on one occasion against Leicestershire as his county fought hard to stave off defeat. Having gloved medium-pacer Terry Spencer to the wicketkeeper and been given not out, a pang of guilt came over him, the feeling that he had let down his fellow professionals. On another occasion, bowling for England against South Africa in 1960, fate conspired against Walker when umpire John Langridge mistakenly gave batsman J.P. 'Pom Pom' Fellows-Smith the benefit of the doubt. At the close of play, Langridge approached Walker and said, 'I'm sorry, Peter, in county cricket, I'm so used to batsmen walking if they edge the ball that when Pom Pom stood there, I thought he couldn't have hit it. But on reflection I was wrong.'

The South Africans and Australians for the most part took the view that, because there was nothing in the laws of the game about walking, the decision should be left to the umpire, and that his word, right or wrong, was final. It was a lesson that the young Alan McGilvray soon learned on his debut for New South Wales against Victoria in 1933/34 when he appeared to have Bill Woodfull caught by wicketkeeper Bertie Oldfield for nought. After Test umpire George Hele ruled Woodfull not out, McGilvray sought out the Australian captain and said, 'I'm sorry about that appeal, Mr Woodfull.' 'Hey, George, I hit that hard,' Woodfull responded to the umpire. 'I was ready to walk when you called not out and I stayed there because I didn't want to offend you.'

Some Australians, notably Arthur Morris, Keith Miller, Neil Harvey and Brian Booth, were walkers, but most believed that their code of leaving it to the umpire was more reliable than the English one, which allowed batsmen to become sporadic walkers. When England were battling to save the first Test against Australia at Brisbane in 1962/63, two of their batsmen were given not out to balls they appeared to have hit, prompting Australian captain Richie Benaud to say to Slasher Mackay, 'And they blame us for not walking.'

This clash of codes surfaced on MCC's tour of South Africa in 1964/65. On the opening day of the third Test at Cape Town, the failure of South African opener Eddie Barlow to walk for a slip catch that came off his boot upset the England team, especially bowler Fred Titmus. Neither his fifty nor his hundred were applauded by the players, a breach of cricketing etiquette which caused much resentment among the host nation.

Barlow's failure to walk was given added piquancy by the belated decision of England's premier batsman, Ken Barrington, to walk on 49 for a catch at the wicket having been given not out by umpire John Warner. To the South African team and the crowd, Barrington's gesture of walking was a highly principled one, a measure of the man, but to others it reeked of double standards. 'Perhaps Barrington imagines he was making a magnificent gesture by signifying that he got a touch to the ball when the catch at the wicket was made,' wrote Paul Irwin of the *Rand Daily Mail*. 'If so, his ideas of cricket don't coincide with mine. All Barrington succeeded in doing was to hold the umpire up to ridicule and contempt.'[148]

'To insist he was out when the umpire said he was not out might appear at first to be sporting,' concurred J.L. Manning, sports editor of the *Daily Mail*, 'but a moment's reflection shows how wrong that is when the whole series of incidents is considered. His exhibition was too ostentatious to be convincing. It smacked of "We chaps know how to play the game – even if you lot don't".[149]

Despite continued suspicions that English batsmen didn't always live up to their ideals, most walked until the early-to-mid-1970s, by which time a cultural change was coming over the game. In a more competitive world, where money and winning became ever more important, the old amateur ethos gave way to something harder. Even a committed Christian such as Alan Knott refused to walk in a Test match, on the premise that if one side walked and the other didn't, the former would cede victory to the latter. When David Constant began umpiring in 1969, he reckoned that about 90 per cent of batsmen in the county game still walked, whereas by the end of the following decade that figure had declined to about 10 per cent. On seeing Somerset's Nigel Popplewell walk in a championship match at the end of the 1970s, Bob Willis reckoned it was some time since he had seen an opposing batsman act in such a manner.

Those who continued to walk, such as Chris Tavare, Geoff Cook and Geoff Miller, came under pressure from their England team-mates on the 1982/83 tour of Australia to change tack to boost their chances of winning. In 1992, Tim Munton's gesture of walking against Pakistan at Headingley elicited some frowns from team manger Micky Stewart, and, in 1998, England debutant Steve James caused consternation with his intention to walk, prompting his captain, Alec Stewart, to explain to the team that that was the way he played the game.

Whether the failure to walk was the cause or the result of mass appealing, even when fielders knew the batsman wasn't out, is a matter of conjecture, but certainly by the mid-1970s the trust between batsman and fielder had broken down. It was a far cry from the time when Trevor Bailey, that most competitive of cricketers, walked for a catch in a Test that Ray Lindwall appeared to have taken on the bounce. 'Did it carry?' Bailey's team-mates asked him as he returned to the pavilion. 'I wasn't sure,' Bailey replied, 'but you know Lindwall, if he said it carried, it carried.'

Malcolm Marshall had never come across any form of gamesmanship until he played his first Test in India in 1978/79, when he was given out caught off his pad on a vociferous appeal. 'I assumed, obviously wrongly, that Test cricket was played in the best of spirits. I had never known cheating or gamesmanship in club, schools, or, in my limited experience, first-class cricket.'[150] Just over a year later, he was suspended for one match by the West Indian management for abusing Geoff Boycott for not walking in the first Test at Trent Bridge, by which time he was becoming inured to modern cricketing ethics.

If the umpiring had been flawed at Trent Bridge in 1998, it was even worse in the final Test at Headingley, where Steve Dunne's replacement, Pakistan's Javed Akhtar, was thrust into a critical Test on the back of one rain-affected second XI match. On a typical Headingley pitch with the ball moving about, Akhtar and his partner, Peter Willey, were kept busy with the frequency of appeals. Both sides suffered some rum decisions, especially South Africa, all of which turned the atmosphere poisonous so that even the religious beliefs of certain South Africans such as Jonty Rhodes became the cause for snide comment. 'England really climbed into us, and the aggro was worse than any match I've ever known against Australia, the disciples of hard cricket,' recalled Allan Donald. He admitted that neither side had helped the umpires at all in that series, and that they had got what they had deserved. 'There was so much appealing that there were bound to be some bad decisions.'[151]

Having secured a narrow lead of 22, South Africa were set 219 for victory. With several umpiring decisions going against them, they were soon 27/5 before they rallied through Brian McMillan and Jonty Rhodes, only for England to come good at the end to win by 23 runs and take the series 2–1. Having been the better side for much of the series, the South Africans found defeat hard to swallow and attributed it to the umpiring, while umpire Willey confessed that Headingley had left him bruised. 'The pressure when I started doing Tests three years ago was high. But now with the constant TV examination it is ridiculous. It is no fun umpiring on TV any more.'[152]

Controversy flared once again when England toured South Africa 15 months later. Defeated in the first Test, England struggled to draw the second at Port Elizabeth after being on the receiving end of some poor umpiring by the South African Rudi Koertzen. The most contentious decision occurred in South Africa's second innings when their leading batsman, Jacques Kallis, at a critical stage of the match, edged Phil Tufnell to Chris Adams at gully. Adams confirmed that the catch was clean, but Kallis cast doubt on his claim, and angry words were exchanged between him and the close fielders. With neither umpire sure that the ball had carried, the decision was referred to the third umpire, who, faced with inconclusive evidence, gave it not out, despite the more sophisticated technology available to Sky Sports showing that it was out. 'Refusing to take the word of your opponent in a game like cricket is a serious matter,' wrote Simon Barnes. 'It means that the last area for trust has been squeezed out and that the umpire must now decide absolutely everything.'[153]

As Koertzen received a pasting in the British media, Willey came to his defence. 'I know Rudi and he is a super bloke. He is a very honest man,' he told BBC Radio Five Live. Whatever mistakes he might have made, he had a thankless task given the willingness of the players to manipulate and undermine the umpire. He reminded his listeners that he, Willey, had officiated in the Headingley Test the year before when England had received all the breaks, and no one had complained then. 'The attitude is that it's all right for me to cheat the opposition but it's not all right the other way. I get cheesed off with everybody writing about the poor old umpires. Let's talk about the honesty and integrity of players. They just want to cheat each other.'[154]

Yet player chicanery aside, the sheer number of dubious or plain wrong umpiring decisions in recent encounters between England and South Africa – the *Sunday Times* cricket correspondent Simon Wilde put it at 26 in the last six Tests – was affecting the way the game was being played and exacerbating the antipathy between the two sides. Like the players, television was adding to the pressure on umpires, its ever-improving technology laying bare their frailties. Given these developments, Wilde contended that more power should be handed to the third umpire. 'The International Cricket Council needs to wake up to the issue, if necessary giving fresh powers to match referees to curb on-field excesses. Captains must be reminded of their responsibilities and fined or suspended if their players indulge in excessive cheating, for that is sometimes not too strong a word for it.'[155] It was to become a familiar refrain over the next couple of years.

Chapter 12

Muralitharan's Elbow

THE admission of Sri Lanka to international cricket in 1982 seemed a welcome throwback to a more genteel age of smiling faces, classic stroke-players and subtle wrist-spinners. The game there was based very much around a handful of elite schools that modelled themselves on the English public school tradition, which helped account for their graceful deportment on the field. Regarded as a soft touch in those early years of Test cricket, the Sri Lankans were shocked by the vitriol they encountered from other sides, and in time they vowed to get even with their tormentors. 'At first we never took the sledging seriously and stuck with our own game,' recalled Arjuna Ranatunga, Sri Lanka's captain between 1988 and 1999. 'But when teams didn't stop, we decided to give it back.'[156]

Hailing from a political family, Ranatunga extended the game beyond the Colombo elite and helped promote a new national consciousness through the exploits of the cricket team. Under his forceful captaincy, Sri Lanka began to play a more aggressive brand of cricket that stretched the laws to the limit and alienated many of their opponents. 'They dine out on a reputation as the charming minnows of cricket,' wrote Bob Simpson, 'but only the naïve really believe that; the fact is that Sri Lanka are as quick to cause trouble as they are to complain about it.'[157]

Sri Lanka's new, uncompromising approach stemmed in part from their 1995/96 tour of Australia. The tour was an unmitigated disaster from start to finish, their 3–0 loss in the Test series overshadowed by disputes with officialdom, especially the no-balling of Muttiah Muralitharan, their 23-year-old off-spinner and leading wicket-taker.

For the previous two years there had been doubts about Muralitharan's freakish action, caused by a deformity that prevented him from straightening his arm naturally. In 1993, match referee Peter Burge spoke privately to members of the Board of Cricket for Sri Lanka (BCCSL) after their series against India, and in March 1995 his colleague Barry Jarman expressed similar concerns following Sri Lanka's win in New Zealand. That October, following the Singer Champions Trophy in Sharjah, umpires Darrell Hair, Tony McQuillan and Nigel Plews conveyed their reservations to match referee Raman Subba Row, who passed them on to the BCCSL; then, at the end of November, McQuillan and another umpire, Martin Whitby, questioned the legitimacy of Muralitharan's action in their report of Sri Lanka's match against Queensland. Finally, after umpiring a one-day international between Australia and Sri Lanka, Hair told match referee Graham Dowling that from his observation there had been no change in Muralitharan's action since Sharjah.

While Muralitharan escaped censure in the first Test at Perth, in which Sri Lanka were comprehensively outplayed, the team was wrongly accused of ball-tampering, an umpiring error that led to a fulsome apology by the ICC on the eve of the second Test at Melbourne. There, in front of a 55,000 Boxing Day crowd, Muralitharan was no-balled by Darrell Hair, standing at the bowler's end, seven times in three overs, the first bowler to be called for throwing in a first-class match in Australia for 32 years.

The decision to call Muralitharan stunned the Australian dressing room and disconcerted the crowd, who sympathised with the off-spinner in his public humiliation. The fact that he was then able to bowl at New Zealander Steve Dunne's end for a further 32 overs without incident only added to the confusion. Hair did try to persuade Dunne to call Muralitharan, but Dunne refused. Although foiled in the short term, Hair had the final say when he told the Sri Lankan management at tea on the second day that should Muralitharan bowl in the final session, he would call him. Ranatunga kept him out of the attack.

A renowned stickler for the rules, Hair's abrasive style grated with many of the players, not least with the touring South Africans in Australia two years earlier, but no one ever doubted his courage and integrity. The ICC supported him and rejected Sri Lanka's request to make a final ruling on Muralitharan's action, since that would be tantamount to instructing umpires not to call him. It was up to the BCCSL to 'take corrective action'.

The decision of the Sri Lankan management to keep playing Muralitharan was a risky one, given the reservations of many an umpire. He survived the scrutiny of two Test match umpires, Terry Prue and Steve Davis, in a one-day international at Hobart, but in the next match, against the West Indies at Brisbane, he was called seven times in three overs by Ross Emerson, a former policeman, standing at the bowler's end. Four of those calls followed Muralitharan's switch to bowling leg breaks, something that he could accomplish only with a straight arm. The Brisbane crowd were unimpressed with this further humiliation, and they booed the umpires from the field as they left with a police escort.

Given these distractions, Sri Lanka did well to reach the final of the triangular series, but the offensive language of both sides and a couple of contentious decisions against Sri Lanka in the first final contributed to a bad-tempered decider in Sydney. At the end of a rain-affected match, marred by McGrath clashing with Sri Lanka opener Sanath Jayasuriya, claims of Sri Lankan time-wasting and Ranatunga feigning injury so that he could use a runner, the defeated tourists refused to shake hands with the Australians, a gesture that riled the home team.

Australia's refusal to play in Sri Lanka weeks later during the World Cup, because of recent terrorist outrages there, did nothing to strengthen relations between the two sides. It said much for the Sri Lankans that they quickly regrouped, and, playing some scintillating cricket, they won the World Cup, beating Australia in the final at Lahore.

That win transformed Sri Lanka and brought them added stature. No longer the paupers of international cricket, they played with a greater swagger and gave no quarter in the dark arts of gamesmanship compared with their opponents. That said, a return to Australia in January 1999 to participate in the triangular one-day series against the host country and England would be no sinecure, given the continued doubts about Muralitharan's action. For while the ICC had given him the all-clear in 1996 after a biochemical analysis by scientists in Australia and Hong Kong, England coach David Lloyd had cast aspersions about his action after he had bowled Sri Lanka to victory at the Oval in September 1998.

Before the Sri Lankans landed in Australia, Darrell Hair had raised the stakes by describing Muralitharan's action as diabolical in his autobiography and indicating his willingness to call him again unless he moderated it. Under pressure from the Sri Lankans, the ACB encouraged Hair to withdraw from the umpiring panel for that summer, but Muralitharan remained a marked man. With Australian crowds now heckling him every time he bowled and match referee Peter van der Merwe admitting that his action was suspect, the potential for another showdown was looming, especially since Emerson was due to take charge of Sri Lanka's match against England on 24 January.

Batting first at the beautiful Adelaide Oval, England had made their way to 97/1 when Muralitharan entered the attack in the 18th over. His first over and a half proved uneventful, but on his tenth ball he was called for throwing by Emerson, standing at square leg. While commentators Tony Greig and Ian Botham denounced Emerson for being out of order, a furious Ranatunga engaged him in a finger-jabbing altercation, before making for the boundary to consult with his manager and board officials back in Colombo.

When play resumed 15 minutes later, Muralitharan switched ends and Ranatunga insisted that Emerson stand right up to the stumps so he couldn't call Muralitharan again. Unnerved by the confrontation, Emerson began making mistakes, and the match descended into near-anarchy as Sri Lanka chased 303 to win.

Amid plenty of invective from both teams, Sri Lankan batsman Roshan Mahanama clearly obstructed England opening bowler Darren Gough as he ran a single, and captain Alec Stewart barged Upul Chandana. With two balls to go, Muralitharan of all people won the match for Sri Lanka, but their celebrations proved short-lived, since Ranatunga was summoned to appear before the match referee to answer five charges of misconduct. Van der Merwe also conveyed his concern to the England management about the general atmosphere of the match, and although he didn't charge any of the Englishmen, believing it would have an adverse effect on the game, this made him look biased in the eyes of the Sri Lankans.

Unrepentant about the stand he took on behalf of his bowler, whom he felt had been sorely provoked, Ranatunga armed himself with expert legal opinion when he met van der Merwe at Adelaide two days later. Informed that the four umpiring charges were invalid because they weren't lodged within the necessary time frame, and that the Code of Conduct was legally flawed, van der Merwe had no choice but to adjourn the hearing and seek legal advice himself. The same day, it emerged that Emerson had been off work with a stress-related illness for the previous eight weeks, without the knowledge of the ACB, and that he wouldn't be officiating again that season.

When the hearing reassembled at Perth, Ranatunga now faced the one major charge of bringing the game into disrepute; but, threatened with an immediate legal challenge should the Sri Lankan captain be banned and the tour placed in jeopardy, van der Merwe was forced to bow to reality. He banned Ranatunga for a maximum six games, suspended for 12 months, and fined him 75 per cent of his match fee.

Although he was imposing the heaviest penalty yet, the highly respected match referee, in a sombre statement, suggested that Ranatunga had escaped on a technicality. 'The code of conduct was drawn up by cricketers to be administered by cricketers. In this instance it was a great disappointment to find that legal people were prominent in this hearing.'[158] In a very public dressing down, he told Ranatunga that he had lost the respect of the cricket community and his team had become the least popular in world cricket.

While Ranatunga's lenient sentence was greeted with jubilation by his team and with relief at home, it was bitterly denounced elsewhere. According to the *Advertiser* [Adelaide], the Sri Lankans' 'shameful' disregard for the spirit of cricket was a greater sin than bodyline.

'Cricket becomes a dangerous and unattractive game if captains are allowed to confront umpires, tell them where to stand, poke them in the chest and threaten to take them off the field when decisions go against them,' opined the *Sydney Morning Herald*. 'This is what Ranatunga did.' He deserved the severest censure. 'The bedrock of cricket's credibility is the acceptance by players that the umpire's word is final.'[159]

'In threatening to take legal action against the very governing body which Sri Lanka fought hard and long to join,' declared Andrew Ramsey in *The Australian*, 'Ranatunga has ensured the sense of propriety and gentility which has characterised cricket through the past 120 years is officially dead.'[160]

Regardless of the wisdom of Emerson's decision which triggered his outburst, Ramsey continued, Ranatunga's attempt to subvert the ICC's Code of Conduct through the courts had shown abject contempt for the game. By successfully legally defending what was morally indefensible, Ramsey believed, Ranatunga had impoverished the once-proud game of cricket.

With the Adelaide match still fresh in the memory, the England tour to Sri Lanka in February 2001 was never going to be for the faint-hearted, given the preponderance of turning wickets, mystery spinners and vociferous close-in fielders. The warm-up matches provided an early warning of the storm to come. Gough clashed verbally with two opponents, England complained that Craig White was racially abused by all-rounder Ruchira Perera and the standard of umpiring left much to be desired.

With two inexperienced officials, Peter Manuel of Sri Lanka and Arani Jayaprakash of India, in charge of the first Test, both teams were warned by match referee Hanumant Singh, the former Indian batsman, to conduct themselves in the right spirit. England toiled for the best part of two days in searing heat at Galle while Sri Lanka compiled a formidable 470/5. Exposed to Muralitharan and his fellow spinner Jayasuriya on a turning wicket and fielders screaming themselves hoarse, they then fell victim to some rank umpiring. Stewart was adjudged lbw to a ball that pitched six inches outside the leg stump, Atherton was given out to a bump ball without reference to the third umpire, and Graeme Hick went caught behind to a ball he missed by a mile. At the end of a match in which England lost by an innings, the umpires left to a chorus of jeers from the travelling supporters, and few pleasantries were exchanged between the two teams. Botham called the umpiring the worst he had ever seen at Test level, and Hanumant Singh fined four Sri Lankans for excessive appealing. According to Michael Henderson of the *Daily Telegraph*, 'Sri Lanka's conduct in this match was nothing less than a deliberate and concerted assault on the fabric of the game, that unspoken law that enables players to rub along together in professional solidarity if not complete amity.'[161]

With Sri Lanka unlikely to let up on their aggression, England were in no mood to turn the other cheek. Their captain, Nasser Hussain, pledged a hard, confrontational style in the Australian mould, and Stewart justified appealing at all costs. 'It might not sound nice and the way people think the game should be played. But it is how the game is played at the highest level.'[162] The appointment of the Sri Lankan B.C. Cooray and the South African Rudi Koertzen to officiate at Kandy did little to inspire confidence, since neither had done England any favours in South Africa the previous year. Their failure to exert any authority helped account for a venomous atmosphere in which verbal abuse, blatant cheating and gratuitous dissent abounded. This time it was England who benefited from umpiring errors, especially from Cooray, who the local papers accused of aiding the tourists. Hussain was fortunate to survive two bat-and-pad catches on his way to a dogged century as England gained a valuable first-innings lead of 90.

All the simmering tension of this toxic encounter boiled over at the start of Sri Lanka's second innings as they slumped to 3/3. Particularly controversial was the dismissal of Jayasuriya at third slip off a clear bump ball. Given out after both umpires had conferred, the irate Sri Lankan captain stalked off, flinging his helmet at an advertising board, an act of pique that brought him a fine from the match referee. When the young Sri Lankan wicketkeeper-batsman Kumar Sangakkara complained to Alec Stewart about the injustice of Jayasuriya's dismissal, Stewart told him that 'What goes around comes around.' Sangakkara responded by branding the England team cheats, a jibe that provoked the normally phlegmatic Atherton to fury, understandable given his conduct during the series. (The victim of a dubious caught-behind in the previous Test, he had requested an adjudication over a catch he had taken in the current Test, believing that it might not have carried.) He waved his fingers at Sangakkara and remonstrated with umpire Koertzen, an outburst that earned both him and Sangakkara a stern reprimand from the match referee. At the end of a tumultuous day's play in which Sri Lanka limped to 98/6, Cooray was given a police escort as local supporters chanted 'cheat' and 'thief' at him.

When taxed about the players' behaviour, both coaches were adamant that they would continue to play in the same vein. England coach Duncan Fletcher said that if the code was fairly administered there would be fewer problems of discipline. 'If only,' wrote Michael Henderson. 'Until the players, including some of his own, prefer honesty to duplicity, and value what is right more than what is possible, then the game will become worthless.' What was the point of having a code, he wondered, unless the match referee was prepared to use it? 'Once again, Singh, despite his amiable public manner, has proved wretchedly ineffective. Jayasuriya should have been banned, full stop.'[163] 'What we have seen over these past three days is as near to lawlessness on an international cricket field as there can ever have been,' concluded his fellow columnist Mark Nicholas.[164]

The tension continued the next day as Sri Lanka, led by a defiant 95 from Sangakkara, fought their way back into the match, taking their total to 250. Set 161 to win, England finished that evening at 91/4. It needed a further two-and-a-half hours of gripping cricket before Craig White and Robert Croft guided England to a three-wicket victory, one of England's most satisfying, but their success couldn't obscure the discordant atmosphere, the most unpleasant Test that both Atherton and Stewart had ever encountered. 'Ultimately, it is the players' game,' wrote Atherton, 'and although I have been critical of some umpiring here, I believe that it is the players' responsibility to clean up the game. Each plays to his own set of principles but I believe that dissent, abusing umpires and clear cheating, such as scooping a catch on the half-volley, has no place in the game.'[165]

Atherton's honesty was applauded by Michael Parkinson in the *Daily Telegraph* days later, but he regretted his omission of walking. He accepted that staying put and leaving the decision to the umpire was the rule rather than the exception. 'But because everyone is at it doesn't make it acceptable. It simply underlines the moral confusion existing in the modern game.'[166] It implied that some cheating was more acceptable than others.

After the battle of Kandy, Cooray was replaced for the final Test at Colombo by South African Dave Orchard, a man not to be trifled with. It proved a judicious move, because both he and his partner, former Sri Lankan leg-spinner Asoka de Silva, performed admirably and the match passed off without serious incident. England won and took the series 2–1, but the Tests had emphasised the need for an elite panel of umpires with the power to hand out more severe penalties, and for more technology to help them with difficult decisions. 'If anybody doubts that cricket has reached a point of no return with the regard to the way the game is adjudicated,' wrote Simon Wilde in the *Sunday Times*, 'then these past few weeks in Sri Lanka should have settled the debate.'[167] With adherence to the laws at an all-time low and acrimony at an all-time high, Wilde thought it imperative that the ICC act. Fortunately, with a new chief executive about to take over, help was at hand.

Chapter 13

An Oriental Superpower

AS CRICKET lost its innocence during the 1970s, the one country that remained most attached to Corinthian values was India. WSC had largely passed it by, intimidatory bowling held out little appeal in a land that produced few fast bowlers, and sledging offended its cultural sensitivities. Yet appearances could be deceptive, because India's transition from cricketing backwater to global superpower began in earnest the moment they won the World Cup in 1983. Sensing the vast commercial potential that lay in Indian cricket, the Board of Control for Cricket in India (BCCI), led by their treasurer Jagmohan Dalmiya, a wealthy Bengali building magnate, combined with Pakistan to bid to host the 1987 World Cup; and, with support from 21 voting Associates, they were successful.

Contrary to expectations, they made a great success of it as the subcontinent took the one-day game to its heart, and in 1993 they stole a march on England by successfully bidding for the 1996 World Cup. That same year, Dalmiya, now secretary of the BCCI, won a protracted legal battle against the state broadcaster Doordarshan for permission to sell television rights to cable broadcasters. As television spread in India, so did cricket's prominence, and, aided by a record-breaking deal for television rights, the 1996 World Cup proved a commercial triumph, netting the ICC some US$50 million.

Having brought unprecedented wealth to the BCCI, Dalmiya now wanted to wrest control of the global game from England

and Australia. Exploiting his support from within the Asian bloc and the Associates, Dalmiya was unanimously chosen to succeed Clyde Walcott as president of the ICC in 1997. By overseeing a proliferation of one-day tournaments in Asia that generated millions of dollars in sponsorship and television rights, the ICC prospered under his leadership. Some of these tournaments, however, gave rise to allegations of match-fixing, culminating in the downfall of South African captain Hansie Cronje, in 2000, following his admission of accepting substantial sums from an Indian bookmaker. (This book doesn't cover the corrupt practice of match-fixing and spot-fixing, for while these scandals have flouted the spirit of the game, they are basically matters of individual gain rather than collective gamesmanship to steal an advantage over the opposition.) The failure of Dalmiya to fully appreciate the gravity of these allegations tainted his final days in office and brought him into conflict with his English and Australian counterparts.

India's rise to global prominence wasn't matched by the performance of its cricket team, especially away from home, something that Sourav Ganguly, Dalmiya's protégé from Bengal, aimed to rectify on becoming captain in 2000. A ferocious competitor, Ganguly was adept at getting under the skin of his opponents and instilling into his players a new-found steeliness. This uncompromising attitude took Steve Waugh's Australians by surprise when they toured India in March 2001. From the moment Ganguly turned up late to toss with Waugh and walked off by himself, a distinct *froideur* existed between the two sides. During the first Test at Mumbai, Michael Slater claimed a low diving catch against India's Rahul Dravid, and when the video evidence proved inconclusive, a furious Slater not only remonstrated with the umpires, he also berated Dravid for not taking his word. 'It was the last thing I wanted to see,' recalled Australian captain Steve Waugh, 'particularly as we'd regularly talked about our on-field behaviour and wanted to change the long-held perception of many that we were "ugly".'[168]

'It was poor behaviour from a senior player,' declared Malcolm Conn, the chief cricket writer for *The Australian*. 'How would Slater have felt late on the first day if India's wicketkeeper Nayan Mongia had confronted him after it appeared that Slater had been caught behind off a solid edge but given not out?'[169]

Slater was summoned to a meeting with match referee Cammie Smith, the former West Indian opening batsman, but, to general amazement, he was let off with a mere warning because of his previous unblemished record. The fact that Smith later fined him after Slater had proclaimed his innocence on Australian radio did little to placate his critics. His leniency was recalled later that year when the Indians, on tour in South Africa, ran into trouble with match referee Mike Denness.

In July 2001, former ACB chief executive Malcolm Speed became the chief executive of the ICC, determined to lay down the law against gamesmanship and ill-discipline. 'We have got to become more pro-active in stamping out some of the behaviour because, quite frankly, it is inexcusable. Players are doing the game an enormous amount of harm.' He proposed an elite panel of umpires and younger referees willing to take a more robust line against misconduct, and wrote to all boards outlining his tougher stance. This stance was to be fully tested in South Africa.

One down in the series and trailing by 162 runs on first innings in the second Test at Port Elizabeth, India had fought their way back into the match by taking three quick wickets at the start of South Africa's second innings. Their frequent and intense appealing caused the two inexperienced umpires, Ian Howell and Russell Tiffin, to feel intimidated, and they reported four of the players to Denness, by now a senior match referee. Denness fined three of them 75 per cent of their match fees and banned the fourth, Virender Sehwag, a centurion on debut in the previous Test, not only for charging the umpire but also for dissent. In addition, he fined the captain, Ganguly, for failing to control his players and examined television footage of Sachin Tendulkar cleaning the grass off the ball when bowling his medium-pacers. Although the umpires hadn't seen anything untoward and his bowling had little impact on the match, Denness concluded that Tendulkar's interference with the ball without the umpires' knowledge had transgressed the letter of the law. He fined him and gave him a one-match suspended ban, a sanction Tendulkar thought highly inappropriate. He told Denness he objected to being labelled a cheat and that he was in no mood to hold his peace.

While there were those such as Steve Waugh who thought that Tendulkar's ban was justified, since no player, whatever his reputation, should be above the game, his revered status and impeccable disciplinary record meant that it sparked outrage in India. Banners denouncing racism in cricket and Denness were unfurled in the streets, and former team-mates of Tendulkar's rushed to proclaim his innocence. Not only was the television footage inconclusive, the umpires hadn't complained about the state of the ball. In Parliament, 50 Hindu nationalist MPs led by Kirti Azad, the former Test player, agitated against Denness, whom the media portrayed as a Victorian imperialist with an outdated sense of fairness. Why had he punished the Indians for excessive appealing when the South Africans had been just as culpable and their bowlers had constantly abused the Indian batsmen, footage of which was repeatedly replayed on Indian television?

Shocked by the scale of the sanctions and fully aware of the Indian players' sense of grievance, Dalmiya, the recently elected chairman of the BCCI, threatened to call off the third Test unless Denness was removed as match referee. Feeling unappreciated for his presidential legacy of greatly increasing ICC wealth through television deals, he was further aggrieved that much of that largesse was now subsidising the system of neutral umpires and match referees, which discriminated against India and Pakistan, since their players constituted most of those who had been charged. Consequently, he was only too ready to lead an insurgency movement against the way the ICC operated.

Even if Denness had been inconsistent in his use of sanctions, the idea that he was racially biased hardly squared with the facts. A former captain of England and a man of great integrity, his appointment had been overseen by Sunil Gavaskar, one of the giants of Indian cricket, and he had never reported any

Indian during the nine previous occasions he officiated them. According to Malcolm Speed, he had been a model of fairness who had followed all the correct procedures. Neither India nor South Africa had objected to his appointment when it had been mooted that September, and no cricket board had the right to remove him. To do so under this kind of pressure would be to disregard the rules agreed by all member countries and set an unacceptable precedent.

Speed's words fell on deaf ears, as the multi-racial United Cricket Board of South Africa chose to join with the BCCI in defying the ICC. Aside from the loss of around £1 million that would accrue to sponsors and broadcasters should the Test be cancelled, the board was instructed by its government, loath to upset India, its major trading partner, to replace Denness for the third Test. When Denness refused to cave in to this pressure, it fell to Gerald Majola, the chief executive officer of the board and former anti-apartheid activist, to bar him access to Centurion Park and replace him with Denis Lindsay, a respected ICC match referee.

Confronted with this challenge to its authority, the ICC responded by declaring the Test match unofficial, a decision supported by cricket-loving Australian prime minister John Howard, the TCCB and the Western media, which saw third-world politicians meddling unacceptably in cricketing matters. 'How on earth could India have the temerity to suggest a match referee be replaced,' declared Australian cricket writer Robert Craddock in the *Courier-Mail*, 'and, even more incredibly, how could South African cricket officials be spineless enough to accede to their request, even if they were pressured by their government? And how could a match referee, Denis Lindsay, who is appointed by the International Cricket Council, be weak enough to snub his bosses and accept an appointment in a match where one of his fellow referees has been sacked? Does anybody involved in world cricket have a backbone? The replacement of Mike Denness is a black mark on the credibility of both nations that will linger not just for the summer but for years to come.'

As an Australian, Craddock accepted that his countrymen had been guilty of persuading Darrell Hair to stand down from matches involving Sri Lanka following clashes between the two, but he still thought this was poor form. It was no coincidence that the two countries involved in the current fracas were complicit in the recent match-fixing scandal, and he thought that the 'same lethal cocktail of weak or misguided administration and cocky players is at play here'.[170]

Some Indians were uneasy about their officials playing the race card. 'Challenging unfair decisions is one thing, said *The Hindu*, 'it is another to browbeat a system, howsoever victimised a nation feels. On all counts, cricket administrators of South Africa and India have not acquitted themselves well by replacing the match referee, Mr Mike Denness.'[171]

As for the ICC, they restated their right as the world governing body of cricket to appoint referees and umpires, and for those officials to make decisions that were respected by both players and boards. Without this right, the sport could descend into anarchy.

Attention now switched to Sehwag. The BCCI claimed that the Centurion Test was official and his omission from the Indian team qualified him to play against England at Mohali the following week on India's return from South Africa. The ICC insisted that Sehwag wasn't eligible, since it had decreed that the Centurion Test be unofficial and warned that further defiance would render the Mohali Test unofficial too. With Dalmiya apparently set on confrontation, the president of the England and Wales Cricket Board (ECB), Lord MacLaurin, rallied to the support of the ICC, warning that England wouldn't play a team with a banned player, even if that meant cancelling their tour of India.

On 27 November, the ICC set an ultimatum of noon on 30 November for Sehwag's withdrawal from the Mohali Test, which was to begin three days later (they feared a last-minute withdrawal would incite the large crowd). The BCCI rejected the ultimatum and continued their brinkmanship until, after several days of intense negotiations, they backed down, acknowledging that most Indians wanted reform of the ICC through deliberation rather than open confrontation. The unofficial status of the Centurion Test, won by South Africa, stood, and the ban on Tendulkar wasn't revoked; but, in a bid to placate Dalmiya, the ICC set up a referees' commission to investigate the possibility of appeals against the type of sanctions issued by Denness.

When the new three-man commission was appointed, the BCCI weren't impressed. They objected to one of its members, former Pakistan captain Majid Khan, because of his comments about match-fixing, and to the chairman, Justice Albie Sachs, because they believed there should be no contributions from representatives of the countries involved in the Denness affair. With the Asian bloc and South Africa rallying behind India, the ICC was forced to postpone the workings of the commission, much to the consternation of ICC president Malcolm Gray.

In the meantime, the announcement of a new elite panel of match referees comprising an Indian, Gundappa Viswanath, a Pakistani, Wasim Raja, a Sri Lankan, Ranjan Madugalle, a West Indian, Clive Lloyd, and no Englishman or Australian, helped defuse any tension prior to the ICC meeting at Cape Town on 16 March 2002.

In an impressive display of unity, the ICC agreed to impose a stringent new Code of Conduct with the umpires, not the match referee, now responsible for laying charges – a power also granted to the chief executive of any country's board and the chief executive of the ICC. They also introduced a right of appeal for serious offences, a revamped three-man appeals commission to be drawn from the ICC executive board, and a disputes resolution committee to investigate the charges brought by Denness. In the event, this new committee never met, after Denness underwent heart surgery in June 2002.

In retrospect, these reforms, not least the new Code of Conduct and new elite panel of match referees, in addition to the elite panel of umpires, proved of some significance, since they began the long road back towards restoring order and discipline to a game that had lost its ethical bearings.

Chapter 14

Mental Disintegration

FOLLOWING Mark Taylor's retirement as Australian captain in January 1999, the mantle of leadership passed to his deputy, Steve Waugh. While lacking his predecessor's tactical innovation and flair for diplomacy, Waugh compensated with his strength of character and uncanny ability to exploit any weakness in his opponents. Fortunate to lead such an outstanding team, Waugh amassed a tally of victories, 41 in 57 Tests, that ranks with the very best – but, in their restless drive for domination, the team once again overstepped the boundaries of acceptable conduct.

The trouble began in Waugh's first series as captain, against the West Indies, when Glenn McGrath was fined for spitting on the wicket during the Antigua Test; nine months later, he was reprimanded for giving Sachin Tendulkar a hostile send-off in the third Test at Sydney. According to Peter Roebuck, 'It did not seem much of a way to treat a batsman of any sort, let alone a champion. Nor was it much of a way to treat a guest or a visiting captain.'[172] A year later, a stump microphone caught Shane Warne making an obscene outburst against Zimbabwe's Stuart Carlisle in a one-day international at Sydney after he had been hit for three. Neil Harvey described it as 'abominable' and called on the ACB, the umpires and Waugh to clean up their act, a call that went unheeded as Australia embarked upon a tempestuous tour of India. They began impressively enough with a ten-wicket victory in the first Test at Mumbai, extending their run of successive victories to

16, but that triumph was overshadowed by Michael Slater and his disputed catch, described in the previous chapter. Later, after losing the Test series, McGrath and wicketkeeper Adam Gilchrist were fined for dissent and abusive language respectively in the one-day internationals. Under pressure from the ICC as part of its drive to clean up world cricket, and keen to eradicate his team's unwholesome image, Waugh pledged that they would observe the spirit of cricket on their upcoming 2001 tour of England. He proved as good as his word as they romped to a 4–1 series win. Later that year, in the home series against New Zealand, the halo began to slip following an unseemly send-off by fast bowler Brett Lee after dismissing Shane Bond, another fast bowler, in the final Test at Perth. For using offensive gestures and crude language, Lee was fined 75 per cent of his match fee.

After drawing against New Zealand, Australia returned to winning ways against South Africa, beating them comprehensively in back-to-back series, but once again they took their aggression to excess. In the third Test at Sydney, Justin Ontong, the young Cape-Coloured debutant, was mercilessly taunted for his controversial selection on racial grounds. Then, following the return series in South Africa, another debutant, Graeme Smith, a precocious 20-year-old not averse to saying his bit on the field, told *Sports Illustrated* magazine how he had been subjected to a barrage of obscenities in the second Test at Cape Town. At one point during this non-stop rant, he turned to umpire Rudi Koertzen, who just shrugged his shoulders as if to say, 'Welcome to Test cricket.'

Smith's allegations, far from embarrassing the Australian team, brought defiance. They claimed it was part of the game, and the sooner he realised it the better. But, not surprisingly, the game's authorities saw matters in a different light. The ICC told Australia that they had the second worst disciplinary record in international cricket (after India), and James Sutherland, the ACB's new chief executive, warned that it was up to umpires and captains to combat abuse. Later that year, Brian Booth, writing in *Wisden Australia*, deplored sledging as unsportsmanlike. 'It is bad manners and an example of discourtesy in sport. It is an admission by those who use it that they do not believe they can win fairly. There are more positive ways of getting the mental edge over opponents that are in keeping with the spirit of cricket.'[173]

He recalled how, at a recent awards night, his critique of some of the Australian team's behaviour had won spontaneous and sustained applause from young and old alike. Sledging in its modern form, as a premeditated and accepted practice, didn't exist in his day.

This was the nub of the problem. Post-1970s Australia, raised in a more confrontational environment, placed great emphasis on what Waugh called 'mental disintegration' to try to unsettle the opposition, and no amount of criticism would persuade them to change tack. At the end of a feisty 2002/03 series against Nasser Hussain's England in which they easily retained the Ashes, they dropped their guard in the final Test and lost by 225 runs. Beset by some indifferent umpiring, opener Matthew Hayden was fined 20 per cent of his match fee for breaking a dressing-room window following his dismissal in the second innings, and Adam Gilchrist was reprimanded for showing dissent. 'Like it or not, the days when we could have the glories of a great innings unsullied by too-frequent petulant displays of anger at bad luck or poor umpiring are long gone,' commented an editorial in *The Australian*. The change had as much to do with the pressures of modern society as with the onset of professionalism in cricket, it said. Thirty years earlier, Australia had been a more relaxed and comfortable place. Since then, the demands of the global economy had forced Australians to work harder and perform better. 'That same commitment to winning shapes the way Australians play elite sport. They train intensively and have the mental toughness to stay focused on winning. Sometimes the tension gets to them, and they behave badly.'[174]

A week later in a one-day international against Sri Lanka at Brisbane, Australian batsman Darren Lehmann was guilty of a racist obscenity outside his dressing room after being run out at a crucial stage in the game. His remarks were heard by members of the Sri Lankan tour party, and their manager made an informal complaint to match referee Clive Lloyd. Because Lehmann, a highly regarded player, appeared full of remorse and apologised after the match to each Sri Lankan player, Lloyd chose to let him off with a severe reprimand. There the matter would have rested had it not been for the intervention of Malcolm Speed. Conscious of the likely reaction worldwide to Lehmann's remarks, he was determined to bring him to book by charging him with a serious breach of the ICC Code of Conduct.

Speed's uncompromising approach was broadly welcomed, in contrast to the repeated failure of the ACB to uphold standards on and off the field. (Their reaction to Lehmann's offence was that he should undergo counselling.) According to Mike Gibson of the *Daily Telegraph* (Sydney), the boorish attitude of the Australian team had been a sore point with many cricket fans for years.

'The churlish manner in which they treat opponents, the arrogance they display and the foul-mouthed sledging that has become their trademark, have seriously damaged our sporting image. It was bad enough when we were winning. Now we are beginning to lose a few, it has grown worse.'

The damage done by Lehmann was inestimable. 'To followers of the game on the subcontinent – where cricket is king – his ignorance and obscene remark will only confirm their suspicions that Australia is largely populated by racist bullies.'[175]

At his three-hour hearing before Lloyd in an Adelaide hotel immediately before the christening of Lehmann's twins, his solicitor apologised for his slur and made much of his previous impeccable record. Others, including Sri Lankan coach Dav Whatmore, appealed for leniency, but they failed to prevent Lehmann's five-match ban for racial vilification – the first time anyone had been suspended for such an offence, and the most serious penalty imposed by the ICC.

Lehmann's ban made him ineligible for much of the 2003 World Cup in South Africa, but despite his absence and that of Shane Warne, serving a year-long suspension for drug abuse, Australia won easily. They kept up the good work in the Caribbean, winning the first three Tests against the West Indies before heading for

Antigua for the final Test. Yet what had been a friendly series suddenly exploded into acrimony.

The spark was ignited in the West Indies' first innings by umpire Venkat's belated decision to give their opener Devon Smith out caught at the wicket. Smith's failure to walk earned him a wigging from Hayden, which so incensed Brian Lara, the incoming batsman, that he immediately made his feelings known to the feisty Queenslander. A not-out decision in Lara's favour when he was on 15 only added to the tension. Having clashed with several Australians, the West Indian captain then found himself engaged in a major spat with Steve Waugh, who accused him of being a selective walker.

This fiery exchange on the second day was but the prelude to an even more heated one on the fourth evening as the West Indies chased 418 to win. A gritty fifth-wicket partnership of 123 between Ramnaresh Sarwan and Shivnarine Chanderpaul had given the home side a sporting chance, and, as the Australians wilted in the heat, tempers became frayed. A late arrival for the tour because of his wife's treatment for cancer at home, McGrath was struggling to find his best form, and, after absorbing some punishment from Sarwan, he taunted him for supposedly having an intimate relationship with Lara. Sarwan, unaware about Jane McGrath's condition, suggested that it was she, not he, who was close to Lara, at which point McGrath erupted in fury. He spun round and, towering over his diminutive opponent, threatened to rip his throat out if he ever mentioned his wife again. It needed the intervention of umpire Shepherd to cool emotions, and when Sarwan reached his century shortly afterwards, he was congratulated by several of the Australians. Following the match's conclusion – the West Indies having won by three wickets, thereby breaking the record for a winning final-innings score in Test cricket – both sides played down the incident as McGrath and Sarwan made up over a glass of rum. Match referee Mike Procter confirmed that no action would be taken, implying that a touch of gamesmanship in Test cricket made for great theatre – remarks which seemed out of kilter with most cricket lovers, not least in

Australia itself. Within hours of the altercation, James Sutherland rang Waugh and told him to control his players. The television footage of the giant McGrath squaring up to the diminutive Sarwan made him look like a bully, and once again Australia's reputation for sportsmanship had been sullied. Paul Sheahan, the former Australian batsman and headmaster of Melbourne Grammar School, declared that for the first time in his life he was ashamed of an Australian side, and Malcolm Gray, the Australian president of the ICC, admitted that his compatriots were disliked the world over because of their sledging. While criticising the umpires for their failure to act, he also called on national bodies to bring about a change in culture in their cricket teams. 'The ACB tells Waugh and his men to clean up their act, McGrath continues to be contrite after repeated indiscretions,' opined *The Australian*. 'The ACB notes the bulging coffers and remains mostly mute.'[176]

It wasn't just the ACB in the firing line. According to Ian Chappell, the ICC, by failing to clamp down on sledging, was eroding one of the basic tenets of the game. The batsman was entitled to a bit of peace out in the middle. 'Australian teams have been the instigators in the increased level of chatter on the field. It's a dangerous ploy because most players who indulge in it find it difficult to cope when they are at the receiving end.'[177]

Aside from flak in the media, the ACB, soon to become Cricket Australia (CA), were deluged with telephone calls, emails and texts from cricket lovers outraged at what they had seen. In Sutherland's opinion, the players were in denial because they were insulated from the Antigua backlash. At a CA function in Sydney in July, he took Waugh, Ponting (the one-day captain) and McGrath aside to confront them with the footage of recent incidents, along with comments from sponsors unhappy to be seen supporting such behaviour. Most pertinently, they heard directly from the CA receptionist, a female cricket lover who had been reduced to tears by fielding so many angry telephone calls from the public. Finally seeing the light, Waugh and Ponting resolved to work closely with CA to clean up their act. The upshot was the Spirit of Cricket project, which refined its guidelines on player conduct. The

Australian team pledged to respect umpires' decisions and their opponents, but on the vexed question of sledging they gave only limited ground: while they promised to eliminate personal abuse, they made no such concession to 'competitive banter'. According to Malcolm Knox in his book *The Greatest*, the problem with these guidelines lay in their subjectivity, since the players were judge and jury of what comments were deemed acceptable. 'Under Waugh's captaincy, the truth of the matter was that Australian sledging was very often not humorous by anyone's definition, nor acceptable, nor inoffensive, nor impersonal. It wasn't just "gamesmanship". Nor was it very clever.'[178]

Despite continued reservations, the Spirit of Cricket pledge brought about an improvement in Australia's conduct over the next couple of years, with no player being reported in their next 28 Tests and only one reported in their next 96 one-day internationals. Ironically, that player was Adam Gilchrist, who the previous year had won worldwide acclaim during the World Cup in South Africa for his decision to walk, a policy he continued to follow thereafter.

In the recent 2002/03 series against England, the vexed question of walking had, not for the first time, sparked some controversy. In the first innings of the second Test at Adelaide, Michael Vaughan remained unmoved by Justin Langer's assurance that he had caught him low at point on 19. Because umpires Steve Bucknor and Rudi Koertzen were unsure, they consulted the third umpire, Steve Davis, and the video replay suggested that the ball had touched the ground. Given not out, Vaughan's reprieve infuriated Langer, and he proceeded to lambast Vaughan for not accepting his word throughout his sublime innings of 177. His grievance received short shrift from sports journalist Peter FitzSimons in the *Sydney Morning Herald*. He pointed out that Langer hadn't taken Brian Lara's word at the SCG, early in the previous year, when Lara had made the same claim.

A similar incident occurred in the fourth Test at Melbourne, when Nasser Hussain clipped leg-spinner Stuart MacGill to mid-on where Jason Gillespie claimed a diving catch. Hussain, then on 14, survived as once again the video evidence proved inconclusive.

It was Hussain's refusal to walk that apparently shaped Gilchrist's decision to start walking. His new resolution became evident in Australia's 2003 World Cup semi-final against Sri Lanka. Attempting to sweep off-spinner Aravinda de Silva, he got a thick bottom edge on to his pad and was caught behind. Given not out by Rudi Koertzen, he walked, much to the astonishment of the opposition, the crowd and his team-mates. With Australia struggling at 51/3 and 144/5, Gilchrist later admitted to having doubts as to whether he had acted judiciously, but these doubts diminished as his team went on to win comfortably. After the game, Ponting, now the captain, stressed that he wouldn't be encouraging his players to follow Gilchrist's example, a policy with which Gilchrist was quite happy to comply. The irony was that, while he attracted great acclaim from the world's press for his sportsmanship, he was no paragon. Already cited twice by the ICC for dissent, he was to receive further fines for the same offence in 2004 and 2006. He also became embroiled in a heated altercation with New Zealand's Craig McMillan in the first Test at Brisbane in November 2004 following the latter's failure to walk for a caught-behind off Jason Gillespie. Given not out by umpire Bucknor and admonished by Gilchrist for staying put, McMillan shot back, 'Not everyone is a walker, Gilly. Not everyone has to walk, mate.' After the match, which Australia won by an innings, McMillan told Gilchrist he thought he was 'being a little bit righteous'. He was supported by his captain, Stephen Fleming, who accused the Australian wicketkeeper of pressurising opponents into joining a walking crusade. Ponting, for his part, tried to placate the New Zealanders by emphasising that, because he didn't expect his own team to walk, he could hardly expect it of his opponents.

Some Australians warned Gilchrist of double standards. Former captain Kim Hughes thought he left himself open to accusations of hypocrisy if he demanded that opponents should walk but said nothing about the failure of his team-mates to do likewise. According to Ian Healy, his predecessor as wicketkeeper, if Gilchrist was adamant about playing the part of the honest broker, he should never appeal if he knew someone wasn't out – a probable reference to Brendon McCullum's dismissal in the second innings, given out caught behind to a ball he clearly hadn't hit.

While Australia modified their aggression, England, under charismatic new captain Michael Vaughan, had added a harder edge to their game. After convincing wins against the West Indies, New Zealand and South Africa during the previous year, they keenly anticipated the 2005 Ashes, confident that they could emerge victorious after eight successive series losses. Their new-found confidence and aggression was visible in the two one-day tournaments preceding the Tests. In the first of these, a throw from fast bowler Simon Jones, destined for the wicketkeeper, accidentally hit opening batsman Matthew Hayden in the chest. Hayden was understandably affronted by such tactics and admonished Jones, whereupon several England players quickly moved in in support of Jones and told Hayden to back off. England lost the NatWest Challenge series, the second one-day tournament, and Duncan Fletcher thought his players had been too genial, especially at Lord's, when several of them had complimented Australian captain Ponting on his century. As far as he was concerned, England needed to be aggressive to prove they wouldn't be intimidated.

With the crowd right behind them, England began the first Test at Lord's meaning business. In a highly charged atmosphere, Steve Harmison's second ball struck Justin Langer on the elbow. Several overs later, Langer's partner, Hayden, was hit on the helmet, and within the hour Ponting was also hit on the elbow, a blow that elicited minimal concern from the fielding side, much to Langer's disgust. 'This isn't war,' he commented to one of his opponents.

With England's four-man pace attack of Harmison, Matthew Hoggard, Andrew Flintoff and Simon Jones on the money, Australia were dismissed for 190, but McGrath struck back in exemplary fashion and England could manage only 162 in reply. From then on, Australia never lost control of the match and went on to win by 239 runs – but, while disappointed by their defeat,

England remained confident for the second Test at Edgbaston. Taking advantage of McGrath's absence through injury, they took the fight to their opponents by scoring over 400 runs on the first day. Australia fought back in style and, having dismissed England for 182, needed 282 to win. By the end of the fourth day, they appeared down and out, but, in a game that ebbed and flowed, their ninth-wicket pair of Shane Warne and Brett Lee added 59. Even after Warne was out, Lee, partnered by Michael Kasprowicz, inched ever nearer until, with only three needed to win, Kasprowicz was given out caught behind down the leg side as he ducked a Harmison bouncer. As Edgbaston let out a collective roar of triumph, Lee sunk to his knees in dejection, at which point England's hero Flintoff approached him and placed a consoling arm around him. If a picture tells more than a thousand words, that one defined the spirit of that series, at least from an English perspective.

For amid the chivalry and good cheer, resentment had been growing in the Australian camp regarding England's tactics of using highly athletic substitutes to replace their pace bowlers while they enjoyed a rub-down and massage. It was a practice that infringed the spirit of the game, and Ponting wasn't slow to convey his annoyance to match referee Ranjan Madugalle before the beginning of each Test, but nothing was done to bring England into line.

After Australia escaped with a draw in the third Test at Old Trafford, they batted abjectly in the fourth at Trent Bridge and followed on. They made a better fist of things in their second innings, with Ponting and Damien Martyn leading the way until the former was brilliantly run out by substitute fielder Gary Pratt, fielding legitimately for Simon Jones, who had twisted his ankle. Frustrated and irritated in equal measure as he walked off to the raucous celebrations of the home crowd, Ponting erupted in fury at the sight of Duncan Fletcher smiling at him from the balcony, and he directed some ill-chosen words at him in full earshot of the members, a rant that cost him 75 per cent of his match fee. A competitor to the peak of his baggy green cap, Ponting was the essence of grace at the end of the match, in which England scraped home by three wickets, and again at the Oval, where a draw enabled England to regain the Ashes after 16 years.

The Australians returned home to a country bereft at the loss of the Ashes, and to the familiar charge from some ex-players that they had been too friendly with the opposition. The intensity of the post-mortems convinced Ponting that the team had to regain their winning formula. An easy win over the West Indies was to be expected, but the real test would come against South Africa. Graeme Smith, their young captain, stirred the pot with some bullish statements about Australia having lost their aura; and the Australians, still smarting from Smith's exposure of their sledging in 2002, weren't shy in returning his barbs in kind, so much so that Malcolm Speed appealed for calm.

After a draw in the first Test at Perth, marred by racist taunts from sections of the crowd towards the South Africans, Australia won convincingly at Melbourne, and again at Sydney, in a rain-affected match that did little for the standing of the game. At issue was the vehemence of Australia's appealing and their lack of respect towards the umpires, neither of whom had their best game. 'Australia have taken their appealing to such ridiculous lengths in this series that, at best, it is gamesmanship,' reported Geoffrey Dean in *The Times*. 'Many fair-minded people would view it as just another form of cheating.'[179] Brett Lee was reprimanded for dissent and McGrath for obscene language towards an opponent, the sixth time he had been guilty of such an offence in his career, but, while James Sutherland expressed disappointment with Australian players being punished, he said he was generally satisfied with their conduct.

His view didn't correspond with those of former Australian players and officials, especially after Gilchrist was fined for dissent in the first one-day international against South Africa. Bob Simpson accused Australia of behaving like 'small children', remarking that sledging had reached 'epidemic proportions' at junior level; Colin Egar said that player dissent was degrading the game, while his former colleague Lou Rowan, in a letter to CA, condemned the side's bully-boy tactics towards the umpires.

> The standard of conduct that was commonplace in my time has been contemptuously trampled underfoot by certain Australian players who cannot grasp the significance of the honour bestowed on them by the baggy green cap. The ever-present and accepted practice of sledging, obscenities, excessive appealing, the questioning of the umpires and the accompanying dissent leaves our Australian team quite correctly dubbed 'the ugly Australians'.[180]

According to Robert Craddock, the Australian team might rue the day when they signed the self-righteous Spirit of Cricket, since they learned from their subdued performance in England in 2005 that they played their best cricket when they were aggressive and mildly confrontational. 'It's not pretty to watch – but it works. Since returning from England, Australia have got their collective grunt back.'[181] The jousting continued when the two teams resumed combat in South Africa. Australia's truculence was rewarded with victories in the first two Tests, but, according to Tony Greig, their sledging had reached unacceptable levels. 'I have never heard anything like it. We turned that stump mike up and we could hear every word out in the centre and it was unbelievable. The whole thing is getting out of hand and the time has seriously come for the authorities in the game to start to rethink the question of what players are allowed to say on the field.'[182]

With England in Australia later that year, Sutherland warned his team about their behaviour – but, buoyed by their return to winning ways, they were in no mood to give ground. Ponting instructed his players to keep their distance from their opponents off the field and to call them by their proper names rather than their nicknames, a tactic the English actively disliked. According to their batsman Kevin Pietersen, the 2006/07 series had a nasty edge that hadn't been there before. At one point during the first Test at Brisbane, his good friend Shane Warne enraged him by nearly hitting him when throwing the ball back aggressively to the wicketkeeper.

England, handicapped by injuries and loss of form, were a pale shadow of the formidable outfit they had been a year or so earlier. Under Flintoff's faltering leadership, deputising for Vaughan, they were comprehensively beaten 5–0, the first time they had suffered such a reversal against Australia since 1920/21. Their lack of resolution under fire, with only Collingwood standing up to the aggression, upset Fletcher, but he reserved his greatest contempt for the verbal intimidation from the Australians. 'In fact, you couldn't call it sledging because it was so foul-mouthed as to be a disgrace to the game. It was the sort of stuff that belongs in the gutter and not on a cricket field.'[183]

Such comments could be dismissed as a typical dirge from a coach not on the friendliest of terms with his opponents, but Australia's competitiveness would come back to haunt them the following summer.

Chapter 15

'Monkeygate'

I N October 2007, Australia won a fractious one-day series in India which saw Harbhajan Singh, a temperamental Sikh with a history of needling the Australians, go head-to-head with Andrew Symonds, the flamboyant all-rounder of part Afro-Caribbean descent. In 1998, on his debut as a 17-year-old, Harbhajan had been fined for giving Ponting a hostile send-off on dismissing him, and in the 2001 series he had taken his wicket five times. Now, during the second one-day international at Kochi, he remonstrated with the Australians over his dismissal, so much so that umpire Steve Bucknor had to intervene. After the third match, Ponting accused Harbhajan of double standards in reaction to his criticism of the Australians for their aggressive on-field behaviour. During the fifth game at Vadodara, the tension mounted when Harbhajan clashed with Symonds, who was singled out by a small section of the crowd for monkey chants. A similar fate befell Symonds in the next two one-day internationals at Nagpur and Mumbai, the match in which Harbhajan allegedly called him a monkey. While the Indian media and its administrators appeared indifferent to the taunts against Symonds, even denying they took place until photographic evidence was produced, the Australians, recalling the punishment meted out to Lehmann for his racist expletives against the Sri Lankans, were outraged. Symonds, meanwhile, sought out Harbhajan after the final one-day international to convey his abhorrence of racially abusive words such as 'monkey' and was left with the impression that Harbhajan wouldn't use such words again.

Given the furore caused by racist comments from some of the Perth crowd towards the South Africans during their 2005/06 tour of Australia and the recent trouble in India, it wasn't surprising that the ICC were keen to stamp out any lingering on-field racist abuse. Before the beginning of India's tour of Australia at the end of 2007, both teams were warned by the match referee to watch their language.

Heavily defeated in the first Test at Melbourne, the Indians rediscovered their form in the second Test at Sydney and gave a plucky performance in a match marred by poor umpiring. Batting first, Australia were perched precariously on 193/6 when Symonds was given a fortunate reprieve on 30, having edged debutant Ishant Sharma to the wicketkeeper. 'By not walking,' Adam Gilchrist later wrote, 'Symo was giving ammunition to all those who accused Australia of not playing in the right spirit.'[184] The fact that he went on to score 162 and admit to reporters that he was out on 30 did little to soothe Indian sensitivities.

Their patience was further tested by a major contretemps on the third day as they fought their way back into the match. Harbhajan was batting, in partnership with Tendulkar, during the final session, and, having run a single off Brett Lee, he patted him on the backside. His capers failed to impress Symonds and prompted him to renew hostilities with his old adversary, telling him that he had no friends in the Australian side. As the two of them traded insults in mid-pitch, Harbhajan once again called Symonds a monkey – at least that was the opinion of Australia's Michael Clarke, who immediately informed Ponting of what he had heard. With Hayden, Symonds's close friend, corroborating Clarke's claim, Ponting, fully aware of CA's uncompromising approach towards racism, raised the matter with the umpires, who reported it to match referee Mike Procter, as ICC protocol dictated. Procter duly charged Harbhajan with breaching level 3 of the ICC's Code of Conduct and set the hearing for the end of the Test, much to the consternation of Indian captain Anil Kumble, who privately warned Ponting of the ramifications should the hearing go ahead.

Thanks to 154 from Tendulkar and 63 from Harbhajan, India secured a first-innings lead of 69, but Australia fought back in their second innings and declared early on the fifth day, setting India 333 to win in 76 overs. Beginning badly, they recovered through a gritty fourth-wicket partnership between Dravid and Ganguly before both departed in controversial circumstances. The former was given out caught behind to a ball from Symonds he wasn't close to hitting, so much so that umpire Bucknor was booed by the crowd as the replay exposed his error, while the latter edged low to slip where Clarke scooped the ball off the ground. Unsure as to whether it had carried, umpire Mark Benson, instead of reviewing it, gave it out when Ponting signalled that the catch was legitimate. Aside from the television replays proving inconclusive, in which case the batsman should have been given the benefit of the doubt, what irked the Indians was Clarke's request to be trusted over the catch when, earlier in Australia's second innings, he had stood his ground after slicing to first slip.

With the Indians hanging on for dear life, the atmosphere became increasingly tetchy during the final session as the Australians, appealing for everything, pressed for victory. With two overs to go, they still needed three wickets, at which point Ponting threw the ball to Clarke, a part-time left-arm spinner, who had never previously taken a Test wicket in Australia. Within six balls he had dismissed Harbhajan, R.P. Singh and Ishant Sharma caught at slip, capping a dramatic finale to an absorbing Test. As the Indian batsmen trooped forlornly from the field, the Australians embraced each other to celebrate their 16th Test win in a row, and Ponting raised his fists in celebration towards the Channel Nine commentary box following criticism from their pundits about his delayed declaration. In his press conference afterwards, he claimed that, one incident aside, the spirit between the two teams in the series had been excellent, an assessment far removed from that of Kumble, the mild-mannered Indian captain. Upset by the umpiring, outraged by the charges against

Harbhajan and disillusioned by his opponents' tactics, he stated that 'only one team was playing within the spirit of the game', echoing Bill Woodfull's famous words during the bodyline crisis. He was going to review the pre-series pact that he had made with Ponting over catches.

Kumble's words won cheers from the Indian press corps and much sympathy from many others. In a trenchant analysis in *The Age* and the *Sydney Morning Herald*, their respected columnist Peter Roebuck lambasted the Australians for their unbecoming behaviour.

> India has been dudded. No one with the slightest enthusiasm for cricket will take the least satisfaction from the victory secured by the local team in an SCG Test match that entertained spectators at the ground, provided some excellent batting but left a sour taste in the mouth. It was a match that will have been relished only by rabid nationalists and others for whom victory and vengeance are the sole reasons for playing sport. Truth to tell the last day was as bad as the first. It was a rotten contest that singularly failed to elevate the spirit.[185]

The following day, in a front-page headline calling for Ponting to be fired, Roebuck, a great apologist for Indian cricket, allowed his emotions to get the better of him with his vitriolic attack on the Australian captain. He accused him of turning a group of professional cricketers into a pack of wild dogs. If CA cared a fig for the tattered reputation of its national team in Australia's national sport, it wouldn't for a moment tolerate the sort of arrogant and abrasive conduct seen from the captain and his senior players at Sydney.

Following the post-match formalities, Procter convened a closed hearing into the allegations against Harbhajan. He called both umpires, Symonds, Ponting, Clarke, Hayden, Kumble, Tendulkar and India manager Chetan Chauhan, who alleged that Australia had concocted the racism incident to get Harbhajan off the tour because he kept getting Ponting out. According to Procter, Tendulkar said he couldn't hear Harbhajan's comments from where he was because of the noise of the crowd, and with India offering little in the way of positive evidence – Harbhajan didn't testify because of his poor English, despite being offered an interpreter – Procter found against them. He declared that he was satisfied beyond reasonable doubt that Harbhajan had racially vilified Symonds, and banned him for three Tests. As Ponting took a taxi back to the team hotel in the small hours, he realised that the suspension would be controversial, but he never envisaged quite how explosive it would be. The Indian team's growing resentment towards the bad umpiring and their opponents' sledging reached fever pitch with the charge of racial abuse against Harbhajan. They made it clear that unless the ban against him was revoked, they would boycott the rest of the tour.

Their indignation was matched by the mood back home. Indian cities were engulfed by demonstrations, some burning effigies of the two umpires, and a poll by the *Hindustan Times* found that 91 per cent favoured an immediate cancellation of the tour. What particularly infuriated them was that, in the absence of any positive proof of a racist slur, since neither the umpires nor the microphones heard anything, the match referee – a white South African – took the word of the Australians over the two Indians, including the revered Tendulkar. The BCCI, declaring Harbhajan's conviction unacceptable and unfair, announced that the tour would be suspended unless the ban was overturned.

India's case didn't lack support elsewhere. Malcolm Speed, on behalf of the ICC, expressed concern about the Australian players' behaviour, and Geoff Lawson, the former Australian fast bowler turned coach of Pakistan, accused the Australian team of being 'arrogant and not well-behaved'. Most striking of all, Neil Harvey, an acerbic critic of contemporary Australian teams, contended that had Ponting kept quiet, none of this would have happened. It was quite unheard of for a captain to report someone in these circumstances, and he hoped that Harbhajan would get off. 'Racism cannot be countenanced,' said David Hopps in *The*

Guardian. 'But it is a rum old world that bans a man for three Tests for calling someone a monkey, yet allows the sort of boorish behaviour that allows first slip to drone on to a batsman that he is shagging his wife, or that convinces any fast bowler with half a brain that personal insults every time a batsman plays and misses are essential for any cricketer of merit.'[186] For too long, in abdicating their responsibility, umpires had played with fire. Now cricket was burning with resentments.

An online poll of nearly 3,000 readers of Sydney's *Daily Telegraph* found that 82 per cent thought Ponting a poor ambassador for cricket and 79 per cent that his team didn't play in accordance with its true spirit. Most Australian talk radio and internet feedback delivered a similar verdict to Kumble's, while abusive telephone calls to Ponting's parents forced them to change their number.

In their failure to anticipate the hostile reaction from many at home, and their insistence that they had played the game in the right spirit, the Australian players, cocooned in their own world, were blind to their failings. Even Sutherland thought the criticism unwarranted. Test cricket wasn't tiddlywinks, he said; it was a tough game out there, and sometimes when emotions spilled over words were said that wouldn't be acceptable in genteel society.

His statement brought a stinging response from Tom Veivers, the Australian off-spinner of the 1960s, writing in the *Courier-Mail*.

> I have no hesitation in being highly critical of Sutherland who has been all over the media defending the way the present team plays the game. ...
>
> Sutherland also has the audacity to say that former Australian teams 'have always played in this tough and uncompromising way' I take strong exception to this statement. While every team I have played in has played it tough, not one has resorted to the unsportsmanlike tactics Mr Sutherland seems to think are OK.[187]

According to Robert Craddock, Australian cricket was in a state of confusion as the national team's hard-nosed tactics contravened its self-appointed role as the game's moral conscience. The outside world could grudgingly accept the arrogance, but could do without the empty posturing and the righteous indignation when anybody took them on at their own game or suggested they'd gone too far. 'The cold hard facts of modern sporting life are that you can be Mike Tyson or Mother Teresa but you cannot be both. And when you try to do both – as Australia will – you get branded "hypocrite" and not without some justification.'[188]

For all the flak thrown at Australia, the Indians were by no means innocent. ICC data showed that since 1997 they had faced more sanctions than any other Test-playing nation. Their batsman Yuvraj Singh was extremely fortunate to have escaped a fine after being cited for dissent in the Melbourne Test, while at Sydney, Harbhajan's celebrations on dismissing Ponting had been excessive, and their batsmen had been guilty of time-wasting on the final day. What's more, the BCCI's threat to pull out of the tour unless umpire Bucknor was replaced for the third Test and Harbhajan's ban was overturned was, according to Craddock, 'a veiled form of blackmail and must be treated with the harsh response it deserves'.

'If the ICC feel Harbhajan was worth suspending,' he continued, 'they must not crumble in the face of a subcontinental blackmail from the world's most powerful cricket nation. India's cricketing wealth may be 50 times that of any rival, but that does not give them the right to run the game. India must be told by Speed in the strongest possible terms to get moving with the rest of the tour and let the ICC worry about Harbhajan.'[189]

When the ICC caved in to BCCI demands by not only suspending Harbhajan's ban but also replacing Bucknor, the New South Wales Umpires' Association took out a newspaper advertisement to express its anger at the decision.

Before the third Test, Ranjan Madugalle, the senior ICC match referee, flew in to Perth to act as mediator. He convened a meeting between the two captains, and although Kumble ended the pre-series pact whereby contentious catches would be settled on the word of the fielder, the two captains shook hands, and India dropped its charge against Australian spinner Brad Hogg for racially abusing Kumble.

With their reputation on trial, a subdued Australian team kept their aggression in check in the Perth Test, a match they lost by 72 runs. After the drawn fourth Test at Adelaide, giving Australia the series 2–1, the appeal hearing took place before Justice John Hansen, a New Zealand high court judge and ICC Appeals Commissioner. While India once again threatened to cancel the remainder of the tour should the charge of racism against Harbhajan be upheld, Harbhajan's willingness to accept a lesser charge of offensive and seriously insulting language caused divisions within the home camp. CA, conscious of the financial repercussions should the tour be cancelled, since they stood to lose US$60 million in television rights, sponsorship agreements and gate receipts, wanted their players to accept the lesser charge, while Ponting insisted that the original charge should stand. Very reluctantly, he backed down on the assurance that Harbhajan's poor disciplinary record would guarantee him a substantial punishment.

These divisions were exposed at the hearing in Adelaide when the Australian and Indian players involved gave evidence. Explaining his intervention under video cross-examination by Indian Board lawyer Vasha Manohar, Symonds declared that a Test match was no place to be friendly with an opposition player. 'If that is his view,' Hansen concluded, 'I hope it is not one shared by all international cricketers. It will be a sad day for cricket if it is.'

It was Tendulkar, something of a silent witness in the original hearing, according to Procter, who now provided the crucial testimony. Strongly objecting to Procter's refusal to accept the Indian version of events, he stated categorically that Symonds had provoked the exchange with Harbhajan and that Harbhajan, while using offensive words in Punjabi, hadn't called Symonds a monkey. Faced with this conflicting evidence, Hansen, taking the side of the Indians, overturned the charge of racial abuse and the three-match ban imposed on Harbhajan. 'But in my view even if he had used the words "alleged" (big monkey) an "ordinary person" standing in the shoes of Mr Symonds who had launched an unprovoked and unnecessary invective-laden attack would not be offended or insulted or humiliated in terms of 3.3 (racist language on the ICC charge sheet).'[190]

Instead, Harbhajan pleaded guilty to the lesser charge of using insulting and abusive language and was fined $3,000, half his match fee. Hansen later admitted that he would have imposed a more severe penalty had he been aware of Harbhajan's previous record of misconduct, information kept from him at the hearing because of problems with the ICC database and human error.

Harbhajan's reprieve (he was later banned for the 2008 Indian Premier League (IPL) by the BCCI for slapping Shantha Sreesanth) was universally condemned by the Australian media, depicting it as another surrender by CA and the ICC to Indian power brokers. 'If this is the way the Indian board intends to conduct its affairs hereafter, then God help cricket,' wrote Roebuck. 'Brinkmanship or not, threatening to take their bat and ball home in the event of a resented verdict being allowed to stand was an abomination. It set a dreadful precedent. What price justice now?'[191]

The decision also left Ponting underwhelmed. 'When Darren Lehmann was suspended for a racist comment in the lead-up to the 2003 World Cup,' he wrote in his autobiography, 'we were criticised as a group for not seeing the seriousness in what Boof [Lehmann's nickname] had done. Five years later, the roles were reversed. I felt that there was a lot of hypocrisy about the "Monkeygate" scandal.'[192]

Yet according to Greg Baum of *The Age*, the longer the aftermath of the Harbhajan Singh affair went on, the less it appeared to have been about the evil of racism and the more it looked to be a desperate scramble for the moral high ground. 'It was a terrible mess, and a situation that Australia's behaviour, or lack of it, throughout the 15 years of its golden age had done much to foment,' wrote Malcolm Knox in *The Greatest*. 'They were reaping what they had sown.'[193]

After a temporary truce in hostilities, the belligerence returned when Australia toured India later that year. India's opening bowler Zaheer Khan was fined for giving Hayden a gratuitous send-off in the second Test at Mohali, and Gautam Gambhir, their young opener, clashed with Shane Watson during the third Test at Delhi. After a series of heated exchanges between the two, the former elbowed the latter while taking a run, an offence that brought him a one-match ban from the ICC match referee. According to the *Sydney Morning Herald*, the Indians were easily the worst-behaved side in international cricket, and Gambhir, with his second physical contact charge within less than a year, should have received at least a two-match ban. 'The reason he probably escaped was down to Sachs's belief that he had been the victim of prolonged and persistent verbal abuse by members of the Australian team, culminating in a moment of anger. To my mind, these "verbals", as they are euphemistically called, whether they involve swearing or not, provide a kind of tension and aggression inconsistent with the spirit of cricket.'[194] Sachs declared that the time had come to consider whether sledging had any part in cricket.

Australia, it is true, were trying to play less belligerently, and in back-to-back series against South Africa in 2008/09 they succeeded. With opposition captain Graeme Smith now grown in stature, there was less animosity between the two sides than in previous encounters, and the good spirit that existed was exemplified by the dismissal of Jacques Kallis in South Africa's second innings in the third Test at Sydney. After he mistimed a drive back to Australian debutant Andrew McDonald, the catch was low enough to enter the realms of doubt. Kallis asked the bowler whether he had caught it, and when he confirmed that he had, he walked off without hesitation. As South Africa battled to save the match – they had already won the series – Smith, out of action since the second day with a broken hand, won the hearts of Australia by coming in at number eleven and resisting for over half an hour before succumbing to fast bowler Mitchell Johnson.

After winning in South Africa, Ponting returned to England in 2009, this time captaining a younger, inexperienced side following the retirement of Warne, McGrath and co. Sharply criticised by former England coach Duncan Fletcher for remonstrating with the umpires in 2005, Ponting was again in combative mood in the first Test at Cardiff, charging the umpire from silly point when claiming a catch off Paul Collingwood as Australia pressed for victory on the final day. His antics won him few friends, and local crowds took to booing him whenever he walked out to bat – an unedifying spectacle he handled with commendable restraint, but it was a rare blemish in an otherwise chivalrous series.

The next year brought Ponting's team a plethora of victories and few confrontations against weak opposition, aside from one explosive game against the West Indies when the old demons resurfaced. In the third Test at Perth, Australia's Mitchell Johnson and Sulieman Benn, the West Indian slow bowler and giant of a man, became entangled as Johnson ran for a short single in Australia's first innings. Johnson's partner, Brad Haddin, took umbrage at Benn's aggression and pointed his bat towards him, leading to a war of words. At the end of the over, Benn stormed down the pitch to eyeball Haddin, and as he gesticulated angrily at him, his arm came into conflict with Johnson, who had stepped in front of his partner. It needed the intervention of umpire Billy Bowden to restore order, and all three combatants were reported to match referee Chris Broad. He suspended Benn for two one-day internationals and fined Haddin 25 per cent of his match fee, while Johnson received a 10 per cent fine.

On the final day of the game, which Australia won by 35 runs, Watson kept the match referee busy by giving Chris Gayle a petulant send-off, a rush of blood that cost him 15 per cent of his match fee. His excuse that Gayle had provoked him brought a tart rejoinder from the West Indian captain. 'When they sledge, and if you give it back to them, they whinge a lot.'

'The Australians have again besmirched a great win with shameful behaviour,' wrote Greg Baum. Watson's behaviour was especially egregious, he argued, because it was premeditated, and fining him a mere 15 per cent of his fee was pitiful. If Benn was volatile, the Australians, you could be sure, hadn't missed an opportunity to provoke him. 'When he reacts, they throw up their arms, as if shocked and affronted, their innocence plain for all to see.'

Some Australians applauded this gladiatorial approach, he conceded. 'But a sizeable proportion of cricket fans were disgusted by Watson's display of triumphalism and discomfited by the brawl over Benn.'[195]

Not everyone agreed. Chris McDermott in the *Sunday Mail* (Brisbane) thought there had been an overreaction to the Benn–Haddin–Johnson altercation. It had been heated rather than nasty, he argued. 'Pressure to be gracious in victory as the Aussies hammered every opponent put before them, has gone too far and their instinctive aggressive nature has been squashed. The game has suffered as a spectacle.'

Sport and cricket demand intense rivalry. 'Tempers fray, blood boils and aggressive confrontations are inevitable. Providing they don't escalate to an unacceptable level, bring it on.'[196]

Ironically, during the Ashes in 2010/11, it was England who appeared the more combative team. At the end of the first day of the second Test at Adelaide, Ponting went head-to-head with his rival captain, Andrew Strauss, about the verbal abuse his batsmen had received from fast bowler James Anderson, a gripe that the England captain scathingly dismissed. Losing by an innings at Adelaide, Australia opted for a more aggressive approach in the third Test at Perth, a ground where England had constantly struggled to cope with the local conditions. They began well, dismissing Australia for 268, but during the later stages of their innings Mitchell Johnson had been upset by some choice words from Anderson. So often a disappointment against England, the tattoo-clad Johnson, goaded by the verbal sparring, rediscovered his form and in a flawless display of swing bowling bowled his side to a 267-run victory. In a Test that witnessed several bruising personal altercations, it was England's turn to complain about sledging, a complaint dismissed as sour grapes in the home camp. According to Paul Marsh, the chief executive of the Australian Cricketers' Association, the Australian team had become victims of their own success. They were winning everything, but that wasn't enough for some people. They had to win in a manner that was different from how previous Australian teams had played over several decades. Consequently, their recent poor form was partly down to their less confrontational style after the 2008 Sydney Test against India. 'Hard, aggressive cricket is in the Australian team's DNA', Marsh said, 'and unfortunately the players started second-guessing their natural instincts in the heat of battle for fear of reprisal from CA or a public backlash from the vocal minority.'[197]

Spurred on by their exploits in Perth, Australia felt confident about the crucial Boxing Day Test in Melbourne, but, in front of an 80,000 crowd, they plumbed the depths. Dismissed unaccountably for 98, they failed to fight back with the ball as England finished the first day on 157/0. As the visitors continued their relentless march towards victory, the out-of-form Ponting, playing with a broken finger, became increasingly frustrated. When Pietersen was given not out to a caught-behind off Ryan Harris at 259/2, the Australian captain could contain himself no longer. Convinced that umpire Aleem Dar had erred, he engaged him and, later, his colleague Tony Hill in a prolonged harangue that earned him a 40 per cent match fee fine for dissent, his fourth such offence in four years, by match referee Ranjan Madugalle.

Ponting's apology wasn't enough to appease his critics. Bill Lawry declared that his dissent was unacceptable, and Ian Chappell called for his suspension, adding that the ICC should have penalised him more heavily for his past indiscretions. As it was, Ponting missed the final Test through injury, and, after Australia lost an Ashes series at home for the first time since 1986/87 and failed to win the 2011 World Cup, he surrendered the captaincy to his deputy, Michael Clarke. An unassuming and gracious person off the field, Ponting's brilliance as a batsman will forever guarantee him a place in his country's pantheon of great cricketers. As for his captaincy, the record is more ambiguous, the many triumphs offset by the indecorous manner in which his team often played the game.

With the captaincy passing to Clarke, Australian cricket entered a quieter period, but, after a disastrous tour to India in the spring of 2013, coach Mickey Arthur was dismissed. His successor, Darren Lehmann, signalled the return to a more confrontational approach, and, after they had lost in England that year, the Ashes were regained in emphatic style months later in Australia (see Chapter 17). 'The Australian team, bullied and browbeaten into submission so many times in the last five years, now has a hard-nosed, take-no-prisoners style,' wrote Ben Dorries in the *Daily Telegraph* (Sydney). 'Clarke doesn't have to carry a red rag in his pocket like Steve Waugh. But opposition teams now know that sledging him or his players is like waving a red rag to a bull.'[198]

Australia continued their winning form in South Africa weeks later. They won the first Test at Centurion on the back of some venomous fast bowling by Johnson, but South Africa won the second at Port Elizabeth, fuelling Australian suspicions that the home side had resorted to ball-tampering, an offence for which they had twice been penalised over the previous year. Opener David Warner's allegations to this effect on Sydney radio earned him an ICC fine and heightened tension before the final Test at Cape Town. Winning the toss, Australia immediately took charge and never relinquished it throughout the match. Requiring a nominal 511 for victory, South Africa began the final day at 71/4, but their cussed resistance throughout the day contributed to the fractious atmosphere between the two teams. Much of the Australian ire was directed at South African batsman Faf du Plessis, who had questioned their ability to achieve reverse swing in the first innings and likened their fielding to 'a pack of wild dogs'. Consequently, he was greeted with howls and barks and taunted mercilessly for his ball-tampering charge of a few months earlier.

As Australia appeared all but home, a stubborn eighth-wicket stand between Vernon Philander and Dale Steyn kept the champagne on ice. With an hour to go, the former was given out caught at short leg off Johnson, only for the decision to be overturned on review, the third umpire ruling that the batsman's right hand was off the bat as the ball brushed his glove. Philander's reprieve infuriated the Australians and embroiled Steyn in heated exchanges with fast bowler James Pattinson and Michael Clarke, who so offended Steyn that he had to be restrained by South African twelfth man Alviro Petersen. At the end of the match, deservedly won by Australia with 27 balls to spare, Clarke apologised to Steyn, but the ill-feeling lingered on a night when the two teams drank separately. 'There was lots of personal stuff and certain guys take it in a different way,' commented South African batsman A.B. de Villiers, who described the abuse in that series as the worst he'd ever encountered. 'I can see that it's part of the game ... but they can't expect us to be mates with them off the field then, if they get very personal' – words which once again refuted the age-old claim that sledging was essentially harmless.[199]

Chapter 16

Ball-tampering

FEW issues have proved more taxing to the cricketing authorities than ball-tampering because once again the laws are ill-defined, a point starkly illustrated by the libel case brought by Ian Botham against Imran Khan in 1996 for allegedly accusing him of ball-tampering. At the centre of the case lay a hazy line as to whether ball-tampering was accepted practice or cheating.

Certainly, lifting the seam or applying illegal substances had occurred since time immemorial. Arthur Mailey, the renowned Australian leg-spinner of the 1920s, used to put resin into the ball to get a better grip; Jack 'Farmer' White, the England slow left-armer who helped win the Ashes in 1928/29, raised the seam; and Keith Miller used Brylcreem. Later, scratching or gouging the ball became more commonplace in England after the TCCB reduced the seam in 1981, and again in 1990.

What brought ball-tampering to international prominence was the rise of reverse swing, a technique invented in Pakistan which enabled conventional swing to overcome a local environment of flat, grassless wickets and hard, bare outfields where balls soon lost their shine. The man most credited with its innovation was the mercurial Sarfraz Nawaz, a supremely talented fast bowler who played 55 Tests for Pakistan between 1969 and 1984. Learning the art on matting wickets by keeping the ball rough and dry on one side, while weighing down the other with sweat or spit, and by holding the ball in more of a baseball grip, he got it to swing towards the smooth side. Because reverse swing needed a bare pitch and rough outfield and Sarfraz was playing most of his cricket in England for Northamptonshire, he rarely resorted to reverse swing. He kept his secret to himself until divulging it to his fellow Pakistani opening bowler, Imran Khan, who first used it against Australia at Melbourne in 1976/77. In time, Imran taught it to his protégés Wasim Akram and Waqar Younis, two exceptional fast bowlers who used it to great effect when playing for Pakistan in the late 1980s and 1990s.

Reverse swing was an innovation of ingenuity, and perfectly legal, but the freakish nature of its success – an old ball swinging at pace – gave rise to allegations of ball-tampering, since any tampering would hasten the wearing process and allow the ball to start reverse swinging earlier than if left to deteriorate naturally.

In the Sussex–Hampshire match of 1981, Imran later admitted to roughing up a ball with a bottle-top, a device to swing the old ball – but, as nobody detected anything untoward, nothing was said. Two years later, after a game between Sussex and Warwickshire in which Imran took 6–6 in 23 balls in Warwickshire's second innings, umpires Don Oslear and Bill Alley wrote in their match report that the ball had been scratched and torn. It was the first of five reports that Oslear sent in about ball-tampering over the next nine years.

One of them implicated the 1990 Indian touring team in their game against a TCCB under-25 XI. The following year, the TCCB received a series of reports about illegal interference of the ball involving Lancashire, Hampshire and Surrey, all sides containing a Pakistani fast bowler. Oslear wrote three reports in one month about Surrey, a county that had been reported for the same offence the previous year by umpire Chris Balderstone in a match against Gloucestershire at Cheltenham. Despite the TCCB's apparent concern about Surrey's 'very serious breach of the laws', they merely warned them confidentially in August 1991 about further transgressions, much to Oslear's disillusionment. 'I had done everything required of me, but the support could not even be termed "weak-kneed", it was non-existent,' he later wrote in his book

Tampering with Cricket.[200] According to his co-author, Jack Bannister, the former Warwickshire fast bowler turned cricket journalist and broadcaster, it was difficult to refute Oslear's contention that the English cricket authorities ran for cover whenever an unpleasant issue arose. Cases of alleged ball-tampering appeared to frighten officialdom more than any other breach of cricket regulation. The legal implications of accusing an alleged ball-tamperer of cheating seemed to inhibit them from acting.

Test cricket was also affected. In 1982 Botham, playing against Pakistan at Lord's, noticed during England's first innings that the quarter seam had been picked at and showed the ball to the umpires. In his 1993 autobiography, David Gower accused India of ball-tampering in the Oval Test in 1990,[201] and South Africa, on their return to international cricket in 1991/92, made similar allegations against the Indians – both accusations were indignantly denied. When New Zealand toured Pakistan in 1990 and lost all three Tests, primarily because of their inability to cope with Wasim and Waqar, their captain, Martin Crowe, complained about ball-tampering by the Pakistani bowlers. In the third Test at Karachi, New Zealand's Chris Pringle, a journeyman of a bowler, took 11 wickets in the match and later admitted to deliberately gouging the ball with a soft drinks bottle. Crowe recalled how, during Pakistan's first innings, one of the umpires, bemused by the amount of swing extracted by his bowlers, demanded an inspection of the ball. 'He looked at it, then threw it back saying "same for both sides".'

Next it was the turn of the West Indies, who were touring Pakistan after the New Zealanders, to voice similar concerns. On the opening morning of the second Test at Faisalabad, their captain and opening batsman Desmond Haynes drew the umpires' attention to the state of the ball, alleging that the Pakistan bowlers had been scratching it with their fingernails. The Pakistani authorities denied any impropriety and suggested that the West Indian bowlers weren't exactly innocent of such an offence.

Ball-tampering was but one of a series of controversies that dogged Pakistan's tour of England in 1992. Because the memories were still raw from the confrontation between Mike Gatting and Shakoor Rana, the British media were in no mood to forgive and forget. They were quick to pounce on any Pakistani duplicity, real or imagined, and exploit it for all that it was worth. This applied particularly to ball-tampering in a Test series England lost 2–1.

According to Oslear, it was during the fourth one-day international, played after the final Test, that the festering sore of ball-tampering finally erupted following years of suspicions regarding the Pakistanis. In a match lasting two days because of bad weather, England, needing 204 for victory, reached 140/5 at lunch. Prior to this, Allan Lamb, one of the not-out batsmen, surprised that the ball had started to swing excessively, picked it up and showed it to umpire Ken Palmer. On one side of it there were big scuff marks, which had grown ever bigger. Having accused the Pakistanis of ball-tampering during the second Test earlier in the summer, Lamb told team manager Micky Stewart of his suspicions at the lunch interval. Stewart went to see the umpires, and they sought out match referee Deryck Murray, the former West Indies wicketkeeper. They told him that they wanted to change the ball under Law 42.5 – illegal interference with the ball – a request with which Murray fully concurred. Murray then sent for the Pakistan manager Intikhab Alam, and informed him that the condition of the ball had been altered and it would have to be changed. Intikhab denied any impropriety but agreed to the change. He selected a replacement ball, which subsequently swung more than the original one, helping Pakistan to a surprise three-run victory. At a meeting between the leading officials of both sides, Intikhab insisted that there be no mention of Law 42.5 included in the ICC statement explaining why the ball had been changed. He was supported by Murray, who also insisted that he would make no further statement on the matter.

While the ICC opted for a policy of silence, Botham tipped off Chris Lander of the *Daily Mirror* about the chain of events that day. The next day, the media were full of allegations that the ball had been changed under Law 42.5, allegations denied by Intikhab.

Under legal advice, the ICC refused to make any further statement, prompting ridicule from the press, which sought to uncover the truth. Because the TCCB, under orders from the ICC, wouldn't reveal the full facts about ball-tampering, the *Mirror* published a two-page article featuring claims by Lamb that the Pakistan bowlers had been complicit in it all summer. His revelations won much support from rival newspapers and many England cricketers past and present. It also cost him a hefty fine of £5,000 by the TCCB, who later that day gave Surrey a suspended £1,000 fine after the county admitted to ball-tampering the previous season – a case of grave injustice according to Lamb. 'I had written about it and copped a £5,000 fine…, but they had been caught and "reported" four times in two years and got a fine of what amounted to about £90 for each player and even that was suspended for two years.'[202] He appealed, and the TCCB, accepting his logic about Surrey, reduced his fine by half.

Lamb now had to contend with a libel action by Sarfraz Nawaz because of his statement that the methods used by the Pakistan bowlers were the same as the one first shown to him by Sarfraz at Northampton. The case went to the High Court in November 1993, and although Lamb felt miffed that the TCCB made little effort to help him, Botham, Robin Smith and Oslear were among those who agreed to testify on his behalf, Oslear confirming that the ball at Lord's in August 1992 had been changed under Law 42.5. Before he could be cross-examined, Sarfraz agreed to drop the case, apparently satisfied with Lamb's admission that he had never seen him cheat on the cricket field.

That wasn't the end of the affair, however. Imran's confession of ball-tampering in his authorised biography by Ivo Tennant, published in 1994, caused some consternation in cricket circles. Believing the reaction to be excessive, Imran allegedly claimed in an interview with *India Today* that Botham and Lamb's criticism of ball-tampering stemmed from racism and a lack of breeding; then, in a second interview in *The Sun,* he accused all England's great bowlers, along with bowlers everywhere, of practising ball-tampering at some stage. No names were mentioned.

Although few took the allegations seriously, Botham and Lamb felt strongly enough to sue Imran for libel, despite Imran's assurance to them that he'd been misquoted. The case was held at the Royal Courts of Justice in July 1996, and, after claim and counterclaim by cricketers past and present as to what constituted ball-tampering, the jury found in favour of Imran on the premise that he had been misquoted and had never meant to impugn Lamb and Botham personally.

Having led the moral posturing against Pakistan, English cricket was to be suitably embarrassed when similar allegations were made against its captain, Michael Atherton, in the first Test against South Africa at Lord's in July 1994, an occasion marking South Africa's return to Test cricket in England after 29 years. On the third afternoon, as England struggled to stay in the match after conceding a first-innings lead of 177, television cameras caught Atherton rubbing something from his pocket on to the ball. The third umpire, Mervyn Kitchen, witnessed the incident and informed both the umpires and match referee Peter Burge. Burge summoned Atherton after close of play that evening to explain himself. Atherton assured him that he hadn't put anything in his pocket, and Burge accepted his explanation that nothing untoward had occurred.

The next morning's Sunday papers weren't so convinced, and, after they had published damning photos of the incident, Ray Illingworth, the chairman of selectors, took it upon himself to investigate further. Atherton admitted to him that he had had dust and dirt in his pocket and that he had misled the match referee. Accepting that his captain hadn't tampered with the ball – he was simply drying his hands with the dirt to free the ball from sweat so it could swing – Illingworth, anticipating a punitive sanction from the match referee, acted peremptorily by fining Atherton £1,000 for putting dirt on the ball and £1,000 for misleading the match referee. It did the trick in that Burge took no further action, but it didn't stop him describing Atherton's behaviour as 'foolish in the extreme and infringing the spirit of cricket', or stop the media, led by BBC cricket correspondent Jonathan Agnew, from waging an all-out war against him.

'If the captain of England's cricket team fails to uphold the values of his society or the values to which his society aspires,' declared *The Times*, 'he is unworthy of that uncommon honour which the captaincy represents. He should be replaced.'[203]

Atherton's steely character and his contention that he had never tampered with the ball enabled him to ride out the storm.

In 1997, in an incident not revealed at the time, Burge's colleague Barry Jarman, overseeing a one-day international between South Africa and India, instructed the umpires to change the ball because he had noticed two South Africans tampering with it. The decision upset the South African coach, Bob Woolmer, but he soon backtracked when Jarman told him who the offenders were. In 2000, Waqar Younis became the first player to be banned for a match for ball-tampering, in a triangular one-day tournament against South Africa; in 2003, Pakistan fast bowler Shoaib Akhtar was similarly penalised after two ball-tampering offences in successive years; and in 2005, Surrey were penalised eight points for twice picking the quarter seam in a county championship match against Nottinghamshire.

Further allegations about ball-tampering blighted Pakistan's tour of England in 2006, although the situation was very different from 1992. Since that ill-fated tour, relations between the two countries had greatly improved, and any animosity displayed by the Pakistan team in 2006 was primarily directed at the umpires. At 2–0 down and with the series lost, the tourists reserved their best cricket for the final Test at the Oval. Having bowled England out for 173 with some skilful swing bowling, they established a lead of 331, and the home side replied with 82/1 by the end of the third evening. During that period, the England dressing room seemed exercised by the amount of swing on parade, reviving talk of ball-tampering by the Pakistanis during the previous Test.

The next morning, Duncan Fletcher, the coach, visited the umpires' room and asked whether he could inspect the ball, a request that third umpire Trevor Jesty declined. Later, Fletcher recalled being accosted by umpire Darrell Hair in the middle. 'I'm not going to show you the ball but we've got a handle on it and are monitoring the situation,' Hair told him. Fletcher went on to say that Hair appeared nervous and asked him not to mention their conversation to the Pakistanis. This may well have had something to do with his testy relationship with them. When England had toured Pakistan the previous winter, he had upset the hosts in the second Test at Faisalabad by referring a run-out to the third umpire as Pakistan captain Inzamam-ul-Haq moved out of his crease to avoid bowler Steve Harmison's throw at the stumps. The third umpire gave Inzamam out, even though the laws of the game state that a batsman shouldn't be given out when taking evasive action to avoid injury. In the same match, Hair reported Pakistan leg-spinner Shahid Afridi for scuffing the pitch with his studs, an act for which he was fined and banned for one Test and two one-day internationals. In the Headingley Test, prior to the Oval, Hair was again in bad odour with Pakistan because of several decisions that favoured England.

On the fourth day at the Oval, England, in more benign conditions, batted with much greater conviction than in their first innings. At first, the Pakistan bowlers extracted little swing until Umar Gul dismissed Alastair Cook at 218/3 with a lethal in-swinging yorker. Twenty minutes later, Hair inspected the ball, then 55 overs old, and was immediately 'horrified' by what he saw. Deep, crescent-shaped scratches had appeared along one quarter section of the ball, and several crescent-shaped indentations were evident on another section of it. As far as Hair was concerned, it looked as if the ball had been attacked with a blunt knife or similar object, and its condition had changed in a short period of time. Such deterioration was not consistent with the way that the game had progressed since Cook's dismissal, as there had only been five scoring shots, one of which was a boundary by Pietersen. Someone must have interfered with the surface of the ball, of that he was certain, Hair later wrote. He showed the ball to his colleague, the West Indian Billy Doctrove, a Test umpire of six years' standing. He, too, was horrified by its condition and agreed that it should be changed. Hair thus asked Jesty to bring out a collection of spare balls and allowed the two batsmen, Pietersen and Ian Bell, to choose another one before awarding England an additional five runs, the first time that this penalty had been imposed in a Test match.

The decision upset Inzamam, but play continued for another 18 overs until bad light forced an early tea interval, by which time England had advanced to 298/4, still 33 runs adrift. On discovering that the ball had been changed, Pakistan bowling coach Waqar Younis visited match referee Mike Procter, and was permitted to inspect the ball. He found nothing wrong with it. Highly sensitive to the charge of ball-tampering, a controversy that had dogged him for many years, Waqar interpreted this latest move as a slur on the players. Given their grievances against Hair and that their objection to his appointment for the current series had been overruled – in contrast, he hadn't umpired Sri Lanka since his contretemps with them in 1999 – their patience was close to breaking point.

The chairman of the Pakistan Cricket Board (PCB), Shaharyar Khan, sympathised with the team and suggested that they delay their return to the field by five minutes, while Bob Woolmer, their mild-mannered coach, felt affronted enough to countenance some form of protest. Having asked the whole team to swear on the Koran that they hadn't interfered with the ball, he suggested a brief sit-down in the middle before play restarted, but in that febrile atmosphere the players, led by Inzamam, wanted to go further. They resolved not to play on unless the decision over the ball was reversed and the umpires apologised publicly, and although Woolmer tried to restrain them from anything so extreme, the players were immune to his reasoning. When play restarted at 4.47pm, the Pakistanis remained huddled in their dressing room. After several minutes in the middle waiting for them to appear, the umpires returned to the pavilion. Proceeding straight to the Pakistan dressing room, Hair asked them if they were coming out, to which Inzamam wanted to know why the ball had been changed. 'I am not here to answer these questions,' replied Hair. 'If you don't come out, I shall charge you again.' The impasse continued so that when the umpires returned to the field at 4.55pm, followed by the

England batsmen, the Pakistanis, by now changed into tracksuits, once again failed to appear, and after two minutes the umpires lifted the bails and awarded the match to England.

There then followed a series of emergency meetings between English and Pakistani officials, after which the Pakistan team agreed to resume the match. At 5.23pm, they came out, to jeers from a capacity crowd, but when there was no sign of the umpires they trudged back again after two minutes. It wasn't until 6.11pm that the crowd, who had been kept in the dark about developments, were finally informed that there would be no further play for the day.

At 7pm, Procter convened a meeting of the representatives of the ECB and PCB, the coaches, the captains and the umpires, at which the latter resisted all attempts to restart the match, insisting that the rules were sacrosanct. Incensed by Inzamam's aggressive questions about the ball, Hair walked out, bringing proceedings to an abrupt end.

Because the match referee lacked the authority to reverse the umpires' decision, Procter now sought the help of Malcolm Speed in getting the match restarted, but Speed proved no more successful in persuading Hair to reconsider. Bowing to the inevitable, the ICC, ECB and PCB issued a statement that night confirming that Pakistan had forfeited the match, the first time a team had done so in 129 years of Test cricket. The next day, the ICC charged Inzamam with ball-tampering and bringing the game into disrepute. He replied defiantly on Pakistani television that if he were found guilty his team would go home and not compete in the one-day internationals.

While students burnt effigies of Hair in the streets of Rawalpindi, Islamabad and Lahore, the country's elite voiced their disdain in the media. Ramiz Raja, the former Pakistan captain and respected Sky television commentator, contended that Hair's arbitrary, insensitive style of judgement had caused a needless controversy and tarnished the pride of an entire people; Pakistan president General Pervez Musharraf contacted the team to say that he was insulted by the claims and backed their struggle; and

Shaharyar Khan declared, somewhat improbably, that Hair had inflamed relations between Christians and Muslims at a time when the British security forces were on high alert against Islamic terrorists. According to the *Pakistan Observer*, Hair belonged to that rare breed of men who had inherited the West's age-old burden to civilise the others through acts of punishment whenever the others tried to excel. An editorial in *The News*, recalling Hair's treatment of Muralitharan, speculated whether he would have acted as he did if the bowler had been from England or Australia.

Pakistani criticism of Hair was echoed to a large degree in Britain. According to Michael Atherton in the *Daily Telegraph*, the crisis was caused by 'the crassest and most insensitive piece of umpiring' he had ever seen. Hair's decision to accuse the Pakistanis of ball-tampering took no account of the history of tension between the two teams. The umpires had inspected the ball 20 minutes earlier upon Alastair Cook's dismissal. Sky Sports scanned their material and found no evidence of ball-tampering with their 26 cameras. They wondered why Hair hadn't taken Inzamam aside and conveyed his concerns, an opinion shared by John Woodcock. According to Simon Barnes in *The Times*, the culture of slavish respect for umpires went back to public school principles. Cricket was a preparation for real life; the boys were required to learn that they were there to serve some greater cause such as the British Empire. But modern professional cricket existed not to teach but to enthral.

'Sport no longer depends on the mystique of an official's position. Sport is not heading into anarchy as a result. Sport is merely in the middle of a changing relationship between match officials and players, in which officials are becoming more the servants of the game than its masters. The idea of unthinking respect for authority no longer sits comfortably with us. We are none of us to be judged any more on who we are. We must be judged instead on what we do.'[204]

By no means were all pundits critical of Hair. Former Pakistan fast bowler Aqib Javed admitted that Hair had acted correctly; Aleem Dar, the respected Pakistani umpire, thought his countrymen were wrong to have taken the law into their own hands; and Javed Miandad worried that the team had come across as bad ambassadors. John Reid, the president of New Zealand Cricket and former ICC referee, said that umpires didn't need to witness any tampering to decide whether a ball had been interfered with, and Barry Jarman revealed details of the alleged ball-tampering by South Africa at Karachi when Woolmer had been their coach.

In Australia, there was much indignation at the way that Hair had been treated. Steve Waugh and Mark Taylor both paid tribute to his integrity, his fellow Test umpire Simon Taufel opined that Hair had little option but to follow the letter of the law, and Kim Beazley, the leader of the Australian Labor Party, declared that Pakistan should have accepted the umpire's decision.

Many a cricket correspondent extolled Hair's courage and ability as an umpire, depicting him as a victim of power politics. The idea that he was simply an old-style colonial out of sympathy with the developing world wasn't borne out by the facts. Aside from his friendship with subcontinent umpires such as Peter Manuel, B.C. Cooray and Aleem Dar, he didn't reserve his ire solely for Indians, Pakistanis and Sri Lankans. In 1994, he had reported South Africa's Peter Kirsten for dissent; in 2000, he had called Zimbabwe's Grant Flower for throwing; and in 2003, he had reported South Africa's Shaun Pollock for dissent and his teammate Mark Boucher for verbally abusing a Pakistani batsman.

'If there were a few more Hairs available to stand in matches around the world then cricket would be in less of a mess than it is right now,' commented Patrick Smith in *The Australian*.[205] According to Smith's colleague Malcolm Conn, Hair should be considered a hero not a liability because the cricket authorities believed his relationship with Sri Lanka and Pakistan untenable. Inzamam failed the game at its most fundamental level, he said. 'The spirit of cricket is central to the well-being of the game and Inzamam crushed that spirit by refusing to play.'[206]

On Friday, 25 August, the saga took a bizarre turn when Malcolm Speed astounded a press conference at a London hotel with the revelation that Hair had offered to retire in return for £265,000, to be paid by 31 August, to cover the loss of earnings until his contract expired on 31 March 2008. Apparently weighed down by the constant treadmill of international cricket and keen to take the heat out of the current dispute, Hair discussed his future with Doug Cowie, the ICC's head of umpires, after the Oval Test. Cowie told him that his offer had some merit and advised him to put his proposal in writing. Hair duly did, and Cowie passed it on to his superiors.

Disconcerted by the content of the email, Speed sought legal advice as to how he should deal with it. He was advised to make it public because it could be relevant to the disciplinary case against Inzamam. Stressing that there was nothing dishonest or malicious in Hair's intention – he had written under duress – Speed nevertheless branded his email misguided as the ICC, keen to restore its tattered authority, exploited his travails to its advantage.

The revelations certainly delighted Pakistan, because Hair's lack of judgement appeared to have boosted Inzamam's chances of being exonerated on ball-tampering charges. According to Geoff Boycott, writing in the *Daily Telegraph*, it made Hair a laughing stock and weakened his case considerably because it smacked of somebody just interested in money.

On 27 and 28 September, Inzamam's Code of Conduct hearing was held at the Oval, with Ranjan Madugalle in the chair. The fact that none of the four umpires either saw ball-tampering or had any video footage or other photographic evidence undermined their case. Boycott and Simon Hughes, the Middlesex seam bowler turned cricket analyst, appearing for the defence, said that the ball hadn't been tampered with, and former Test umpire John Hampshire said that Hair's decision to act immediately on his suspicion that the ball had been interfered with was 'pedantic'. According to Madugalle, there was not sufficient, cogent evidence that the fielding team had changed the condition of the ball. 'In my judgement, the marks are as consistent with normal wear and tear of a match ball after 56 overs as they are with deliberate human interventions.'

While Inzamam could legitimately claim that the slur on the team and the nation had been removed, the judgement had far-reaching repercussions for umpires. Derek Pringle, the cricket correspondent of the *Daily Telegraph*, wrote, 'One of the fundamental pillars of cricket is that the decision of the umpire is final, even if it is wrong, but yesterday's judgement by Madugalle has toppled that. What now prevails – for a dangerous precedent has been set – is that the umpire's opinion is inviolable except in sensitive matters that may provoke national outrage, in which case hard evidence is now required.'[207]

On the wider question of bringing the game into disrepute, Madugalle found Inzamam guilty and banned him for four one-day internationals, the minimum penalty for this offence. 'Mr Ul-Haq's conduct undermined one of the fundamental principles of cricket – that players led by their captain, must abide by the decisions of the umpires, however much they may disagree with them, and whether or not they have good reason for disagreeing with them.'

Madugalle was also damning of the umpires for enforcing a forfeit when it became obvious that both teams wanted to play. Player management and effective communication were crucial to good umpiring. If a similar situation occurred again, 'the umpire should do everything possible to try and defuse tensions and to ensure the resumption of play'.[208]

The hearing announced that Hair wouldn't stand in the forthcoming ICC Champions Trophy on the subcontinent, where feelings ran high. Pakistan also lodged a formal written complaint about Hair's demeanour at the Oval and insisted that they wouldn't play under his auspices again. At the ICC board meeting at Mumbai at the beginning of November, the Asian bloc, supported by South Africa, the West Indies and Zimbabwe, voted 7–3 to remove Hair from the elite panel of umpires, despite Malcolm Speed's protestations on his behalf. Confidential ICC files ranked him as its second equal best umpire (the best for decision-making), and lauded him for his strong sense of fairness and consistency.

In Australia, the reaction was highly critical of the ICC, Richie Benaud alleging that it had stabbed Hair in the back. His former team-mate Neil Harvey called his dismissal disgusting, and CA wanted the ICC to review its management of umpires to ensure transparency and fairness. It was imperative that umpires made decisions without fear or favour. According to Robert Craddock, Hair's ousting set a chilling precedent, as other umpires would now be running scared of offending any or all of the four subcontinental nations, 'who might, at any time, loathe each other, but invariably work together on important issues. Having seen how brutally abandoned Hair has become after his tough call, only a brave or foolish umpire would be courageous enough to throw themselves into the lion's den.'[209]

Affronted by his treatment, Hair filed a lawsuit against the ICC in February 2007 for racial discrimination, but when it collapsed later that year he underwent an ICC rehabilitation programme, before returning briefly to officiate two Test matches in 2008 prior to his retirement.

As for the Oval Test itself, the ICC raised eyebrows the following year by changing the result to a draw, a decision that angered MCC, the guardian of the Laws of Cricket, who accused the governing body of setting a 'very dangerous precedent'. In 2009 the ICC then reverted to its original decision, a victory of sorts to Hair and all those who valued the integrity of the game.

Since 2006 ball-tampering has remained something of an intermittent curse. In the Cape Town Test of January 2010, South Africa raised concerns with match referee Roshan Mahanama about the England bowlers altering the condition of the ball. England coach Andy Flower vehemently denied the allegations, and the match referee chose not to take any action, a touch of good fortune according to former captain Michael Vaughan. In 2013, England were again suspected of ball-tampering after the ball was changed in their Champions Trophy match against Sri Lanka at the Oval, just when their bowlers were beginning to make it reverse swing. Former England captain and Sky Sports commentator Bob Willis accused one unnamed player of deliberately scratching the ball, a charge categorically refuted by team manager Ashley Giles. He explained that the ball had been changed because it had gone out of shape, an explanation accepted by the ICC, who decided not to investigate the matter any further.

The ICC did ban Pakistan's Shahid Afridi for two Twenty20s after he admitted biting the ball in a one-day international against Australia at Perth in 2010, and fined South Africa's Faf du Plessis half his match fee for altering the ball in the second Test against Pakistan at Dubai in 2013, a sanction that the Pakistanis thought too lenient. Given what had happened to Afridi, they couldn't understand why du Plessis hadn't also been banned, a view with which others such as Michael Vaughan concurred.

The following year, South Africa were again in the dock when their talented all-rounder Vernon Philander was fined 75 per cent of his match fee for scratching the surface of the ball in the first Test against Sri Lanka at Galle; then, on their tour of Australia in 2016/17, television footage emerged of du Plessis, the stand-in captain, applying saliva to the ball with a mint during the second Test at Hobart. He was fined 100 per cent of his match fee. Eighteen months later, there was a far more serious case of ball-tampering by Australia in South Africa, as discussed in Chapter 18.

With the game increasingly loaded in the batsman's favour with flatter wickets, more powerful bats and shorter boundaries, many former fast bowlers, such as Imran Khan, Richard Hadlee and Allan Donald, support the legalisation of ball-tampering. Others in the trade, such as Waqar Younis and Angus Fraser, take the opposite view, believing that the ball would swing to excess, and it is this view that prevails as bowlers continue to find ingenious ways of interfering with the ball.

Chapter 17

England Bare
Their Teeth

AFTER years in the shadows, England's cricket revival began under Nasser Hussain and Michael Vaughan, reaching its apogee under Andrew Strauss when the team topped the world rankings. Their success won acclaim from their loyal supporters, but the manner in which they played their cricket left something to be desired. When Kevin Pietersen accused some of his England team-mates of promoting a culture of bullying in his 2014 book, *KP: The Autobiography*, former opponents such as Ricky Ponting and Graeme Smith were quick to identify with his claims, most notably the abuse directed towards those who dropped catches. 'We do have a win-at-all-costs mentality now,' admitted Stuart Broad in August 2013. 'I think we are an unpleasant team to face. Teams will not enjoy the experience of playing against us, and that is what we want.'[210]

Such an attitude might have seemed out of place with the general tenor of Alastair Cook's captaincy. Cook, who succeeded Strauss on the latter's retirement in 2012, seemed the last person to preside over a culture of hard-nosed cynicism, especially since his own conduct appeared impeccable, but this is perhaps to underestimate the approach to modern international cricket. Amid the furore over the James Anderson–Michael Clarke confrontation at Brisbane in 2013, Cook had no complaints about Australian sledging. 'On the pitch it's pretty much a war anyway, so there's always going to be a few battles and a few words. That's the way people want to watch cricket being played; tough, hard cricket.'[211]

The following summer, when Anderson was under intense scrutiny for his hostility towards opponents following his spat with India's Ravindra Jadeja at Trent Bridge, Cook was quick to defend him. 'His popularity, a by-product of his modesty and obvious work ethic, is ironic given that under his captaincy England have become the team everyone loves to hate,' wrote Michael Calvin about Cook in the *Independent on Sunday*.[212] In their defence, England would probably point to the intense Australian aggression they were subjected to during the Border-Waugh era, and more recently under Ponting. 'They were at our throats,' Pietersen wrote in the aftermath of their 2006/07 whitewash in Australia, 'and now that is what we want to do to other teams we have to come up against.'[213] When Peter Moores was appointed coach in April 2007, he tried to instil a more ruthless streak in England's cricket, especially with the selection of the vocal Matt Prior as wicketkeeper, a policy that brought them into conflict with India later that summer.

Although nothing like the cold war that had developed between India and Australia, England's relations with India had deteriorated over the years as both sides had adopted a harsher edge to their cricket. After England had the better of a draw in the first Test at Lord's in 2007, they were accused by Dinesh Karthik, the young Indian wicketkeeper, of sledging him just as he was about to face the bowling. His allegations were dismissed by Vaughan, who was involved in a heated exchange with Sourav Ganguly over the treatment of Karthik. 'We are trying to play our cricket with a real intensity and that involves being a little bit aggressive.'[214]

The hostility lingered throughout the second Test at Trent Bridge as India dominated throughout. What brought the tension to the surface was the notorious jelly bean incident on the third evening, when India's Zaheer Khan came in to bat and found a couple of jelly beans left on the pitch. Insulted by this treatment, he branded his bat at Pietersen, who told Zaheer that he was targeting the wrong man. Tempers became so frayed that the umpires had to intervene to calm things down.

After close of play, Prior insisted that England played in the right spirit while looking to 'get one up on your opponent', 'but that is the attitude of a professional habitually pushing the Laws to the limit', suggested David Hopps in *The Guardian*.[215]

Fired up in a way that his captain, Rahul Dravid, had never seen before, Zaheer proceeded to rip the heart out of the England batting with 5–75 in their second innings, setting up an Indian victory by seven wickets. Their triumph was marred, however, by the intemperance of their fast bowler Shantha Sreesanth, who, besides bowling a beamer at Pietersen for which he apologised, deliberately shoulder-charged Vaughan, an offence that led to him being fined half his match fee.

After the match, Vaughan apologised to Zaheer for the jelly beans, and Moores, while defending England's general aggression, admitted there had been a couple of times when they had 'gone over the top'. His solution to curbing the insults and profanities was to turn down the volume on the stump microphones, inviting the response that if sledging was harmless, why should the players be concerned about being overheard on the microphones?

Overall, the truculence of the England players drew a lot of flak from the critics. David Lloyd called the jelly bean incident 'juvenile rubbish', Stephen Brenkley, the cricket correspondent of *The Independent*, found them boorish and unattractive to watch, and Simon Barnes lambasted them for 'defending such idiocy'. 'The whole business of taunting, putting off, insulting – all the things that go under the name of sledging – has become a battleground in which ugliness and inanity struggle for supremacy.' The England cricket team were suffering from confusion. 'The players believe to a man that behaving like an arsehole makes you a better cricketer. The fact is that it doesn't. It only makes you an arsehole.'[216]

Their attitude was again under the spotlight the following summer when they entertained New Zealand. Relations between the two teams had become strained after England's time-wasting in the rain-affected second one-day international had denied New Zealand a possible win. (They were one over away from the match being decided under the Duckworth–Lewis method.) After their defeat in the third match, captain Paul Collingwood declared that England needed to show a greater ruthlessness, something they overdid in the next game at the Oval. With New Zealand needing 26 to win off five overs and with three wickets left, Grant Elliott pushed Ryan Sidebottom to the off side and set off for a quick single, only to collide with the bowler and fall to the ground. As he struggled to his feet and tried to continue his run, Ian Bell collected the ball and lobbed it to Pietersen at the bowler's end, and he removed the bails. Because there was no deliberate obstruction, umpire Mark Benson had little hesitation in giving the batsman out on appeal, but encouraged Collingwood to withdraw his appeal as Elliott received treatment for his injured thigh.

With support from most of his team-mates, Collingwood insisted that the original appeal be upheld, much to Elliott's bemusement and the crowd's disapproval. As he hobbled off to the pavilion accompanied by a chorus of jeers directed at the England team, the New Zealand players, led by captain Daniel Vettori, gave vent to their anger, and even the warm glow of victory for them off the last ball of the match did little to quell the tempest. Vettori refused to shake Collingwood's hand, and only the England captain's later admission that he had made the wrong decision brought some form of reconciliation.

Apologies aside, Collingwood's tactics received a pasting from the British media. Paul Newman of the *Daily Mail* thought it the worst incident to sully English cricket since Mike Gatting's stand-off with Shakoor Rana, and *The Independent*'s Angus Fraser declared that England, for the second time in eight days, were guilty of betraying the spirit of cricket. From a New Zealand perspective, Ian Smith, their former wicketkeeper turned Sky Sports commentator, compared the Elliott run-out to Trevor Chappell's underarm delivery in 1981.

To add insult to injury, Collingwood was charged with overseeing a poor over rate and was banned for four one-day internationals by the ICC, the first England player to be so penalised. Months later, he resigned the one-day captaincy, and the next year, ironically, he was the beneficiary of a sporting gesture by Vettori. Batting against New Zealand in the Champions Trophy at Johannesburg, he wandered out of his crease after playing a ball, and wicketkeeper Brendon McCullum took off the bails. The television umpire confirmed he was out, but Vettori retracted the appeal.

After their capitulation in Australia in 2006/07, England experienced mixed results at Test level over the next couple of years. In 2009 the captaincy passed to Andrew Strauss, and he, along with new coach Andy Flower, set about reviving the team's fortunes. Back-to-back series against the West Indies proved valuable preparation for the much-anticipated Ashes series, and with Australia rebuilding after the retirement of so many of their leading players, there seemed little to choose between the two sides.

England started well in the first Test at Cardiff by scoring 435 in their first innings, but Australia replied with 674/6 and quickly disposed of the home team's upper order on the final morning. After sinking to 159/7, they rallied through a stubborn half-century by Collingwood, and then, after he was out, the last pair of James Anderson and Monty Panesar, against all expectation, held out for the final 45 minutes, much to the frustration of the Australians. What particularly riled them was the sight of the twelfth man appearing twice in two overs with a change of batting gloves for Anderson, the second time accompanied by the physiotherapist for a non-existent injury. Ponting vented his fury at the physio, and later described England's time-wasting as 'pretty ordinary' and against the spirit of the game. The Australian press corps adopted a similar line, and Nasser Hussain called their tactics 'village green stuff'.

The fact that Australia had been reprimanded many times for time-wasting since 2005 and that Ponting had quibbled with several umpiring decisions on the final day brought counter-charges of hypocrisy. For the rest of the summer, he was greeted with boos whenever he came out to bat, but fortunately this breach of sporting etiquette didn't detract from the spirit for the rest of the series. At the beginning of the third Test, England won points by allowing their opponents to change their wicketkeeper after the toss when Brad Haddin broke his finger in the warm-up; then Australia repaid the compliment in the fourth Test by agreeing to delay the toss to enable Matt Prior, who had sustained a back spasm in practice, to have a fitness test.

The atmosphere was less benign when England won in Australia in 2010/11 (see Chapter 15), but any fears that their home series against India the following summer would be equally tetchy were scotched by an act of sportsmanship by the latter. It took place in the second Test at Trent Bridge as England built a match-winning lead in their second innings around a century by Bell. In the final over before tea on the third day, his partner, Eoin Morgan, clipped Ishant Sharma towards the square-leg boundary and ran an easy three, whereupon Bell, believing the ball had gone for four, jogged down the pitch to the non-striker's end, despite Morgan indicating that he should return to his crease. At this point, Praveen Kumar, the fielder, returned the ball to wicketkeeper M.S. Dhoni, who relayed it to substitute fielder Abhinav Mukund, who removed the bails at the striker's end. After skipper Dhoni informed umpire Marais Erasmus that he didn't wish to rescind his appeal, Erasmus gave it out and third umpire Billy Bowden confirmed it, much to the crowd's disgust. Boos rang out as the players and umpires left the field for tea.

During the tea interval, the England captain, Strauss, and coach Andy Flower went to the Indian dressing room and asked their opponents to reconsider, since Bell hadn't been trying to get a run. Their argument initially made little impression on Dhoni and India coach Duncan Fletcher, but following a telling intervention by Sachin Tendulkar, Dhoni had second thoughts. He agreed to rescind their appeal. The umpires consented and the Indians took the field after tea to jeers, the crowd unaware of Bell's reprieve. It was only when Bell re-emerged that the jeers turned to cheers. Without regaining his previous flair, he added another 22 before he was out for 159. As he departed to the pavilion, he shook hands with Dhoni and several other fielders.

Dhoni's gesture was greeted with approval at home and by most of the English media. Yes, Bell had been naïve for trotting down the pitch to greet Morgan, declared Angus Fraser, 'but to me there is a line of what is an acceptable form of dismissal and what is not'.[217] Others adopted a different view. 'Laws are not there to be pushed aside when it suits the prejudices of any particular audience,' wrote his colleague James Lawton. 'The truth is that when cricket was asked a basic question yesterday it blinked in an entirely unsatisfactory way.'[218] The appeal was revoked because England, backed by a large and partisan crowd, pleaded their case.

David Gower, Nasser Hussain and Michael Atherton also argued for the law. 'Dhoni will be congratulated for his sportsmanship,' wrote the latter. 'It was certainly a magnanimous gesture, and one that took the sting out of the situation, but he would have been well within his rights not to have withdrawn his appeal regardless of the unpopularity and possible ramifications that would have inevitably followed.'[219]

Trent Bridge was the scene for further controversy two years later in the first Test between England and Australia. In 2009, after a trial period the previous year, the Decision Review System (DRS), a technology-based system to review the percentage of correct decisions made by the on-field umpires, was introduced, with each side permitted two unsuccessful reviews. The system helped to increase the number of correct decisions, but, in the Trent Bridge Test in 2013, a number of injudicious reviews by the Australians meant it couldn't help them when, in England's second innings, Stuart Broad edged spinner Ashton Agar to skipper Michael Clarke at slip via the pads of wicketkeeper Haddin. Although the catch appeared an absolute formality, Broad, playing on his home ground, stayed put, and umpire Aleem Dar, to general astonishment, gave him not out. His let-off proved a crucial turning point in the match, because he was on 37 at the time and went on to score 65, a vital contribution to England's victory by 14 runs.

Although the Australian team refused to criticise Broad in public for not walking – umpires were there to make decisions and players accepted them – there was much indignation in private, not least from the coach Darren Lehmann. It wasn't simply the fact that Broad was a polarising figure who enjoyed riling his opponents, it was his total lack of remorse for not walking for such an obvious catch. Even his father, Chris Broad, an ICC referee who had recently fined West Indian wicketkeeper Denesh Ramdin for claiming a catch that hadn't carried, wondered how he had managed to keep a straight face.

While the Trent Bridge crowd remained right behind their man judging by the enthusiastic ovation they gave Broad when he resumed his innings the next morning, the critics were more divided on the matter. According to Botham, Broad was entitled to stay put and he in no way influenced the umpire. 'If you're going to start banning and taking action against players who don't walk, then Australia wouldn't have a cricket team.'[220] 'Non-walking was introduced to cricket by the Australians, and yesterday they became victims of its charms offensive,' concurred Atherton.[221] As far as Boycott was concerned, the rules stipulated that it was the opinion of the umpire that mattered and not the spirit of the game. Bowlers didn't recall a batsman if he had been adjudged lbw to a ball that was missing leg stump.

'The problem with having a line-up [of television analysts] solely consisting of ex-professionals is that, to a man, they take the pragmatic rule,' noted Martin Samuel in the *Daily Mail*. 'There was nobody to stick up for the spirit of cricket yesterday, just a lengthy procession of mealy-mouthed justifications, the sort that would have played through Broad's mind in the middle.'[222]

'For far too long, the mantra of "it is up to the umpire to determine if I nicked it" has reigned in cricket,' wrote Matthew Syed in *The Times*. 'As a moral position, it is clearly suspect. It is not terribly dissimilar to "it is up to the umpire to determine if I have tampered with the ball" or "it is up to the authorities to determine if I have taken drugs". We cannot abrogate all responsibility for our actions; we cannot justify deceit by claiming that it was up to the umpire to spot it.'[223] The reality was that rules on their own were never sufficient to police behaviour. There were always grey areas.

From a neutral perspective, Sky Sports commentator Michael Holding argued that Broad should be suspended for breaching the spirit of cricket, as Ramdin had been during the Champions Trophy. 'Two years ago, the England team invoked the spirit of cricket to ask that a legitimate run-out dismissal of Ian Bell – as per the laws of the game – be overturned. When you do that one day, you can't turn around and hide behind the laws on another. That's called hypocrisy.'[224]

While the rest of the series was free of major controversy, Australia objected to their opponents' time-wasting and sledging. The traditional end-of-series celebrations between the two sides were kept to a minimum, and the subsequent urinating on the Oval field by several of the England players seemed rather typical of a side that lacked class. 'While Alastair Cook's side savour the satisfaction of a 3–0 series win,' wrote Oliver Brown in the *Daily Telegraph*, 'they ought to reflect upon how their uncompromising, occasionally cynical style of play denies them the acclaim that would otherwise be their due.'[225]

With the return series following in Australia three months later, there was no time to let bygones be bygones, and the home team were intent on revenge. Lehmann accused Broad of blatant cheating at Trent Bridge and encouraged the Australian crowds to harangue him whenever possible; Mitchell Johnson threatened to target throats and fingers; and the local media went to town on England, with Broad singled out for vilification. With the crowd patently hostile, the tourists walked into a cauldron at Brisbane, the venue for the first Test, and, after a promising first day in the field, they wilted thereafter as Johnson pulverised them with blistering pace and bounce. According to Australian opener David Warner, England were scared of Johnson, and he described the dismissal of Jonathan Trott in the second innings as 'pretty poor and weak', remarks that had CA's media officer wincing. When it was later revealed that Trott was flying home immediately to cope with depression, Warner stood accused of undue insensitivity.

As Australia stood on the brink of a crushing victory in the first Test, another exchange took place which seemed to encapsulate the lack of respect between the two sides. James Anderson, a bête noire with the opposition, took exception to some barbs from debutant George Bailey, standing at short leg, and reciprocated in kind, whereupon skipper Clarke told Anderson to get ready for a broken arm. His expletive-ridden threat was picked up by the Channel Nine microphone, and he was fined 20 per cent of his match fee.

Delighted with the intensity with which Australia had played, Clarke remained unrepentant about his remark and promised more of the same for the rest of the summer. 'Through my career there's always been banter on the cricket field. I cop as much as I give. That's part and parcel of the game, and I've copped my fair share.' His bullishness was supported by Lehmann, who rejected Andy Flower's proposal of a get-together to try to establish some form of pact. While few in Australia lost sleep about England's plight, they did find an unlikely ally in Ian Chappell. If the ICC didn't stop all the chatter, he declared, it would end up in fisticuffs. 'I was delighted that Jimmy pulled away and went over to speak to George Bailey. The only thing that disappointed me was that it took a No 11 to stand up for his rights.'[226] As a batsman, you were entitled to peace and quiet.

Yet while this latest chapter of Ashes rancour shocked many back home, England, according to Matthew Syed, couldn't claim the moral high ground. 'They have also bought heavily into the culture of sledging, baiting opponents, shouting abuse and using the area near to the bat to make crude insinuations. Anderson, as many Australian pundits have pointed out, is one of the worst culprits.'[227] The Ashes should be played with the sharpest of competitive edges with the players giving their all, he argued, but teams should demonstrate these attributes through the quality of their play rather than the nastiness of their abuse.

England's failure to change tack led to two ill-tempered series at home the following summer against Sri Lanka and India, the latter culminating in a prolonged spat between James

Anderson and Ravindra Jadeja, India's colourful all-rounder. Once again Trent Bridge, that most friendly of grounds, was the venue. The trouble began on the second morning of the first Test as the Indians took advantage of a docile wicket to accumulate a useful first-innings total. When Jadeja came to the wicket, he was given an unfriendly greeting by Anderson, so much so that umpire Bruce Oxenford told him to calm down. He did, only to let fly again after Jadeja survived an appeal for caught behind in the last over of the morning session. The insults continued as the players left the field for lunch, right into the pavilion corridor, at which point Anderson was alleged to have pushed Jadeja. The altercation so upset the Indians that they chose to lay a level 3 charge under the ICC Code of Conduct against Anderson that could have landed him a four-match ban if found guilty.

Surprised by the charge, and thinking it a ploy to keep Anderson out of the rest of the series, England countered by pressing charges against Jadeja, which led to him receiving a level 1 fine imposed by match referee David Boon. Now it was the turn of the Indians to express shock, and their lawyers compelled the ICC to waive their own rules and allow Jadeja to appeal.

With Dhoni determined to see Anderson in the dock, partly because of what he saw as the latter's history of antagonism towards his team, all attempts at mediation failed, and a hearing was fixed for the day after the end of the third Test at Southampton.

After a six-hour hearing before ICC judicial commissioner Gordon Lewis, a retired Australian judge, via a video link to Melbourne, it took Lewis just ten minutes to find both players not guilty of their respective charges because of the lack of video evidence.

'That a barely disguised mutual distrust and secret loathing should have been allowed to descend into the litigious farce that was concluded in Melbourne via a Skype connection to Southampton reflects badly on the game,' claimed Stephen Brenkley. 'What took place at Trent Bridge did not merit the money or the ill-feeling that was wasted on it.

'Of much more relevance to the average spectator is the way in which players conduct themselves. Whatever Anderson did or did not do in Nottingham it had been clear for a little while that he is [a] tricky blighter on the field. He sledges and swears constantly and he never appears to be doing much for fun.

If Test cricket really is not for cissies nor should it be for the curmudgeonly and the embittered.'[228]

Smile or not, Anderson cut a much more restrained figure during the final two Tests without in any way diminishing his performance. Indeed, he had rarely bowled better and was deservedly named man of the series as England beat India 3–1. It was the beginning of a less strident era for English cricket.

Chapter 18

McCullum's Crusade

FOR all the misfortunes that have befallen the game, nothing could equal the tragedy that occurred at the Sydney Cricket Ground on 25 November 2014. The Australian batsman Phillip Hughes, playing for South Australia against New South Wales, had made his way to 66 when he tried to hook a bouncer from fast bowler Sean Abbott. Fractionally late with the shot, he was struck on the neck, causing a vertebral artery dissection and massive bleeding on the brain. Hughes collapsed on the spot, never regained consciousness and died in hospital two days later. His death devastated Australia and the cricket world. Aside from the loss of a popular young man cut down in his prime, it was a stark reminder that cricket, for all its charm, could be a brutal game. As the nation rallied around the Hughes family in an endearing show of unity, its team's captain, Michael Clarke, spoke movingly at the funeral about his friend's life and legacy. 'His spirit, which is now part of the game for ever, will act as a custodian of the sport we all love. We must listen to it. We must cherish it. We must learn from it.'

'With those words,' wrote Mark Nicholas, 'Clarke has thrown down the gauntlet.' Stop the rancour, stop the sledging, applaud your opponent and do not be afraid of kindness. Playing hard didn't mean a lowering of standards. Cricket deserved more than had come its way of late. It was a game at the crossroads, and where the players took it now would define its future forever. 'None of these ideals can bring Phillip back but they can begin the path of his legacy.'[229]

Because of the exceptional circumstances surrounding Hughes's death, India, then touring Australia, agreed to the postponement of the first Test, but that was the final gesture of goodwill in another fractious series between these two sides. In the first Test at Adelaide, Australia's David Warner and India's Shikhar Dhawan and Virat Kohli were penalised for verbal exchanges, and in the second at Brisbane, Ishant Sharma was fined for giving Steve Smith a hostile send-off. In the third Test at Melbourne, Kohli was embroiled in constant run-ins with Brad Haddin and Mitchell Johnson amid the many insults emanating from both sides. According to Warner, who participated in several verbal exchanges during his second innings of 40, Australia were 'still going to be playing in-your-face cricket as we normally do but we won't be stepping across that line'. Asked by an Indian journalist what constituted the line, Warner appeared bemused. 'It's just a figure of speech which we use all the time.'[230]

Warner crossed the line weeks later, when he was fined for telling Rohit Sharma to speak English in a one-day international during an altercation over whether the Indians should have gone for a single off an overthrow. Frustrated by his constant breaches of discipline, CA's James Sutherland told Warner 'to stop looking for trouble'.

Australia's failure to rise to the occasion and act on their best intentions by eradicating the posturing and abuse left the BBC's Jonathan Agnew unimpressed. 'Michael Clarke said very clearly that Hughes' memory would run through the team, and would be in the way they would play their cricket. Well, I haven't seen evidence of that. I really hoped that out of this tragedy might have come some good, but the players haven't behaved any better and I think that's a real disappointment.'[231]

Agnew's words attracted opprobrium with Hughes's team-mates, but according to Tom Ryan in the *Sydney Morning Herald*, Australia's harassment of the opposition equated to schoolyard bullying transformed to the sporting field.

In contrast to Australia, brighter skies were dawning across the Tasman Sea, where New Zealand, under Brendon McCullum, were playing a style of cricket that blended chivalry with entertainment. Always the poor relation of international cricket, New Zealand had endured a particularly lean few years before McCullum assumed the captaincy in 2011. A battler from humble origins in Dunedin, the muscular McCullum had featured in a few scraps during his time, but captaincy seemed to bring the best out of him. As a swashbuckling batsman who had excelled at the one-day game, he wanted to revive popular interest in cricket at home by getting his team to play with a smile. 'For a long time we were searching for a bit of soul about our team and we stumbled on the fact that sledging had never worked for us,' he later explained. 'We're not very good at it and we're not skilled enough to take our eye off the ball.'[232]

This philosophy really came into its own following the tragic loss of Phillip Hughes. On hearing the news during a Test against Pakistan in the United Arab Emirates, the New Zealanders suddenly saw the game in a new light. As a mark of respect for their fallen colleague, they shunned their usual preparations, they bowled no bouncers, and they celebrated no wickets in a match they won by an innings. Paradoxically, they found this less intense approach to be positively liberating, and they continued in the same vein during the 2015 World Cup, where, in front of their enthusiastic home crowds, they carried all before them by playing some vibrant cricket. Having defeated England and Australia, they beat South Africa in the semi-final by the closest of margins, their hero being Grant Elliott, who, having despatched Dale Steyn for six to win the match, helped the distraught bowler off. It was the prelude to South African captain A.B. de Villiers leading his men into the New Zealand dressing room to offer their congratulations.

Buoyed by their success to date, New Zealand flew to Australia for the final in confident mood, only then to fall to earth in spectacular fashion. Batting first in front of over 90,000 at the MCG, they didn't show up and, after making only 183, were defeated by seven wickets. Australia had won their fourth World Cup in five attempts, but their triumph was overshadowed by the graceless manner in which they had conducted themselves, especially the boorish send-offs of three of the New Zealand batsmen, including Daniel Vettori in his final international. When questioned about this on radio the following day, wicketkeeper Brad Haddin said that their opponents had deserved it because they had been too nice to them during the earlier qualifying game in New Zealand. 'I said I'm not playing cricket like this. If we get another crack at these guys in the final, I'm letting everything out.'

While New Zealand kept a diplomatic silence about the antics of the victors, other than to congratulate them on their victory, their sportsmanship won them a following the world over. 'The Kiwis played as true gentlemen and rightly proved that cricket is a game played by gentlemen,' wrote Dinesh Weerawansa in the Sri Lanka *Daily News*. 'They valued principles in sports and the spirit of the game more than winning.'[233]

With encomiums such as this two a penny, New Zealand carried on their crusade for brighter cricket on a brief tour of England soon afterwards. Unlike so many Tests at Lord's in May, the first Test was a classic, with five days of fluctuating, attacking cricket played in the best of spirits. Behind by 134 runs on first innings, England were indebted to a magnificent century by all-rounder Ben Stokes to turn the tables on their opponents and guide them to a 124-run victory with nine-and-a-half overs to spare. Disappointed but not depressed, the New Zealanders joined England in the dressing room for a post-match drink, and the good-natured rivalry continued at Headingley for the second Test, with the tourists this time victorious by 199 runs. 'What McCullum and his men were doing didn't seem false or forced in the least,' wrote Stuart Broad. 'They seemed genuinely decent fellas who were happy to play their cricket hard but in the right spirit. It was very refreshing.'[234]

The scintillating cricket continued in the one-day series, won by England 3–2, and although New Zealand returned home empty-handed, they left behind a host of new friends. 'When England played New Zealand recently, it was not just cricket that was elevated, it was everyone who watched the matches,' reflected

Matthew Syed. 'The contest showed that it was possible to strive to expose every weakness in an opponent's game while clapping him to the crease and not feeling an urge to insult his mother.'[235]

McCullum had set the bar for the summer and was later rewarded with the CMJ Spirit of Cricket Award for 2015. When even James Anderson expressed appreciation of the mutual respect during the New Zealand series, cricket lovers hoped for something similar for the Ashes. The Australians publicly disabused such hopes, but appeared to follow suit, and with England on their best behaviour, the series was the most harmonious between the two sides for many years. England won 3–2, and Australian captain Michael Clarke was the soul of graciousness in defeat. The only minor squall came in the second one-day international at Lord's, when Stokes was given out after putting his hand in the way of the ball, which had been hurled at the stumps by bowler Mitchell Starc in an attempted run-out. While the English press debated the merits of the decision, McCullum wasn't impressed. Writing in the *Daily Mail*, he branded one-day captain Steve Smith's refusal to recall Stokes immature, an intervention which prompted the Australians to accuse McCullum of speaking out of turn. 'At the end of the day you are not playing for the spirit of cricket award,' declared David Warner, the new Australian vice-captain. 'You are playing for a series.'

Australian irritation with McCullum's hypocrisy, as they saw it, added frisson to their three-match Test series at home against New Zealand in November 2015. Desperate to make up for their World Cup defeat and show that their positive approach could pay off, the visitors experienced the worst possible start in the first Test at Brisbane. Flagging under a bombardment of attacking shots from Australian openers David Warner and Joe Burns, they never recovered as the home side rattled up 556/4 declared in their first innings. With the weather closing in on the final day, New Zealand's one hope of saving the match rested on a gritty 80 from McCullum until his luck deserted him. While clearly upset to be the victim of a serious umpiring error, caught at slip off his pad, he was magnanimous towards the umpires afterwards. As for the

Australians, they derived great satisfaction from the margin of their victory. 'It's all very well being nice, making a beeline to shake the hand of another Australian century-maker as part of their spirit of cricket pact,' commented sportswriter Jon Pierik in the *Sydney Morning Herald*, 'but if it comes at the expense of the necessary grunt required to win Test matches, it's time for a rethink.'[236]

After an inconclusive draw in Perth, Australia took the series by winning a low-scoring match at the Adelaide Oval in the first day-night Test. In reply to New Zealand's first-innings score of 202, the home side were struggling at 117/8 when Nathan Lyon's attempted sweep against spinner Mitchell Santner struck the shoulder of the bat and looped to slip. He was given not out by umpire Sundaram Ravi, but New Zealand referred the decision to third umpire Nigel Llong, who ignored a clear mark on Lyon's bat and upheld the on-field decision. Llong's error, later confirmed by the ICC, had an important bearing on the match, as Lyon added 74 for the ninth wicket with wicketkeeper Peter Nevill to give Australia a valuable lead of 22, helping them to an eventual three-wicket victory. After the match, McCullum admitted to great frustration about Lyon's reprieve, but refused to blame the umpire and looked forward to gaining revenge against his opponents in New Zealand later in the summer. It wasn't to be. Playing the better cricket, Australia won both Tests comfortably despite the fastest Test century on record by McCullum in his final Test.

Following in McCullum's footsteps was Misbah-ul-Haq, who was appointed captain of Pakistan at a critical stage in his country's history. A horrific attack on the Sri Lankan cricket team bus at Lahore in 2009 had consigned them to playing all their matches in exile; then, the following year, the Pakistan tour to England was tainted by the spot-fixing scandal, which led to the imprisonment of captain Salman Butt and two of his team-mates. Stepping into this void, the 36-year-old Misbah proved equal to the challenge. Employing his natural unflappability and gravitas to great effect, he fashioned a new pride and mutual respect in his team, so much so that by September 2016 they'd risen to the top of the ICC international rankings. More pertinently, this success was enhanced by the chivalrous manner in which they played the game. His retirement at the end of the West Indies–Pakistan series in May 2017, the latter's first series win in the Caribbean, leaves a rich legacy for his successor to build on.

The gentle breezes in the Caribbean followed something more heated in India, where the host nation once again went head-to-head with Australia in March–April 2017. A series of compelling cricket, won 2–1 by India, was overshadowed by personal barbs and slights both on and off the field. The situation turned particularly nasty in the second Test at Bangalore when India took exception to Australian captain Steve Smith seeking help from the dressing room on whether he should take a review, in breach of DRS rules. After his side lost by 75 runs, Smith apologised for his error but strongly refuted post-match allegations by his Indian counterpart, Virat Kohli, of systematic cheating by his team. After a meeting between the two boards in Mumbai, the BCCI withdrew a report filed to the ICC charging Smith and batting partner Peter Handscomb with abusing the spirit of cricket. The good work was undone, however, by a snide comment by James Sutherland about Kohli, and the BCCI's decision to post a video clip of two Indian players boasting about their sledging of David Warner. After two more Tests of personal run-ins, one of which embroiled Smith in a loose rant against Murali Vijay for claiming a catch, he redeemed himself with a gracious apology at the end of the series. He paid tribute to India's talent and looked forward to sharing a drink with them, an offer brushed aside by Kohli, who professed that the Australians were no longer his friends.

A year later, Australia lacked friends everywhere following a ball-tampering scandal on their controversial tour of South Africa. Ever since South Africa's readmission to international cricket in 1991, there had been little goodwill between them and Australia, and the legacy of past discord cast a pall over their meeting in 2017/18. The first Test at Durban, convincingly won by Australia, featured a fracas in the pavilion on the fourth day between David Warner and South African wicketkeeper Quinton de Kock, as the two traded insults. Such was the former's anger at an alleged slur by the latter regarding his wife that he had to be physically restrained by his team-mates. Both were fined by the match referee – Warner 75 per cent of his match fee, de Kock 25 per cent – as was Nathan Lyon for his indecorous celebration of A.B. de Villiers's second-innings dismissal. After Cricket Australia had rebuked their team and James Sutherland had spoken to Steve Smith, the captain remained unfazed about his team's combative approach. 'I think that the way we play our best cricket is when we're aggressive. We're in the fight together, we're hunting as a pack, we're working for each other and backing our mates on the field ... that's part of being an Australian in my opinion.'

His words did nothing to quell the animosity that blighted the second Test at Port Elizabeth. Warner, who prior to the match had accused de Kock of making vile comments about his wife, thereby flouting the Australian mantra of 'what happens in the middle, stays in the middle', now increasingly found himself the object of derision. Aside from facing unsubstantiated allegations of ball-tampering from his opponents, he had to endure offensive allusions to his wife's past personal life from the crowd, unsavoury behaviour which drew an apology from the president of Cricket South Africa.

In a riveting game, an 11-wicket haul by South Africa fast bowler Kagiso Rabada led his team to a highly satisfying six-wicket victory, but his efforts were overshadowed by being found guilty of two charges of misconduct – shoulder-charging Smith and shouting in Warner's face on dismissing him. Given his record as a serial offender, these latest sanctions qualified him for an automatic two-Test ban, a body blow to South Africa's chances of winning the series. He appealed, and because the ICC's judicial commissioner, Michael Heron QC, found no conclusive evidence that his contact with Smith was deliberate, his offence was downgraded, enough to overturn the ban. His surprising reprieve, while delighting all South Africans, irked Smith, not least because his opinion hadn't been sought, and his mood was barely brightened by an alleged tweet from Vernon Philander accusing him of faking the contact.

The strife continued in the third Test at Cape Town, with Warner once again in the line of fire. A South African spectator hounded him on his dismissal in the first innings, and the abuse of the crowd towards the Australians was such that Cricket Australia lodged a complaint with their South African counterparts. 'It has been disgraceful,' fulminated coach Darren Lehmann. 'You are talking about abuse of various players and their families,' an understandable enough refrain, but this from the man who'd told Australian supporters in 2013 to harry Stuart Broad until he cried.

Alone and unloved in a foreign land, Australia resolved to fight back as they fell behind on first innings and failed to make a significant breakthrough in South Africa's second. At lunch on the third day, Warner, with Smith's approval, hatched a plan to use sandpaper to rough up the ball to get it to reverse swing and entrusted Cameron Bancroft, one of the most inexperienced players in the team, to execute it. Bancroft was later caught on camera doing the deed and then trying to hide the sandpaper (which he later claimed had been adhesive tape) down his trousers. After feigning innocence when challenged by the umpires, he and Smith admitted to premeditated cheating at a press conference that evening, although Smith seemed more contrite about getting caught than about the offence itself. Their mea culpa unleashed an outcry across the cricket world, not least in Australia, where cricket as the national game holds a special place in the popular consciousness. Prime minister Malcolm Turnbull branded the team's behaviour 'beyond belief' and called on Cricket Australia to put their house in order. They obliged by sending home Smith, Warner and Bancroft in disgrace, and banned Smith and Warner from first-class cricket for a year and Bancroft for nine months. In addition, Smith and Bancroft were banned from holding all leadership positions from 12 months after completing their one-year ban, while Warner was banned from all leadership positions for life. At the same time, they exonerated Lehmann, who many hold responsible for his team's cynical reputation, though he would resign soon afterwards.

It was this 'earthquake of arrogance', as *The Australian* dubbed it, that helps explain the febrile reaction to what, in ICC terms, was a relatively minor level 2 offence (level 4 is the most serious) with its maximum one-match ban. Aside from the disgust at the way in which captain and vice-captain orchestrated such a brazen conspiracy and left it to the inexperienced Bancroft to carry the can, the incident was yet a further stain on the team's chequered reputation. Robert Craddock wrote in the *Courier-Mail*: 'But the tampering affair was not a moment of madness. It was the culmination of a grubby-win-at-all- costs culture deliberately crossing the line between self-righteous rule-bending into a world of shameless bald-faced cheating. Having teased and taunted and demeaned opposition sides for years, Australia developed such a shallow respect for the game that it decided a little bit of cheating would not go astray.'[237]

Others were of a similar view. According to Gideon Haigh, the public had already wearied of the players' 'unapologetic truculence' and their self-justifying protestations that they just played cricket the 'Aussie way', while to Jason Gillespie, 'The brutal reality is that this team are seen as arrogant and all too quick to dictate the line to others.'[238]

And yet, for all their shame, it isn't only Australia who need to take a long, hard look at themselves. During the same week as that Cape Town Test, England fielded a player against New Zealand charged with affray following an incident outside a Bristol nightclub the previous September, and, days earlier, the Bangladesh Cricket Board apologised for the unacceptable conduct of two of its players in a match against Sri Lanka. If David Lloyd, the former England player, first-class umpire and Sky Sports commentator, is correct when he says that behaviour on and off the field has sunk to an all-time low, then the cricket authorities the world over have helped bring this on themselves by their failure of leadership. Whether this latest crisis in the game finally persuades the ICC and others to act remains to be seen, but, if nothing else, it has been a telling reminder that, despite all the efforts to restore the spirit of the game, there is still some way to go.

Conclusion

LIKE the unwritten British constitution, the conduct of the game of cricket has rested more on a series of conventions than the actual laws, presenting a basic dilemma should those conventions be breached. This was most evident during the bodyline series, when Douglas Jardine was prepared to antagonise a nation by physically intimidating its batsmen, so they could contain Don Bradman and win back the Ashes. After allegations of poor sportsmanship, bodyline was banned, but its legacy lived on in the form of intimidating bowling. Bradman thought nothing of letting Lindwall and Miller loose on Hutton and co post-war, and, although opponents bristled at the number of short-pitched balls, they were afforded little protection from the umpires, a pointer to the all-out bouncer war of the 1970s and 1980s.

If the throwing controversy of the late 1950s and early 1960s lacked the devastating impact of bodyline, it seriously flouted both the laws and the spirit of the game. With the burden of proof falling very much on the umpires, few felt able to assert themselves, ensuring that the problem continued to fester. It was only after England's ill-fated tour to Australia in 1958/59 that the legislators faced up to their responsibilities and consigned that generation of throwers to oblivion. When in time the issue resurfaced in the 1990s, most notably in the action of Muttiah Muralitharan, the task of determining whether he threw or not proved highly complex and was never entirely resolved.

Other examples of gamesmanship have littered the game, most notably scuffing the pitch, lifting the seam and, increasingly, time-wasting. Even the revered Frank Worrell slowed down the game when it suited him, most notably at Lord's in June 1963 when England were chasing victory, so that when Brian Close was stripped of the England captaincy in 1967 for Yorkshire's time-wasting in a county match, Keith Miller thought the punishment risible. Writing in the *Daily Express*, he admitted to committing the same offence and numbered Bradman and Hutton, both knighted for their services to cricket, among his list of perpetrators.

Yet while cricket was never the moral crusade that the game's literary elite would have us believe, it would be wrong to dismiss its conventions and etiquette as mere hypocrisy. In the 1945–70 era, most players adhered to the ethic of fair play, walking when they were out caught (though a different ethos applied in Australia), and refraining from bowling bouncers at tail-enders and claiming spurious catches; above all, they respected the authority of the umpire.

This ethic of fair play, which made such an impression on C.L.R. James when he was growing up in early 20th-century Trinidad, continued to win a following in parts of the former Empire after it had been discarded elsewhere. The memoirs of Viv Richards, Gordon Greenidge and Malcolm Marshall all tell of their consternation when exposed to the cheating of other Test-playing countries. It was an experience later shared by Sri Lanka on their introduction to Test cricket in the 1980s. Chastened by this rude awakening, they soon changed tack, and, under the pugnacious leadership of Arjuna Ranatunga, they became as uncompromising as the next team.

If sport mirrors life, the onset of 1970s materialism, which placed ever greater value on winning, exposed the fragility of the old conventions that underpinned the game. Nothing better illustrated the transition to a more hostile era than the escalation in unrelenting speed in the 1970s, with no batsman, not even the most hapless of tail-enders, spared the onslaught. Leading the charge was the four-man West Indian pace attack that dominated Test cricket for the best part of two decades. Battered into submission by Lillee and Thomson in 1975/76, the West Indies soon learned the new rules of engagement and established an aura of superiority over all comers.

While fast bowlers had always used intimidation as part of their armoury, the brutal nature of the sustained West Indian assault introduced what John Woodcock called a new and chilling dimension to the game as the number of serious injuries multiplied. When confronted with this criticism, the West Indians depicted it as a white man's lament commensurate with his new inferior post-colonial status. Racial issues aside, they placed their defence on the authority of the umpire, knowing full well that most umpires had opted out of applying Law 42, especially since there was some dispute as to what constituted a bouncer as opposed to a short rising ball. In time, the ICC brought some clarity to the confusion by limiting the number of bouncers to two an over. Umpires remain the arbiters of what passes for intimidatory bowling, but offer little protection for non-recognised batsmen, who, armed with helmet and armguard, are now expected to face the music. Captains, out to exploit every advantage, have little time for sentiment, as Steve Waugh displayed against South Africa at Adelaide in 2001. That year, the South Africans arrived in Australia intent on displacing the Australians as the world's best team and boasting a fiery young fast bowler called Nantie Hayward. Determined to preserve his team's domination and inflict a few mental scars on this young upstart, Waugh instructed his fastest bowler, Brett Lee, to give Hayward, a genuine number eleven, the full treatment when he came in to bat in the first Test. Lee promptly bowled three fiendishly quick bouncers: two of them struck Hayward on his helmet, and the third had him running for cover. 'Through the grille of his helmet, I saw a man totally rattled, unable or unwilling to take a few deep breaths and regain focus, so he could help his team get its first-innings total reasonably close to ours,' Waugh later recalled. 'While it was a little disconcerting to see an international cricketer unable to stand his ground, the duel for the Number 1 title can often hinge on moments such as these.'[239]

The following year, Lee floored England's Alex Tudor with a bouncer in the Perth Test and turned deathly pale when he saw the bloodied Tudor in real trouble. 'Therein lies the contradiction at the heart of targeting a tail-ender, albeit one with a top score of 99 not out,' wrote Rob Bagchi in *The Guardian*. 'Bowlers launch their attack with a kind of barbarous frivolity then once the all too predictable consequences of their actions are revealed contrition strikes home. Tudor left the WACA on a stretcher and, sadly for him as other injuries dogged his career, never played another Test.'[240]

It is a measure of the rift that had evolved between the game's administrators and the players that the values propagated by the former have been increasingly ignored by the latter. Even members of the cricket establishment shed the habits of a lifetime by turning from gamekeeper to poacher when it suited them. On the West Indies tour of New Zealand in 1980, manager Willie Rodriguez blamed the subversive behaviour of his players on the incompetence of the umpires; two years later, on England's 1981/82 tour of India, manager Raman Subba Row publicly protested about the standard of umpiring following their defeat in the first Test. Six years later, in Pakistan, England manager Peter Lush expressed similar allegations about the umpiring, while his captain, Mike Gatting, became embroiled in one of the most unedifying on-field feuds ever seen with an umpire. It was particularly poor form from the nation that preached the values of fair play and respecting the umpire's decision to the rest of the world.

After 20 years of deteriorating behaviour, the ICC introduced an International Code of Conduct and match referees in 1991, in an effort to restore order. It was a sound enough idea, but the referees failed to live up to expectation in bringing miscreants to heel. And when they did assert their authority, as Peter van der Merwe did against Arjuna Ranatunga at Adelaide in 1999, following the latter's harangue of umpire Ross Emerson regarding Muttiah Muralitharan's action, the Sri Lankans resorted to litigation, forcing the match referee to back down. Later, in November 2001, Mike Denness caused such a rumpus by fining six Indians in the Port Elizabeth Test, while allegedly turning a blind eye to various South African transgressions, that his days as a match referee were numbered.

It is true that the appointment of Malcolm Speed as the ICC's chief executive that same year did inject some backbone into an organisation notorious for its lack of steel. At the same time, umpires, once the unrivalled source of authority, increasingly had to contend with political machinations off the field. In August 2006, Pakistan's forfeiture of the Oval Test following a row about ball-tampering led to Darrell Hair, the senior umpire in the match and one of the world's best, being ousted from the ICC umpires' panel on the initiative of the Asian bloc.

India's growing economic clout struck again after the notorious Sydney Test of January 2008 when it claimed the scalp of umpire Steve Bucknor, the veteran of 120 Tests. Bucknor, it must be admitted, hadn't enjoyed one of his better matches, but his summary dismissal from the next Test on pain of an Indian boycott of the rest of their Australian tour gave rise to considerable concern.

It was to reclaim the game's ethos that Colin Cowdrey and Ted Dexter devised the Spirit of Cricket, a preamble that accompanied the laws. Introduced with much fanfare by MCC in 2000, its impact after 18 years remains limited, its principles dismissed as 'well-meaning guff' by Michael Atherton, 'a load of rubbish' by Ian Chappell and 'a morass of double standards' by Steve James. These ex-players, now prominent in the media, probably speak for today's players, yet even in the modern professional game there are certain breaches of cricketing etiquette which are deemed to be off limits.

The Spirit of Cricket comprises three cardinal principles: the authority of the umpire, respect for opponents and the eradication of cheating and sharp practices. While there has been undoubted progress on the first principle, there has been rather less on the other two.

Although a higher standard of umpiring, a stricter disciplinary code and DRS have reduced the amount of dissent, it has by no means been eliminated. To compound matters, some of the worst offenders have been the captains themselves, with Sourav Ganguly, Ricky Ponting and Inzamam-ul-Haq among those frequently up before the bill. In 2011, veteran Australian umpire Daryl Harper retired prematurely following several run-ins with the Indian team in the first Test against the West Indies at Kingston and intense criticism of his performance by their captain, M.S. Dhoni. The fact that the ICC failed to take disciplinary action against Dhoni only added to Harper's disillusion.

For all of the IPL's success in bringing cricketers from different nationalities closer together, and welcome innovations such as giving retiring Test players a guard of honour in their final match, respect for opponents isn't what it should be. While few would expect the modern player to emulate Keith Miller, Gary Sobers or Bishan Bedi by applauding a good shot, the failure to compliment an opponent on reaching a century is a breach of cricketing etiquette that wouldn't have escaped the most competitive of teams in times past. Less excusable is the modern tendency to engage in unsavoury send-offs of dismissed batsmen, as seen in the 2015 World Cup Final when Australia's graceless demeanour towards their New Zealand opponents embarrassed many of their own supporters. Most grievous of all is the blight of sledging, described by Mike Brearley as 'a totally unwelcome aberration in the game, inane, humourless and unacceptable'.[241]

Although the game has never lacked the odd colourful comment, systematic and sustained verbal abuse to intimidate and unsettle opponents has become ingrained since the 1970s. If Australia were the originators of sledging and its main practitioners, other teams have bought into it, either through sheer provocation or because they deem it to be tactically advantageous. While there were those batsmen like Nasser Hussain, Mark Ramprakash and Daryll Cullinan who appeared susceptible to personal goading, others such as Tony Greig, Steve Waugh and Michael Atherton positively relished the cut and thrust of verbal spats, since it spurred them to greater heights. Certainly, the personal duels between Lillee and Greig in 1974/75, Ambrose and Waugh in 1994/95 and Donald and Atherton in 1998 all made for great theatre, but personal animosity isn't an essential component for compelling cricket. The crowds who flocked to watch the Australia–West Indies Tests of

1960/61 or the Ashes series of 2005 saw wonderfully entertaining spectacles in which chivalry triumphed over cynicism. Similarly, the recent revival of Test cricket in New Zealand coincided with a decision by Brendon McCullum's side to play in a positive vein, devoid of personal abuse.

Forced to defend sledging, its advocates would claim that it is part of the game and players need to be resilient enough to withstand the mental pressure. Many trot out clichés about playing 'hard but fair' and 'not crossing the line' – a code for personal abuse – but, contrary to countless denials, that is often what sledging amounts to: Arjuna Ranatunga was stigmatised for his weight, Jonty Rhodes for his religion, Andrew Symonds for his ethnic origins, Muttiah Muralitharan for his bowling action and Justin Ontong for his selection due to racial quotas.

When Graham Thorpe was having marital problems on England's tour to South Africa in 1999/2000, it fell to South African opener Gary Kirsten to dissuade his team-mates from alluding to this in any on-field chatter. The extent of the personal abuse was inadvertently acknowledged by Australian captain Michael Clarke when, following his reprimand for threatening to break James Anderson's arm at Brisbane in November 2013, he claimed that many worse things had been said to him. His comments tallied with Graeme Smith's revelations about the level of personal abuse he had been subjected to on his Test debut in 2002 by the Australians. They berated him for going public about on-field antics, but while this convention held good in the days when close-of-play socialising between the teams helped clear the air, such fraternisation now rarely occurs. Even then, there were players from different cultures who harboured little desire to mix with those who earlier had grossly insulted them. Those who trade in insults and vitriol seem to forget that cricket, for all its fierce rivalries and financial rewards, is at heart a game and should act as a bridge between different nations and cultures. 'The practice of sledging destroys that special bond between players,' wrote Ian Botham in his autobiography, 'and if something is not done about it soon the game will be damaged beyond repair.'[242]

His words resonated at the inquest into the death of Phillip Hughes in November 2016, when allegations were made that sledging had occurred in the minutes leading up to the accident. At the end of the inquest, the New South Wales State Coroner, Michael Barnes, ruled that Hughes's death was entirely a tragic accident, but he did call sledging an unsavoury practice, contrary to the spirit of the game, and made an impassioned plea for it to end.

First-class cricketers might object to being called role models, but inevitably their attitudes, good or bad, rub off on others throughout the game. All too often, churlish behaviour towards the opposition infects league cricket, schools cricket and even the village green, bringing a discordant note to what should be a harmonious occasion. 'I gave up umpiring in the leagues mid-season in 2014 because I had got so fed up with the behaviour of some of the players,' former Test umpire John Holder told his biographer Andrew Murtagh. 'Honestly, Murt, some of the shenanigans that go on have to be seen to be believed. And they seem to get away with it. They shouldn't. The punishments should be tough enough to be effective, like being banned for a match or two. Suspended sentences never work.'[243]

Holder's concerns were amply vindicated by a University of Portsmouth survey in 2015. From data gathered from 763 umpires, the majority serving at recreational level, it found that 56.3 per cent had faced abuse or aggressive confrontation; 3 per cent had suffered physical abuse; and 20 per cent had given up due to the increased abuse. It was primarily to clean up the game at this level that MCC and the ICC approved tough new rules on player conduct, so that, from 28 September 2017, umpires were given the power to eject from the field any player guilty of threats or acts of violence.

Although not everyone in the post-war era was a stickler for walking, it was a convention that the majority adhered to. In time, as the stakes grew ever higher, the Australian practice of leaving all such decisions to the umpire became all-embracing. By acting accordingly, most batsmen claim to have flouted no law, and within the game not walking is deemed less reprehensible than claiming a catch on the bounce, a transgression that led to West Indian wicketkeeper Denesh Ramdin being suspended by the ICC in 2013. Comparing this incident with Stuart Broad's refusal to walk against Australia in the Trent Bridge Test days later, Andrew Strauss wrote that, 'Not walking in cricket is a little like tax avoidance. It is frowned upon to various degrees according to the audacity with which it is applied. Claiming a catch that you know you have dropped is far more like tax evasion, which is against the law, and there have to be consequences for actions of such a devious nature. Neither policy is right morally but one is deemed semi-acceptable.'[244]

And yet batsmen who fail to walk are often the first to cast aspersions at opponents who follow suit. For all the vituperation directed at Atherton for staying put against South Africa at Trent Bridge in 1998, how many South Africans would have walked in those circumstances? Similarly, it is a bit rich for non-walkers who have invoked the authority of the umpire as the final arbiter to challenge that authority when he has ruled against them. 'Players talk about letting an umpire do his job,' observed John Holder, 'but a lot are only happy when it goes their way.'[245]

It used to be said that visiting teams on the subcontinent were often victims of frenetic appealing, especially for bat-pad catches on turning wickets. In time, umpires the world over were subjected to greater pressure from this practice, and although the ICC disciplinary code has helped curb the excesses, it hasn't been eliminated. Bob Woolmer and Mickey Arthur, the respective coaches of the Pakistan and South Africa teams that toured Australia in 2004/05 and 2005/06, spoke of the marginal decisions going against them because of the home side's propensity to strenuous appealing, a ploy that match referee Chris Broad called 'kind of borderline'.

Part of the Indian team's disillusion with Australian gamesmanship in the Sydney Test of January 2008 centred on their failure to honour the pre-series pact regarding catches. While Michael Clarke edged to slip in Australia's second innings and refused to walk – he was given out on appeal – the Australians insisted that his word be accepted in India's second innings when television replays showed that his catch to dismiss Sourav Ganguly was at best inconclusive.

With so many conventions open to conflicting interpretation, it behoves the ICC to legislate against other forms of gamesmanship, as it has done in times past regarding bodyline, throwing and over rates. For instance, the responsibility for ruling whether a batsman at the non-striker's end should be run out for backing up too far should be transferred from the bowler to the umpire after the bowler has given the batsman an obligatory warning. When England's Jos Buttler was given run out backing up in the final one-day international against Sri Lanka at Edgbaston in 2014, the tourists sparked much controversy, despite bowler Sachithra Senanayake having given both Buttler and his partner, Chris Jordan, previous warnings.

And yet rules on their own are never sufficient to police behaviour. In cricket, as in life, it is our spoken customs that determine the larger part of conduct. According to Christopher Martin-Jenkins, the preamble to the laws had its place and 'cricketers from the village green to the Test arena have a shrewd idea, in 99 cases out of 100, what is and is not within the Spirit of the Game. That spirit, distilled, is simply "fair play".'

He also said that the preamble, 'no less clear and concise', left little doubt about what was and what wasn't acceptable. In response to Atherton's concern that the Spirit of Cricket was a grey area and it asked captains to make moral judgements that were sometimes contrary to the laws, Martin-Jenkins saw that as the task of leadership, 'and good captains know almost by instinct when something is right or wrong'.[246] This, surely, is the nub of the matter. If the Spirit of Cricket is to become anything more than fine words, it is up to the captains to take the high road and lead by example. Brendon McCullum and Misbah-ul-Haq have taken the first steps. Are others prepared to follow in their wake?

Bibliography

Books

Allen, David Rayvern, *Jim: The Life of E.W. Swanton* (London: Aurum, 2004).

Alley, Bill, *Standing the Test of Time* (Manchester: Empire, 1999).

Atherton, Michael, *Opening Up: My Autobiography* (London: Coronet, 2003).

Bailey, Jack, *Trevor Bailey: A Life in Cricket* (London: Methuen, 1993).

Baloch, Khadim Hussain, *Imran's Summer of Fulfilment: An Account of the 1987 Pakistan Cricket Tour of England* (St Helens, K.H. Baloch, 1987).

Bannister, Alex, *Cricket Cauldron: With Hutton in the Caribbean* (London: Stanley Paul, 1954).

Bannister, Jack and Oslear, Don, *Tampering With Cricket* (London: Collins Willow, 1996).

Barker, J.S., *In the Main* (London: Pelham Books, 1968).

Bedser, Alec, *The Fight for the Ashes* (London: George G. Harrap and Co, 1959).

Bedser, Alec, *Twin Ambitions* (London, Stanley Paul, 1986).

Benaud, Richie, *Anything But: An Autobiography* (London: Hodder and Stoughton, 1998).

Benaud, Richie, *On Reflection* (London: Collins Willow, 1984).

Berry, Scyld, *A Cricket Odyssey: England on Tour 1987–88* (London: Pavilion Books Ltd, 1998).

Birley, Derek, *A Social History of English Cricket* (London: Aurum Press, 1999).

Birley, Derek, *Playing the Game: Sport and British Society, 1910–45* (Manchester: Manchester University Press, 1995).

Birley, Derek, *Willow Wand: Some Cricket Myths Explored* (London: Queen Anne Press, 1979).

Booth, Brian, *Booth to Bat* (Homebush West: Anzea Publishers, 1983).

Border, Allan, *Beyond Ten Thousand* (London: Souvenir Press, 1994).

Bose, Mihir, *A History of Indian Cricket* (London: Andre Deutsch, 2002).

Bose, Mihir, *Keith Miller: A Cricketing Biography* (London: Allen and Unwin, 1979).

Botham, Ian, *Botham: My Autobiography* (London: CollinsWillow, 1994).

Boycott, Geoffrey, *The Autobiography* (London: Macmillan, 1987).

Brearley, Mike, *The Art of Captaincy* (London: Hodder and Stoughton, 1985, republished Pan Books, 2015).

Brettig, Daniel, *Whitewash to Whitewash: Australia's Years of Plenty and Summer of Plenty* (Scoresby: Penguin Group Australia, 2015).

Briggs, Simon, *Stiff Upper Lips and Baggy Green Caps* (London: Quercus, 2013).

Broad, Stuart, *Broadside: How We Regained the Ashes* (London: Simon and Schuster, 2015).

Cantrall, John, *Farokh Engineer from the Far Pavilion* (Stroud: The History Press, 2004).

Cary, Clif, *Cricket Controversy: Test Matches in Australia 1946–47* (London: Werner Laurie Ltd, 1948).

Chalke, Stephen, *At the Heart of English Cricket: The Life and Memories of Geoffrey Howard* (Bath: Fairfield Books, 2001).

Chalke, Stephen, *Caught in the Memory: County Cricket in the 1960s* (Bath: Fairfield Books, 1999).

Chalke, Stephen, *Micky Stewart and the Changing Face of Cricket* (Bath: Fairfield Books, 2011).

Chalke, Stephen, *Runs in the Memory: County Cricket in the 1950s* (Bath: Fairfield Books, 2002).

Clarke, John, *Challenge Renewed: MCC Australian Tour 1962–63* (London: Stanley Paul, 1963).

Clarke, John, *With England in Australia: The MCC Tour 1965–66* (London: Stanley Paul, 1966).

Close, Brian, *I Don't Bruise Easily* (London: Macdonald and Jane's, 1978).

Close, Brian, *The MCC Tour of West Indies, 1968* (London: Stanley Paul, 1968).

Compton, Denis, *End of an Innings* (London: Oldbourne, 1958).

Compton, Denis, *In Sun and Shadow* (London: Stanley Paul, 1952).

Compton, Denis, *Testing Time for England* (London: Stanley Paul and Co, 1948).

Compton, Denis and Edrich, Bill, *Cricket and All That* (London: Pelham Books, 1978).

Cowdrey, Colin, *MCC: The Autobiography of a Cricketer* (London: Hodder and Stoughton, 1976).

Cowdrey, Colin, *The Incomparable Game* (London: Hodder and Stoughton, 1970).

Coward, Mike, *Caribbean Odyssey: Australia and Cricket in the West Indies* (London: Simon and Schuster, 1991).

Coward, Mike, *Cricket Beyond the Bazaar* (London: Allen and Unwin, 1990).

Coward, Mike, *The Chappell Years: Cricket in the 70s* (Sydney: ABC Books, 2002).

Crace, John, *Wasim and Waqar: Imran's Inheritors* (London: Boxtree Ltd, 1992).

Davidson, Alan, *Fifteen Paces* (London: Souvenir Press, 1963).

Denness, Mike, *I Declare* (London: Arthur Barker Ltd, 1977).

Dexter, Ted, *Ted Dexter Declares* (London: Stanley Paul, 1966).

De Silva, Aravinda: *My Autobiography* (Edinburgh: Mainstream, 1999).

Donald, Allan, *White Lightning* (London: Collins Willow, 1999).

Douglas, Christopher, *Douglas Jardine: Spartan Cricketer* (London: George Allen and Unwin Publishers, 1984).

Edrich, Bill, *Cricket Heritage* (London: Stanley Paul, 1948).

Edrich, Bill, *Round the Wicket* (London: Frederick Muller Ltd, 1959).

Evans, Godfrey, *The Gloves Are Off* (London: Hodder and Stoughton, 1960).

Fazal Mahmood, *From Dust to Dawn: Autobiography of a Pakistan Cricket Legend* (Oxford: Oxford University Press, 2003).

Fingleton, Jack, *Brown and Company* (London: Collins, 1951).

Fingleton, Jack, *Cricket Crisis* (London: Cassell, 1947).

Fingleton, Jack, *Four Chukkas to Australia* (London: Heinemann, 1960).

Fletcher, Duncan, *Behind the Shades: The Autobiography* (London: Simon and Schuster, 2007).

Foot, David, *Wally Hammond: The Reasons Why* (London: Robson Books, 1996).

Fortune, Charles, *MCC in South Africa* (London: Robert Hale, 1965).

Fortune, Charles, *The MCC Tour of South Africa 1956–57* (London: George G. Harrap and Co Ltd, 1957).

Frith, David, *Bodyline Autopsy* (London: Aurum, 2002).

Gavaskar, Sunil, *Runs and Ruins* (India: Rupa and Co, 1984).

Geddes, Margaret, *Remembering Bradman* (Melbourne: Viking, 2003).

Gilchrist, Adam, *True Colours: My Life* (South Melbourne: Affirm Press, 2009).

Giller, Norman, *Denis Compton* (London: Andre Deutsch, 1997).

Gower, David, *The Autobiography* (London: CollinsWillow, 1992).

Graveney, Tom, *Cricket Over Forty* (London: Pelham Books, 1970).

Graveney, Tom, *The Heart of Cricket* (London: Arthur Barker Ltd, 1983).

Greenidge, Gordon, *The Man in the Middle* (Newton Abbott: David and Charles, 1980).

Griffith, Charlie, *Chucked Around* (London: Pelham, 1970).

Grout, Wally, *My County's Keeper* (London: Pelham Books, 1965).

Hadlee, Richard, *Hadlee* (London: Angus and Robertson, 1981).

Haigh, Gideon, *The Big Ship: Warwick Armstrong and the Making of Modern Cricket* (London: Aurum Press, 2005).

Haigh, Gideon, *The Border Years* (Sydney: The Text Publishing Company, 1994).

Haigh, Gideon, *The Summer Game* (Sydney: The Text Publishing Company, 1997).

Hair, Darrell, *Decision Maker: An Umpire's Story* (Australia: Random House, 1998).

Hamilton, Duncan, *Harold Larwood* (London: Quercus, 2009).

Harte, Chris, *A History of Australian Cricket* (London: Andre Deutsch, 1993).

Harvey, Neil, *My World of Cricket* (London: Sportsman's Book Club, 1964).

Hill, Alan, *Bill Edrich: A Biography* (London: Andre Deutsch, 1994).

Hill, Alan, *Brian Close: Cricket's Lionheart* (London: Methuen, 2002).

Hill, Alan, *Jim Laker: A Biography* (London: Andre Deutsch, 1998).

Hill, Alan, *Peter May: A Biography* (London: Andre Deutsch, 1996).

Hill, Alan, *Tony Lock: Aggressive Master of Spin* (Stroud: The History Press, 2008).

Holding, Michael, *Whispering Death* (London: Andre Deutsch, 1993).

Holt, Richard, *Sport and the British* (Oxford: Clarendon, 1989).

Howat, Gerald, *Len Hutton: The Biography* (London: Mandarin, 1988).

Howat, Gerald, *Plum Warner* (London: Unwin Hyman, 1987).

Hutton, Len, *Cricket Is My Life* (London: Hutchinson and Co, 1949).

Hutton, Len, *Fifty Years in Cricket* (London: Stanley Paul and Co, 1984).

Hutton, Len, *Just My Story* (London: Hutchinson, 1956).

Illingworth, Ray, *Yorkshire and Back* (London: Queen Anne Press, 1980).

Imran Khan, *All Round View* (London: Chatto and Windus, 1988).

Jackman, Robin, *Jackers: A Life in Cricket* (Pitch Publishing, 2012).

James, C.L.R., *Beyond a Boundary* (London: Stanley Paul, 1963).

James, Steve, *Third Man to Fatty's Leg: An Autobiography* (Lydney: First Stone, 2005).

Javed Miandad, *Cutting Edge: My Autobiography* (Oxford: Oxford University Press, 2003).

Kay, John, *Ashes to Hassett: A Review of the MCC Tour to Australia, 1950–51* (Altrincham: John Sherratt and Co, 1951).

Knox, Malcolm, *Bradman's War* (London: The Robson Press, 2013).

Knox, Malcolm, *Never a Gentleman's Game* (Melbourne: Hardie Grant Books, 2012).

Knox, Malcolm, *The Captains* (Melbourne: Hardie Grant Books, 2011).

Knox, Malcolm, *The Greatest: The Players, the Moments, the Matches* (Melbourne: Hardie Grant Books, 2010).

Laker, Jim, *Over to Me* (London: Frederick Muller Ltd, 1960).

Lamb, Allan, *Allan Lamb: My Autobiography* (London: Collins Willow, 1996).

Lane, Tim and Cartledge, Elliot, *Chasing Shadows: The Life and Death of Peter Roebuck* (Melbourne: Hardie Grant Books, 2015).

Le Quesne, Laurence, *The Bodyline Controversy* (London: HarperCollins Willow, 1985).

Lewis, Tony, *Double Century: The Story of MCC and Cricket* (London: Hodder and Stoughton, 1987).

Lewis, Tony, *Playing Days: An Autobiography* (London: Hutchinson, 1985).

Lillee, Dennis, *Menace: The Autobiography* (London: Headline, 2003).

Lister, Simon, *Fire in Babylon* (London: Random House, 2015).

Lloyd, Clive, *Living for Cricket* (London: Stanley Paul, 1980).

Mackay, Ken, *Quest for the Ashes* (London: Pelham Books, 1966).

McDermott, Craig, *Strike Bowler* (Sydney: ABC, 1992).

McGilvray, Alan, *The Game Is Not the Same* (Sydney: ABC Books, 1985).

McGrath, Glenn, *Line and Strength: The Complete Story* (London: Yellow Jersey Press, 2009).

McGregor, Adrian, *Greg Chappell* (London: Collins, 1985).

McKinstry, Leo, *Geoff Boycott: A Cricketing Hero* (London: Collins Willow, 2005).

McKinstry, Leo, *Jack Hobbs: England's Greatest Cricketer* (London: Yellow Jersey Press, 2011).

McLean, Roy, *Pitch and Toss* (Cape Town: Howard Timmins Ltd, 1957).

Major, John, *The Story of Cricket's Early Years* (London: Harper Collins, 2007).

Mangan, J.A., *Manliness and Morality* (Manchester: Manchester University Press, 1987).

Manley, Michael, *A History of West Indies Cricket* (London, Andre Deutsch, 1988).

Marshall, Malcolm, *Marshall Arts: The Autobiography of Malcolm Marshall* (London: Macdonald, 1987).

Marshall, Michael, *Gentlemen and Players* (London: Grafton Books, 1987).

Marqusee, Mike, *Anyone but England: Cricket, Race and Class* (London: Two Heads Publishing, 1994).

Martin-Jenkins, Christopher, *Assault on the Ashes: MCC in Australia and New Zealand, 1974/75* (London: Macdonald and Company, 1975).

Martin-Jenkins, Christopher, *Cricket Contest* (London: Queen Anne Press, 1980).

Martin-Jenkins, Christopher, *Testing Time: MCC in the West Indies 1974* (London: Macdonald and Jane's, 1974).

Martin-Jenkins, Christopher, *Twenty Years On: Cricket's Years of Change, 1963 to 1983* (London: Willow Books, 1984).

Martin-Jenkins, Christopher, *World Cricketers: A Biographical Dictionary* (Oxford: Oxford University Press, 1996).

May, Peter, *A Game Enjoyed* (London: Stanley Paul, 1985).

Meckiff, Ian, *Thrown Out* (London: Stanley Paul and Co, 1961).

Meher-Komji, Kersi, *Conflicts and Controversies in Cricket* (London: New Holland Publishers, 2013).

Meredith, Anthony, *Summers in Winter* (London: The Kingswood Press, 1990).

Miller, Douglas, *Charles Palmer: More Than a Gentleman* (Bath: Fairfield Books, 2001).

Miller, Keith, *Cricket from the Grandstand* (London: Oldbourne, 1959).

Miller, Keith and Whitington, R.S., *Catch!* (London: Latimer House, 1951).

Mosey, Don, *Laker: Portrait of a Legend* (London: Queen Anne Press, 1989).

Murtagh, Andrew, *Test of Character: The Story of John Holder – Fast Bowler and Test Match Umpire* (Pitch Publishing, 2014).

Murtagh, Andrew, *Touched by Greatness: The Story of Tom Graveney, England's Much Loved Cricketer* (Pitch Publishing, 2014).

Nicholas, Mark, *A Beautiful Game* (Sydney: Allen and Unwin, 2016).

Noman, Omar, *Pride and Passion: An Exhilarating Half Century of Cricket in Pakistan* (Karachi: Oxford University Press, 1998).

Nourse, Dudley, *Cricket in the Blood* (London: Hodder and Stoughton, 1949).

Oborne, Peter, *Basil D'Oliveira: Cricket and Conspiracy* (London: Time Warner Books, 2005).

Oborne, Peter, *Wounded Tiger: A History of Cricket in Pakistan* (London: Simon and Schuster, 2014).

Pataudi, The Nawab of, *Tiger's Tale* (London: Stanley Paul and Co Ltd, 1969).

Peel, Mark, *England Expects: A Biography of Ken Barrington* (London: The Kingswood Press, 1992).

Peel, Mark, *The Last Roman: A Biography of Colin Cowdrey* (London: Andre Deutsch, 1999).

Perry, Roland, *Keith Miller: The Life of a Great All-Rounder* (London: Aurum Press Ltd, 2006).

Pocock, Pat, *Percy* (London: Clifford Frost Publications, 1987).

Ponting, Ricky, *My Autobiography* (London: Harper Collins, 2013).

Rae, Simon, *It's Not Cricket* (London: Faber, 2002).

Rae, Simon, *W.G. Grace: A Life* (London: Faber and Faber, 1998).

Ray, Mark, *Border and Beyond* (Sydney: ABC Books, 1995).

Reid, John, *Sword of Willow* (Wellington: A.H. and A.W. Reed, 1962).

Richards, Barry, *The Barry Richards Story* (London: Faber and Faber, 1978).

Richards, Jeffrey, *Happiest Days: The Public Schools in English Fiction* (Manchester: Manchester University Press, 1988).

Richards, Viv, *Hitting Across the Line* (London: Headline, 1991).

Richards, Viv, *Sir Vivian: The Definitive Autobiography* (London: Michael Joseph, 2000).

Robinson, Ray, *The Wildest Tests* (London: Pelham Books, 1972).

Roebuck, Peter, *In It to Win It: The Australian Cricket Supremacy* (Sydney: Allen and Unwin, 2006).

Ross, Alan, *Australia 1955* (London: Michael Joseph, 1955).

Ross, Alan, *Cape Summer* (London: Hamish Hamilton, 1957).

Ross, Alan, *Through the Caribbean* (London: Hamish Hamilton, 1960).

Rowan, Lou, *The Umpire's Story* (Sydney: Jack Pollard, 1972).

Russell, Jack, *Jack Russell: Unleashed* (London: Collins Willow, 1997).

Sandford, Christopher, *Godfrey Evans* (London: Simon and Schuster, 1990).

Sandford, Christopher, *Imran Khan: The Biography* (London: Harper Collins, 2009).

Sandford, Christopher, *Tom Graveney* (London: H.F. and G. Witherby, 1992).

Shaharyar Khan, *Cricket Cauldron: The Turbulent Politics of Sport in Pakistan* (London: IB Tauris, 2013).

Shepherd, David, *Shep: My Autobiography* (London: Orion, 2001).

Simpson, Bobby, *Captain's Story* (London: Stanley Paul, 1966).

Simpson, Bob, *The Reasons Why* (Australia: Harper Collins, 1996).

Smith, Robin, *Quest for Number One* (London: Boxtree Ltd, 1993).

Smyth, Rob, *The Spirit of Cricket* (London: Elliott and Thompson, 2011).

Snow, John, *Cricket Rebel* (London: Hamlyn, 1976).

Sobers, Gary, *King Cricket* (London: Pelham Books, 1967).

Sobers, Gary, *My Autobiography* (London: Headline, 2002).

Sobers, Gary, *Twenty Years at the Top* (London: Ebury, 1996).

Stackpole, Keith, *Not Just for Openers* (Abbotsford: Stockwell Press, 1974).

Statham, Brian, *A Spell at the Top* (London: Souvenir Press, 1969).

Steen, Rob, *David Gower: A Man out of Time* (London: Victor Gollancz, 1995).

Stevenson, Mike, *A Biography of Ray Illingworth* (Tunbridge Wells: Midas Books, 1978).

Stewart, Alec, *Playing for Keeps: The Autobiography of Alec Stewart* (London: BBC, 2004).

Stollmeyer, Jeffrey, *Everything under the Sun* (London: Stanley Paul, 1983).

Swanton, E.W., *Gubby Allen: Man of Cricket* (London: Hutchinson/Stanley Paul, 1985).

Swanton, E.W., *Report from South Africa* (London: Hale, 1957).

Swanton, E.W., *Sort of a Cricket Person* (London: Collins, 1972).

Swanton, E.W., *Swanton in Australia* (London: Collins, 1975).

Swanton, E.W., *West Indian Adventure* (London: Sportsman's Book Club, 1955).

Swanton, E.W., *West Indies Revisited* (London: Heinemann, 1960).

Taylor, Bob, *Standing Up, Standing Back* (London: Collins, 1985).

Taylor, Mark, *Time to Declare* (Sydney: Pan Macmillan, 1999).

Tennant, Ivo, *Imran Khan* (London: Gollancz/Witherby, 1994).

Tossell, David, *Grovel! The Story and Legacy of the Summer of 1976* (Studley: Know the Score, 2007).

Trelford, Donald (ed), *Len Hutton Remembered* (London: H.F. and G. Witherby Ltd, 1992).

Turbervill, Huw, *The Toughest Tour: The Ashes Away Series 1946 to 2007* (London: Aurum Press Ltd, 2010).

Tyson, Frank, *A Typhoon Called Tyson* (London: William Heinemann Ltd, 1961).

Tyson, Frank, *In the Eye of the Typhoon* (Manchester: Parrs Wood Press, 2004).

Walcott, Clyde, *Island Cricketers* (London: Hodder and Stoughton, 1958).

Walcott, Clyde, *Sixty Years on the Back Foot* (London: Victor Gollancz, 1999).

Walker, Peter, *It's Not Just Cricket* (Bath: Fairfield Books, 2006).

Wasim Akram, *Wasim* (London: Piatkus, 1998).

Waters, Chris, *Fred Trueman: The Authorised Biography* (London: Aurum, 2011).

Waugh, Steve, *Out of My Comfort Zone* (London: Michael Joseph, 2004).

Wellings, E.M., *Dexter v Benaud: MCC Tour to Australia 1962–3* (London: Bailey and Swinfen, 1963).

Wellings, E.M., *No Ashes for England* (London: Evans Brothers, 1951).

West, Peter, *Denis Compton: Cricketing Genius* (London: Stanley Paul, 1989).

Whitington, R.S., *Captains Outrageous? Cricket in the Seventies* (London: Stanley Paul, 1973).

Whitington, R.S., *Keith Miller: The Golden Nugget* (Sydney: Rigby, 1981).

Whitington, R.S., *Simpson's Safari: South African Test Series 1966–7* (Melbourne: Heinemann, 1967).

Williams, Charles, *Bradman: An Australian Hero* (London: Little, Brown, 1996).

Williams, Jack, *Cricket and England: A Cultural and Social History of the Inter-War Years* (London: Frank Cass, 1999).

Willis, Bob, *Lasting the Pace* (London: Collins, 1985).

Willis, Bob, *The Cricket Revolution: Test Cricket in the 1970s* (London: Sidgwick and Jackson, 1981).

Worrell, Frank, *Cricket Punch* (London: Stanley Paul, 1959).

Wright, Graeme, *Betrayal: The Struggle for Cricket's Soul* (London: H.F. and G. Witherby, 1993).

Newspapers and Annuals

Advertiser (Adelaide)

Age

Australian

Canadian Press

Canberra Times

Courier-Mail

Cricketer

Cricketer Australia

Daily Express

Daily Herald

Daily Mail

Daily Mirror

Daily News (Sri Lanka)

Daily Star

Daily Telegraph

Daily Telegraph (Sydney)

Evening Chronicle (Newcastle)

Evening News (London)

Evening News of Trinidad

Evening Standard

Guardian

Herald Sun (Melbourne)

Hindu

Hindustan Times

Independent

Independent on Sunday

Observer

Pakistan Observer

Playfair Cricket Monthly

Radio Times

Rand Daily Mail

Smith's Weekly

Sun

Sun (Sydney)
Sunday Mail (Brisbane)
Sunday Mirror
Sunday Telegraph
Sunday Telegraph (Sydney)
Sunday Times
Sydney Morning Herald
Sydney Referee
Times
Times of India
Trinidad Guardian
Truth
Wisden Australia
Wisden Cricketers' Almanack
Wisden Cricket Monthly

Online Resources
BBC News Online
Cricket Archive
ESPNcricinfo

Endnotes

1 *Daily Telegraph*, 16 July 2006
2 Derek Birley, *A Social History of Cricket*, p191
3 C.L.R. James, *Beyond a Boundary*, p35
4 Gary Sobers, *Twenty Years at the Top*, p117
5 Quoted in Malcolm Knox, *Bradman's War*, p371
6 *Sunday Times*, 20 April 1986
7 *The Times*, 4 January 1989
8 Graeme Wright, *Betrayal: The Struggle for Cricket's Soul*, p162
9 *Daily Telegraph*, 14 January 2008
10 Jeffrey Richards, *Happiest Days: The Public Schools in English Fiction*, p122
11 J.A. Mangan, *Manliness and Morality*, p244
12 Richard Holt, *Sport and the British*, p263
13 Simon Rae, *It's Not Cricket*, p189
14 Malcolm Knox, *Never a Gentleman's Game*, p3
15 Gideon Haigh, *The Big Ship: Warwick Armstrong and the Making of Modern Cricket*, p4
16 Jack Fingleton, *Cricket Crisis*, p78
17 Quoted in Gerald Howat, *Plum Warner*, p107
18 ibid
19 Fingleton, *Cricket Crisis*, p50
20 ibid, p51
21 Howat, *Plum Warner*, p117
22 ibid, p118
23 Quoted in Birley, *A Social History of English Cricket*, p236
24 Quoted in Birley, *A Social History of English Cricket*, p237
25 Christopher Douglas, *Douglas Jardine, Spartan Cricketer*, p145
26 ibid
27 Laurence Le Quesne, *The Bodyline Controversy*, p92
28 Fingleton, *Cricket Crisis*, p56

ENDNOTES

29 Quoted in Fingleton, *Cricket Crisis*, p108
30 Roland Perry, *Keith Miller: The Life of a Great All-Rounder*, p132
31 *Sydney Morning Herald*, 6 October 2004
32 Charles Williams, *Bradman: An Australian Hero*, p212
33 R.S. Whitington, *Keith Miller: The Golden Nugget*, p114
34 Norman Giller, *Denis Compton*, p141
35 Godfrey Evans, *The Gloves Are Off*, p55
36 *Truth*, 9 March 1947
37 Fingleton, *Cricket Crisis*, p303
38 Knox, *Bradman's War*, p179
39 ibid, p249
40 ibid, p383
41 Julia Gillard, open letter to Arthur Morris, read at Alec Bedser's memorial service, 12 July 2010 (information provided by Rodney Cavalier, sometime president of the Sydney Cricket Ground Trust and good friend of Arthur Morris)
42 *Sydney Morning Herald*, 1 March 1951
43 Alan McGilvray, *The Game Is Not the Same*, p133
44 Peter West, *Denis Compton*, p122
45 Frank Worrell, *Cricket Punch*, p82
46 Quoted in Gerald Howat, *Len Hutton*, p135
47 Clyde Walcott, *Sixty Years on the Back Foot*, p49
48 Bobby Simpson, *Captain's Story*, p44
49 Alan Hill, *Jim Laker: A Biography*, p109
50 Gideon Haigh, *The Summer Game*, p82
51 Margaret Geddes, *Remembering Bradman*, p246
52 Christopher Sandford, *Godfrey Evans: A Biography*, p169
53 Colin Cowdrey, *The Incomparable Game*, p53
54 E.W. Swanton, *Sort of a Cricket Person*, p191
55 Tom Graveney, *Cricket Over Forty*, p33
56 *Daily Telegraph*, 6 July 1966
57 Gary Sobers, *King Cricket*, p107
58 Haigh, *The Summer Game*, p153
59 *Wisden Cricketers' Almanack* 1961, p120
60 *Wisden Cricketers' Almanack* 1962, p111
61 Gary Sobers, *My Autobiography*, p145
62 Clive Lloyd, *Living for Cricket*, p49
63 R.S.Whitington, *Simpson's Safari: South African Test Series 1966-7*, p164
64 ibid, p192
65 Keith Stackpole, *Not Just for Openers*, p50

66 ibid, p84
67 Barry Richards, *The Barry Richards Story*, p96
68 *The Times*, 26 January 1970
69 Ray Robinson, *The Wildest Tests*, p20
70 David Shepherd, *Shep: My Autobiography*, p147
71 Stephen Chalke, *Caught in the Memory: County Cricket in the 1960s*, p212
72 Bob Taylor, *Standing Up, Standing Back*, p66
73 ibid, p65
74 ibid, p143
75 Quoted in Christopher Martin-Jenkins, *Twenty Years On: Cricket's Years of Change, 1963 to 1983*, p118
76 *Wisden Cricketers' Almanack* 1974, p68
77 Pat Pocock, *Percy*, p98
78 Bob Willis, *The Cricket Revolution: Test Cricket in the 1970s*, p65
79 Mike Denness, *I Declare*, p129
80 *Wisden Cricketers' Almanack* 1976, p96
81 Bill Alley, *Standing the Test of Time*, p102
82 Gordon Greenidge, *The Man in the Middle*, p72
83 Viv Richards, *Hitting Across the Line*, p67
84 *The Times of India*, 30 November 2014
85 *Daily Telegraph*, 12 July 1976
86 *Daily Mail*, 12 July 1976
87 Simon Lister, *Fire in Babylon*, p123
88 *The Cricketer*, May 1979
89 Allan Border, *Beyond Ten Thousand*, p127
90 Javed Miandad, *Cutting Edge: My Autobiography*, p43
91 Chris Harte, *A History of Australian Cricket*, p 613
92 Christopher Martin-Jenkins, *Cricket Contest*, p73
93 Richard Hadlee, *Hadlee*, p185
94 Richie Benaud, *On Reflection*, p165
95 *Wisden Cricketers' Almanack* 1982, p89
96 Quoted in Rob Steen, *David Gower*, p183
97 *Sunday Times*, 27 July 1980
98 *Wisden Cricketers' Almanack* 1985, p48
99 Pocock, *Percy*, p130
100 Malcolm Marshall, *Marshall Arts: The Autobiography of Malcolm Marshall*, p168
101 *The Times*, 24 February 1986
102 *Sunday Times*, 20 April 1986
103 Michael Holding, *Whispering Death*, p143

104 *The Times*, 4 January 1989

105 *Sydney Morning Herald*, 31 December 1988

106 ibid, 13 February 1989

107 *Wisden Cricketers' Almanack* 1992, p1042

108 Quoted in Omar Noman, *Pride and Passion: An Exhilarating Half Century of Cricket in Pakistan*, p247

109 Quoted in ibid

110 Javed Miandad, *Cutting Edge*, p51

111 Imran Khan, *All Round View*, p210

112 *The Times*, 8 November 1987

113 *Sunday Times*, 29 November 1987

114 *The Times*, 2 December 1987

115 ibid, 12 December 1987

116 ibid, 23 December 1987

117 ibid, 14 January 1988

118 *Wisden Cricketers' Almanack* 1989, p924

119 *Sydney Morning Herald*, 19 September 1988

120 *Wisden Cricketers' Almanack* 1990, p978

121 Peter Oborne, *Wounded Tiger: A History of Cricket in Pakistan*, p361

122 Mark Nicholas, *A Beautiful Game*, p111

123 Colin Cowdrey, *MCC: The Autobiography of a Cricketer*, p148

124 Quoted in Jack Bannister and Don Oslear, *Tampering with Cricket*, p172

125 Quoted in ibid, p208

126 *The Age*, 20 February 1998

127 *The Hindu*, 3 January 2000

128 *Courier-Mail*, 4 January 2000

129 *The Independent*, 23 March 2003

130 Steen, *David Gower*, p162

131 John Cantrall, *Farokh Engineer from the Far Pavilion*, p57

132 Worrell, *Cricket Punch*, p118

133 *Courier-Mail*, 10 October 2001

134 *Sydney Morning Herald*, 1 February 1991

135 *Wisden Cricketers' Almanack* 1994, p330

136 ibid, p333

137 *The Age*, 9 March 1994

138 *Adelaide* (Adelaide), 1 December, 2013

139 Mark Taylor, *Time to Declare*, p418

140 *The Australian*, 4 February 1997

141 *The Guardian*, 3 February 1999

142 *Sunday Times*, 7 January 1996

143 *Daily Mail,* 28 July 1998

144 *The Sun,* 4 August 1998

145 *Daily Mail,* 5 August 1998

146 *Sunday Times,* 7 December 1969

147 Alan Hill, *Bill Edrich: A Biography,* p203

148 Quoted in Simon Rae, *It's Not Cricket,* p23

149 Quoted in Mark Peel, *England Expects: A Biography of Ken Barrington,* p91

150 Marshall, *Marshall Arts,* p33

151 Allan Donald, *White Lightning,* p259

152 *Independent on Sunday,* 16 August 1998

153 *The Times,* 5 December 1999

154 *The Guardian,* 15 December 1999

155 *Sunday Times,* 19 December 1999

156 *The Independent,* 20 February 2001

157 Bob Simpson, *The Reasons Why,* p160

158 *The Guardian,* 29 January 2001

159 *Sydney Morning Herald,* 30 January 1999

160 *The Australian,* 30 January 1999

161 *Daily Telegraph,* 27 February 2001

162 *The Sun,* 2 March 2001

163 *Daily Telegraph,* 10 March 2001

164 ibid, 11 March 2001

165 *Sunday Telegraph,* 11 March 2001

166 *Daily Telegraph,* 20 March 2001

167 *Sunday Times,* 11 March 2001

168 Waugh, *Out of my Comfort Zone,* p584

169 *The Australian,* 2 March 2001

170 *Courier-Mail,* 24 November 2001

171 *The Hindu,* 24 November 2001

172 *Sydney Morning Herald,* 3 January 2000

173 Quoted in *The Age,* 18 November 2002

174 *The Australian,* 7 January 2003

175 *Daily Telegraph* (Sydney), 22 January 2003

176 *The Australian,* 23 May 2003

177 *Hindustan Times,* 17 May 2003

178 Malcolm Knox, *The Greatest,* p301

179 *The Times,* 6 January 2006

180 *Courier-Mail,* 20 January 2006

181 ibid, 21 January 2006

182 *The Age,* 31 March 2006

183 Duncan Fletcher, *Behind the Shades: The Autobiography*, p330
184 Adam Gilchrist, *True Colours: My Life*, p574
185 *Sydney Morning Herald*, 7 January 2008
186 *The Guardian*, 8 January 2008
187 *Courier-Mail*, 10 January 2008
188 *Daily Telegraph* (Sydney), 8 January 2008
189 ibid, 14 January 2008
190 *The Australian*, 30 January 2008
191 *Sydney Morning Herald*, 30 January 2008
192 Ricky Ponting, *My Autobiography*, p481
193 Knox, *The Greatest*, p378
194 *The Australian*, 6 November 2008
195 *The Age*, 22 December 2009
196 *Sunday Mail* (Brisbane), 20 December 2009
197 *Sydney Morning Herald*, 22 December 2010
198 *Daily Telegraph* (Sydney), 26 November 2013
199 *The Age*, 28 August 2014
200 Bannister and Oslear, *Tampering with Cricket*, p78
201 David Gower, *The Autobiography*, p191
202 Allan Lamb, *My Autobiography*, p192
203 *The Times*, 26 July 1994
204 ibid, 29 September 2006
205 *The Australian*, 30 September 2006
206 ibid, 22 August 2006
207 *Daily Telegraph*, 29 September 2006
208 *The Australian*, 30 September 2006
209 *Sunday Telegraph* (Sydney), 5 November 2006
210 *The Times*, 20 August 2013
211 ibid, 27 November 2013
212 *Independent on Sunday*, 20 July 2014
213 *Daily Star*, 24 June 2007
214 *Evening Chronicle* (Newcastle), 27 July 2007
215 *The Guardian*, 31 July 2007
216 *The Times*, 3 August 2008
217 *The Independent*, 1 August 2011
218 ibid
219 *The Times*, 1 August 2011
220 *Daily Mirror*, 13 July 2013
221 *The Times*, 13 July 2013
222 *Daily Mail*, 13 July 2013
223 *The Times*, 17 July 2013

224 *Evening Standard,* 16 July 2013
225 *Daily Telegraph,* 29 August 2013
226 *The Independent* online, 27 November 2013
227 *The Times,* 27 November 2013
228 *The Independent,* 2 August 2014
229 *Cricinfo,* 4 December 2014
230 *The Times of India,* 31 December 2014
231 *The Australian,* 16 January 2015
232 *Canadian Press,* 4 November 2015
233 *Daily News* (Sri Lanka), 4 April 2015
234 Stuart Broad, *Broadside: How We Regained the Ashes,* p126
235 *The Times,* 8 July 2015
236 *Sydney Morning Herald,* 9 November 2015
237 *Courier-Mail,* 26 March 2018
238 *The Guardian,* 26 March 2018
239 *Advertiser* (Adelaide), 1 December 2013
240 *The Guardian,* 29 June 2012
241 Mike Brearley, *The Art of Captaincy,* p212
242 Ian Botham, *Botham: My Autobiography,* p335
243 John Holder, *Test of Character: The Story of John Holder – Fast Bowler and Test Match Umpire,* p342
244 *Sunday Times,* 17 July 2013
245 *The Observer,* 14 July 2013
246 *The Times,* 12 October 2009

Index

Kallis, Jacques, 167, 207
Kanhai, Rohan, 71, 88-9
Kapil Dev, 146
Karthik, Dinesh, 230
Kasprowicz, Michael, 194
Keating, Frank, 111
Kentish, Esmond, 89
Kidson, Hayward, 74
King, Frank, 113
Kippins, Cec, 49
Kirsten, Gary, 154, 257
Kirsten, Peter, 146, 154, 224
Kirti Azad, 181
Kitchen, Mervyn, 141, 160-1, 218
Kline, Lindsay, 67
Knott, Alan, 72, 87, 89-90, 112, 165
Knox, Malcolm, 22, 37, 191, 206
Koertzen, Rudi, 167, 175-6, 186, 191-2
Kohli, Virat, 242, 247
Kumar, Praveen, 234
Kumble, Anil, 17, 199, 200-1, 203-5
Kureishi, Omar, 127

Laker, Jim, 47, 52-3, 55, 103
Lamb, Allan, 118-19, 152, 216-18
Lance, 'Tiger', 77
Lander, Chris, 216
Langer, Justin, 191
Langridge, John, 162-3
Lara, Brian, 157-8, 189, 191
Larwood, Harold, 24-8, 32-3, 38, 92, 112
Lawry, Bill, 65, 69, 74-7, 85, 151, 210
Lawson, Geoff, 121-2, 202
Lawton, James, 235
Lee, Alan, 136-7
Lee, Brett, 186, 194-5, 199, 253
Lee, Frank, 58
Lehmann, Darren, 17, 187-8, 198, 206, 211, 236-7
Lever, Peter, 93-4
Le Quesne, Laurence, 30
Lewis, Tony, 87-8
Lewis, Gordon, Judge, 239
Lillee, Dennis, 13, 79, 91-3, 95, 105, 107-9, 114, 118, 252
Lillywhite, James, 21
Lindsay, Denis, 74, 182
Lindwall, Ray, 33, 37-8, 40, 42, 45-6, 51, 57, 80, 112-13, 150, 165, 251
Llewellyn-Smith, Julia, 161
Llong, Nigel, 246
Lloyd, Andy, 115
Lloyd, Clive, 14, 73, 96-7, 105, 107, 114, 118, 157-8, 184, 188
Lloyd, David, 172, 231, 250
Loader, Peter, 55, 58
Lock, Tony, 12, 47, 49, 52, 55, 58, 113, 150-1
Logie, Gus, 124
Loxton, Sam, 45, 80, 108
Lush, Peter, 132-4, 254

Lyon, Nathan, 246

MacGill, Stuart, 191
Mackay, 'Slasher', 67
MacLaren, Archie, 22
McCabe, Stan, 26
McCarthy, Cuan, 11, 55
McCool, Colin, 39
McCosker, Rick, 98
McCullum, Brendon, 19, 193, 233, 243-6, 257, 260
McDermott, Chris, 209
McDermott, Craig, 124-5
McDonald, Andrew, 207
McDonald, Colin, 53, 66
McDonald, Ted, 30, 33, 112
McFarline, Peter, 145
McGilvray, Alan, 46, 149, 163-4
McGrath, Glenn, 16, 146-7, 156-8, 171, 185-6, 189, 190, 193-5, 208
McGrath, Jane, 189
McKechnie, Brian, 108
McKenzie, Graham, 68-70
McMillan, Brian, 108
McMillan, Craig, 192
McQuillan, Tony, 170
McWatt, Clifford, 49
Madugalle, Ranjan, 146, 184, 194, 204, 210, 225-6
Mahanama, Roshan, 173, 227
Mahboob Shah, 136-8
Mailey, A.A, 213
Majola, Gerald, 82
Majid Khan, 184
Malcolm, Devon, 140
Mangan, J.A., 20
Manning, J.L., 164
Manohar, Vasha, 205
Mant, Gilbert, 29
Manuel, Peter, 174, 229
Marlar, Robin, 13, 118, 160, 163
MCC, 12, 26, 28-35, 37, 40, 47-8, 51, 54, 59, 60-1, 71, 73, 79, 84, 87, 89, 113, 144, 147, 164, 190, 227, 255, 258
Marsh, Geoff, 157
Marsh, Jack, 22
Marsh, Paul, 209-210
Marsh, Rodney, 79, 98, 108
Marshall, Malcolm, 115-18, 123-4, 166, 252
Martindale, Manny, 31
Martin-Jenkins, Christopher, 105, 120, 260
Martyn, Damien, 194
May, Peter, 52, 56-8, 65, 80, 109, 114, 150
Maynard, Matthew, 153
Mead, Phil, 23
Meckiff, Ian, 12, 56-60, 62, 66
Melford, Michael, 97
Menzies, Badge, 79
Menzies, Robert, 36
Miller, Geoff, 165